# Boundaries of Privacy

SUNY series in Communication Studies
Dudley D. Cahn, editor

# Boundaries of Privacy

## *Dialectics of Disclosure*

Sandra Petronio

STATE UNIVERSITY OF NEW YORK PRESS

Published by
State University of New York Press, Albany

© 2002  State University of New York

For information, address State University of New York Press,
90 State Street, Suite 700, Albany, NY 12207

Production by Cathleen Collins
Marketing by Michael Campochiaro

Cover art: "Evolutionary Boundaries of Privacy" by Mircea Teodorescu.
Used by permission of the artist.

Library of Congress Cataloging-in-Publication Data

Petronio, Sandra Sporbert.
    Boundaries of privacy : dialectics of disclosure / Sandra Petronio.
        p.  cm. — (SUNY series in communication studies)
    Includes bibliographical references and index.
    ISBN 0-7914-5515-7 (alk. paper) — ISBN 0-7914-5516-5 (pbk. : alk. paper)
        1. Self-disclosure. 2. Secrecy. 3. Privacy. 4. Interpersonal communication. I. Title. II.
    Series.

    BF697.5.S427 P48 2002
    302.5—dc21
                                                                            2002021055

10   9   8   7   6   5   4   3   2   1

*To Charles and Kristen, my two anchors*

# Contents

# List of Illustrations

# Foreword

I write this foreword to Sandra Petronio's book shortly after the terrorist attacks on September 11, 2001, when thousands of Americans and foreigners died, an estimated 10,000 children lost a parent, and thousands of family members and friends became living victims of that nightmarish day. All of our lives are now changed forever, it is said, as we in America and, indeed, people throughout the world, face new challenges, uncertainties, and vulnerabilities. Our shock is magnified because the American mainland has not been attacked on such a scale by foreigners since the War of 1812; Americans are not accustomed to facing invisible and amorphous political or warlike threats; we are perplexed by the attack in light of our self-image as a benevolent, freedom-loving, and well-meaning people. And we are unsure about how to cope with the immediate and long-term specter of terrorism. The September 11th catastrophe and subsequent incidents bring to the forefront challenges that we and our children and grandchildren will face in the twenty-first century—issues that link closely with those discussed so well by Sandra Petronio.

Two interwoven features of our lives today and in the future are *technology* and *globalization*. Aside from their obvious economic and political aspects, and their military and scientific offshoots, we have already begun to experience the *personal and interpersonal* opportunities and problems of globalization and technology. The opportunities are spectacular and will surely increase geometrically in the years to come. With computer and internet technology in hand, anyone—adult or child, healthy or ill person, rich or poor—can have unlimited access to information on any subject and from anywhere in the world. Furthermore, *interpersonal* possibilities are limitless, as people join chat groups, listservs, communicate with others everywhere on the globe, carry on e-mail and interactive conversations with distant relatives and friends, and capitalize on educational exchanges with others. Surely, such opportunities will multiply in the years to come in ways that presently are almost unimaginable.

But there is a flip side to these opportunities. Aside from concerns about centralization of political and economic power, and exploitation and abuse of human rights, technology and globalization have begun to generate threats to our personal and interpersonal well-being—several of which link directly to Sandra Petronio's writing. Newspaper headlines, investigative reports, activist groups, and political aspirants clamor against the increasing technological invasions of our privacy. Computerized and live telephone solicitors harangue us daily to buy a multitude of products and services; catalogues and credit offers flood our mailboxes; massive data banks gather and sell information about our medical histories and buying patterns; there is an epidemic of stolen personal identities; our names are on computer listservs we didn't request. And we learn that our DNA, genetic history, and a myriad of personal qualities may someday be stored "somewhere"—for use by who knows whom? Then there are the con artists, purveyors of rumors, hate mongers, and sexual predators attracting adults and children into unhealthy and exploitative interpersonal relationships. Thus, as emerging technology opens up astounding possibilities for education, information, and contacts with people around the world, so it is that our personal lives also can be involuntarily open and accessible to others.

How do we strike a balance between the incredible positive opportunities to reach out to others made possible by modern technology, versus the dangers of losing the ability to control and regulate what others may know or have access to about us? This issue is at the heart of Sandra Petronio's book—how to maintain a healthy and viable balance of our *privacy* and our *disclosure*, to use her terms. Or, as I have stated in my research—how can we achieve "selective control over our *openness* and *closedness* to others"?

Of course, we have always had to deal with this issue in relationships with strangers and friends, intimate partners, family members, coworkers, and social acquaintances. But we now face new challenges in managing privacy and disclosure, or openness and closedness, as a result of globalization and technological advances. And these new challenges are magnified by another contemporary fact of life—the growing *cultural diversity* of the world in which we live. Communication and interaction with people from diverse cultures and backgrounds within and outside our own society is and will be an everyday occurrence. Ethnic, national, religious, and racial diversity are exploding in the United States as a result of immigration and birth rates. And global linkages of all people, as discussed earlier, are also increasing. Although the rich diversity of American society, and of the world at large, has enormous positive potential, so does it present unique challenges. How to engage in positive and constructive communication across language and cultural differences in meaning and style? How to manage the diversity of rules for appropriate privacy and disclosure? How to avoid serious lapses and errors of communication, inappropriate intrusions or disclosures? How to know when and how to protect interpersonal "'secrets" versus disseminating information learned in an interpersonal exchange?

Of course, these communication issues have been part of our every-day life, and we generally understand the "rules," although there are innumerable cases of misunderstanding and conflict. Difficult as it is to function constructively in our own culture, it can be enormously complex in cross-cultural settings. And much of our life in the twenty-first century will be "cross-cultural"—interacting with people from different ethnic, national, and racial heritage within our own society and globally. Add to this the intrinsic challenge of global technological communication discussed earlier, and the possible outcomes vary widely, from very positive to very disruptive.

Sandra Petronio's conceptual framework of dialectic or oppositional processes of interpersonal privacy-disclosure is directly on target to guide us as citizens, teachers, practitioners, and scholars through the maze of interpersonal communication in the twenty-first century.

Petronio is certainly not the first scholar to tackle privacy and disclosure, as she herself notes. However, treating privacy and disclosure as inseparable aspects of a unified dialectical process is a recent idea. In the 1970s I proposed the general idea that research and theory on self-disclosure-openness and on privacy-closedness—previously isolated from one another—could be integrated within a dialectical model. Later, Leslie Baxter, Barbara Montgomery, and others expanded the dialectical approach to interpersonal interaction, and also examined how people cope with imbalances, factors affecting openness-closedness, and related issues. Now, Sandra Petronio offers a comprehensive framework that incorporates systematically many aspects of privacy-disclosure that had previously been neglected, or treated in only a fragmentary way. Her integrative model is an excellent map or guide for students, teachers, practitioners, and scholars to address an array of privacy-disclosure issues. The timing of her conceptual framework with events in the secular world is also fortuitously ideal, making her theoretical contribution an excellent fit with the needs of the times.

What is so constructive about her ideas? Most important, Sandra Petronio proposes a conceptual framework based on an explicit philosophical and theoretical underpinning—a dialectical interplay of forces for people and groups to be simultaneously, but differentially, private and disclosing, depending on a variety of factors. Moreover, the dialectical privacy-disclosure dynamic is viewed as a "boundary regulation" process governed by a set of "rules" and boundary coordination principles. Petronio also describes how, under certain circumstances, boundary coordination processes malfunction, yielding what she terms "boundary turbulence." Each of these and related processes are scrupulously and thoroughly analyzed, yielding a conceptual architecture that is precise, orderly, and systematic. Her framework is also replete with hypotheses and topics for future research that surely will be mined by researchers for years to come. In my view, it is the most comprehensive conceptual framework presently available, and is likely to continue to be so for years to come.

Sandra Petronio also advances our thinking by incorporating different "levels" or combinations of participants in communication processes. Whereas earlier research and theorizing on privacy-disclosure focused on dyads or individuals, Petronio also describes communication within families and between family members and outsiders, within and outside work and social groups, and between many combinations of individuals, dyads, and others within and across social boundaries. A most complicated set of dynamics that is carefully enunciated by Petronio. In addition, her analysis of privacy-disclosure "turbulence," or breaches of desired communication patterns, is articulate and systematic.

Sandra Petronio's treatment of the development of privacy-disclosure rules is also provocative and worthy of further research, as is the application of her conceptual framework to practical issues of medical mistakes, child abuse, and HIV/AIDS. Throughout the book, and wherever possible, she buttresses analyses with extensive reviews of relevant literature, that will be a valuable resource for students, teachers, researchers, and practitioners interested in privacy-disclosure processes.

There is much to be gleaned from this insightful and comprehensive book, not only in academic pursuits, but also in everyday life, as we all struggle to cope with the opportunities and dangers of technology, globalization, and cultural diversity in these uncertain and turbulent years. Thanks to Sandra Petronio for her comprehensive, creative, and constructive analysis of privacy-disclosure processes.

Irwin Altman
Distinguished Professor
Department of Psychology
University of Utah

# Preface

This book presents the theory of Communication Privacy Management (CPM) to study private disclosures. CPM is considered a practical theory and is designed to provide an explanation for communicative issues about privacy that individuals face in the everyday world. The development of this theory has taken approximately 20 years. At this writing, the theory is in its young adulthood and ready to be presented in book format. If this theory is usable, it will continue to grow and change as it is applied to practical problems.

Initially, I began this endeavor out of frustration with finding so few theoretical perspectives to contextualize a way to understand disclosure. Thanks to Irwin Altman, I was able to see how the metaphor of *boundary* might be useful in coming to grips with the disclosure process. His move to use the notion of boundary provided the backdrop needed to cast a frame for studying disclosure. Equally significant, was Altman's focus on privacy. From his works, I realized that many of the early studies implied that private information was a core feature of disclosure; however, privacy did not appear to be identified as central to the study of disclosure. Once a conceptual shift was made to define private information as that which individuals revealed, many more issues about the process of disclosure and its underlying aspect of privacy became apparent. I would like to take this opportunity to thank him for his contribution to this volume and his generous words in the foreword.

I published several studies with coauthors outlining the fledgling principles of the theory early in my career (e.g., Petronio, Martin, & Littlefield, 1984; Petronio & Martin, 1986). Each of these studies challenged me to conceptualize the way people deal with privacy and disclosure as a dialectic. In 1991, I attempted a more comprehensive approach to identify main principles of this theory. Robert Craig, editor of *Communication Theory* in 1991, published that first attempt which deserves a thank you, as do the reviewers. In the initial publication, using the term "Communication Boundary Management," I proposed a micro-theory limiting the ideas of privacy management to a marital dyad (Petronio, 1991). The argument for this first proposal was to examine a specific relationship to reduce the set of circumstances found for privacy management to see where the pieces fit together.

With this micro-theoretical base, each new research project provided further evidence to expand the ideas of privacy management. In the intervening years, the theory has literally mushroomed into a macro-theory with more explanatory power. In this book, the reader will find many ways Communication Privacy Management gives meaning to common everyday practices of managing the dialectic of private disclosures. The theory has been renamed to reflect the central focus on privacy. My hope is that the reader will find a vocabulary to reflect and articulate choices people make when regulating their privacy.

I write this preface shortly after September 11, 2001. I cannot know the ways in which our privacy will be changed in the coming months and years as a result of this tragedy. However, I will put this theory to good use in examining the kinds of changes we will experience.

I would like to take this opportunity to thank a number of people who have helped develop the ideas within this book. Like most creative works, they stand on the shoulders of others whose ideas form the building blocks. Most significantly, I would like to thank my husband, Charles R. Bantz, who tirelessly listened and commented on my considerations concerning this theory. He has offered numerous directions and counterarguments forcing me to really think about the proposals I was making. He is my colleague, friend, and someone I care about deeply. My daughter Kristen E. Petronio also deserves recognition. She has been my inspiration for a number of proposals made in this theory and is a constant source of information. She consistently provides proud moments and always keeps me centered. Besides Charles, she is my other best friend.

I would like to thank Dudley D. Cahn, the series editor, for his continued faith in this project and support during the development of this volume. In addition, there are a number of colleagues and students deserving recognition, but I will start with one of the first graduate students I had at the University of Minnesota, Professor Dawn O. Braithwaite. Her dissertation on privacy and disabilities was an early testimony to the possibility of CPM being a practical theory and she continues to apply CPM to family issues. Dr. Braithwaite has been a trusted friend and advocate of my work on this theory.

Ironically, it was her invitation to teach a Ph.D. seminar on privacy at the University of Nebraska that provided one of the most enjoyable experiences I had in developing the ideas for the macro-theoretical proposal found in this book. Of particular note is Jack Sargent, now a professor at Kean University, who was especially instrumental in bringing issues to light. He completed his dissertation using the theory to examine nonverbal behaviors that accompany explicit and implicit disclosures, a fine example of theory application. Jason Thomas, Jeff Cook, and Ana Cruz pushed and pulled the views I had on CPM around in so many different ways that the theory literally grew before my eyes. A thank you is also in order for John Caughlin. As a faculty member attending that class, he kept me honest by limiting my wiggle room when I had no ready answers, and Bill Seiler, as chair, for his constant support.

During the same summer, I was recognized as the Cowperthwaite Visiting Scholar at Kent State University, where I also taught a seminar on privacy and disclosure. This Ph.D. seminar was as instrumental as the one in Nebraska in stimulating new ideas and inspiring innovative ways to think about CPM. In addition, the Kent State students provided so many stories to illustrate the concepts that I will have a ready storehouse for years to come. I would like to thank Maria Alfano, Angie Planisek, Paula Horvath, Susan Christopher, Sara Cornette, Kyra Rothenberg, Xi Wang, Marcia Everett, Keren Eyal, and Narissra Punyanunt. Finally, Rebecca and Alan Rubin deserve a hearty thank you for their invitation and opening their home.

During the years at Arizona State University, I have worked with many students on this theory. Everyone contributed; however, two stand out. First, I would like to acknowledge Mary Claire Morr, who participated in helping to develop many of the ideas in this book, particularly the dialectical argument. She has an excellent mind and is a delight as a colleague. Along with Mary Claire is Susanne Jones. Now at the University of Wisconsin, Milwaukee, Susanne also is an excellent colleague. She was a coparticipant in developing the ideas about confidants and enthusiastically contributed to many of the concepts of CPM theory.

Now at Wayne State University, I am again fortunate to encounter yet more graduate students who have much to give. In particular, Laura Andea keenly embraced the ideas of CPM and used her math background to suggest applying set theory to describe coordination. She is a valuable colleague who has assimilated the ideas of CPM into her vision of everyday life. David Cichocki, a graduate student at Wayne State, has been a most able assistant. Both Craig Allen Smith, the chair at Wayne State and Dean Linda Moore have provided needed support.

Many of my coauthors are featured in this book and their contributions will become evident as the reader pages through this volume. Thanks to all of them for their undying faith and constant support. A final note of thanks to the artist Mircea Teodorescu for supplying artwork for the book's cover. He is from Romania studying at Wayne State University for his Ph.D. in engineering. Mircea worked hard to capture the sense of ever-changing dynamics of privacy boundaries and his efforts paid off. Thank you Mircea. Finally, thanks to the SUNY editors, Cathleen Collins, Ronald Helfrich, and Priscilla Ross. I wish all an enjoyable and productive read.

# 1

# Overview of
# Communication Privacy Management

> Private life is not something given in nature from the
> beginning of time. It is a historical reality, which different
> societies have construed in different ways. The boundaries
> of private life are not laid down once and for all; the divi-
> sion of human activity between public and private spheres
> is subject to change. Private life makes sense only in rela-
> tion to public life.
> —Prost, *Public and Private Spheres in France*

Private disclosures epitomize the paradox of managing a public persona
while maintaining the dignity of one's private life (Westin, 1970). Talking about our private feelings in public is not always easy. In fact, it is often
risky because we might feel embarrassed, uncomfortable, or somehow
exposed. For instance, a friend of mine recently went to the doctor complaining of chest pains. She felt uncomfortable talking about these pains
because she thought she was too young to have something as dramatic as
a heart condition. Nevertheless, she went at her husband's request. However, when she started telling the doctor the reason for her visit, she
revealed only some of the symptoms, waiting to see if the doctor seemed
concerned. She thought that if the symptoms she disclosed were nothing,
she would not go into depth. In this way, she would avoid the further
embarrassment of giving them too much significance.

To tell or not to tell is a condition that we frequently face, yet the
question is complicated. The question is when to let others know our private side and when to let it stay confidential? As the example above illustrates, revealing private information is never a straightforward decision.
We are constantly in a balancing act. We try to weigh the demands of the
situation with our needs and those of others around us. Privacy has importance for us because it lets us feel separate from others. It gives us a sense
that we are the rightful owners of information about us. There are risks
that include making private disclosures to the wrong people, disclosing at
a bad time, telling too much about ourselves, or compromising others.

On the other hand, disclosure can give enormous benefits. Undoubt-
edly, recent studies on people facing traumas such as sexual abuse,

1

HIV/AIDS, or catastrophic illness all confirm the gains they receive from revealing feelings (Derlega & Barbee, 1998; Pennebaker, 1995). We also may increase social control, validate our perspectives, and become more intimate with our relational partners when we disclose (Johnson, 1974). The balance of privacy and disclosure has meaning because it is vital to the way we manage our relationships. Revealing is necessary, yet we see evidence that people value privacy when they lament its apparent demise. For example, Alderman and Kennedy (1995) state that

> the issues [of privacy] are especially vital today as more and more of our privacy is stripped away. Private individuals join public figures in decrying "tabloid journalism" and complaining that the press can invade lives with impunity. Pro-choice advocates argue that a woman's right to make fundamental decisions is threatened by a hostile and intrusive government. Increasing concern about crime, terrorism, and calls for stricter law enforcement have led to measures expanding the authority of police to enter our homes, search our belongings, and intercept our communication. Moreover, the notion that information can be kept secret to any degree may simply vanish in cyberspace. (p. ix)

Clearly, both disclosure and privacy are important to maintain. Until recently, few theories have isolated a process to understand how people manage the relationship between revealing and concealing. This book presents a theoretical approach that gives us a rule-based system to examine the way people make decisions about balancing disclosure and privacy.

The theory of Communication Privacy Management (CPM)[1] represents a map that presumes private disclosures are dialectical, that people make choices about revealing or concealing based on criteria and conditions they perceive as salient, and that individuals fundamentally believe they have a right to own and regulate access to their private information. In order to fully grasp the nature of private disclosures, we not only have to consider the individual who is revealing or concealing, but we also must focus on how the decision affects other people. Thus, unlike previous research on "self" disclosure, CPM assumes that others are also central to discerning the tension between being public and private.

---

1. The name of the theory has been adjusted in this book from "Communication Boundary Management" to "Communication Privacy Management," better reflecting the focus on private disclosures. Though the theory uses a boundary metaphor to explain the management process, the name change underscores that the main thrust of the theory is on private disclosures.

CPM uses the metaphor of boundaries to illustrate that, although there may be a flow of private information to others, borders mark ownership lines so issues of control are clearly understood. Thus, regulating boundary openness and closedness contributes to balancing the publicness or privacy of individuals. The regulation process is fundamentally communicative in nature. Consequently, CPM theory places communication at the core of private disclosures because it focuses on the interplay of granting or denying access to information that is defined as private.

Before we begin, there is one point of clarification. The term, *private disclosures*, is used to mark a distinction from the more traditional "self-disclosure" literature. CPM refashions the notion of disclosure in three ways. First, the literature on disclosure, from Jourard's inception, principally attends to a process of disclosing that gives less consideration and definition to the content of disclosure. CPM makes private information, as the content of what is disclosed, a primary focal point. In this way, CPM sets parameters and gives substance to the heart of disclosures, that is, what is considered private. Second, CPM continues the tradition of looking at how people disclose; however, it offers a rule-based theoretical system to conceptualize that process. Third, disclosure is not just about the self if it is considered a communicative process. Thus, to fully understand the depth and breadth of disclosure, CPM does not restrict the process to only the self, but extends it to embrace multiple levels of disclosure including self and group. Consequently, CPM theory offers a privacy management system that identifies ways privacy boundaries are coordinated between and among individuals.

Each of us has a mental calculus that we use to decide whether to tell or keep private information. Communication Privacy Management Theory provides a way to understand that calculus (see Figure 1.1). The theory proposes *five basic suppositions* that underpin the *rule management system*. Based on these assumptions, CPM proposes rule management processes for privacy regulation. Five fundamental suppositions define the nature of CPM.

First, the theory concentrates on private information. Second, a boundary metaphor is used to illustrate the demarcation between private information and public relationships. Third, control is an issue for two reasons. One, people believe that private information is *owned* or *co-owned* with others; thus, they desire control over the boundaries. Two, revealing or concealing private information may lead to feeling vulnerable. Consequently, control is also important to ward off the potential for vulnerability. Fourth, the theory uses a rule-based management system to aid in decisions about the way boundaries are regulated. Fifth, the notion of privacy management is predicated on treating privacy and disclosure as dialectical in nature.

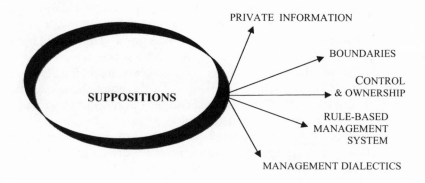

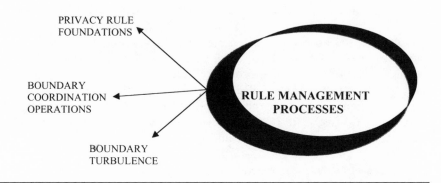

**Figure 1.1**
Overview of Communication Privacy Management Theory

Because CPM is a rule-based theory, it depends on three rule management processes. First, in order to manage privacy boundaries, people exercise control through implementing privacy rule foundations that manage revealing and concealing personally or collectively. Second, because people often co-own private information with others, they need to coordinate their collectively owned boundaries. CPM theory proposes we manage both personal boundaries and collective ones. Thus, we adjust levels of access to privacy boundaries that we own independently of anyone else. In addition, we also find that once disclosure takes place, people become involved in collective management that requires coordination with others.

There is also an overlap in the way that personal and collective privacy boundaries are managed. Both types of privacy management use three rule management operations: (a) boundary linkage, (b) boundary co-own-ership, and (c) boundary permeability. However, the kind of boundary coordination necessary for collective management may vary. Currently, the theory identifies three kinds of collective coordination patterns: (a) inclusive boundary coordination, (b) intersected boundary coordination, and (c) unified boundary coordination. Within the collective privacy patterns, the co-owners of the information determine rules that regulate linkages, control permeability, and determine the extent of ownership.

Third, though coordination is an objective, there are times when asynchrony is an outcome rather than achieving effective management. When coordination is less than smooth, boundary turbulence is a possibility. Discordant coordination often means that owners or co-owners of private information need to take corrective action to return boundary management back to a more synchronous level.

## THEORETICAL SUPPOSITIONS

### Supposition 1: Private Information

When we reveal, we disclose private information. Thinking about disclosure in this way is not new. In 1974, Goodstein and Reinecker suggested,

> while some information about one's self is rather public . . .
> there is other information about one's self that is rather private
> or intimate and is disclosed under special circumstances. This
> private, intimate information about the self ought to be the
> focus of both research and theorizing about self-disclosure. If
> this is not done, the term "self-disclosure" becomes vague and
> general . . . losing any special meaning. (p. 51)

Making *private information* the content of disclosure allows us to explore the way privacy and intimacy are separate but related fundamentally to the act of disclosure. Parks (1982) argues that in a vast number of studies and among textbook writers, self-disclosure is often equated with intimacy. In shifting the emphasis to private information, intimacy may be redefined as one possible outcome of revealing the self to others instead of being synonymous with self-disclosure. Attaining intimacy, that is, achieving a close personal relationship where the individuals are mutually dependent and engage in joint actions is more than sharing private information (Braiker & Kelley, 1979). Intimacy reflects all of the aspects of a close relationship. Disclosing private information may be one way that intimacy is established, but it cannot substitute for all of the dimensions of an intimate relationship. Hence, disclosure is not the same as intimacy, and not all of private information (even at its most risky) leads to intimacy.

Intimacy is the feeling or state of knowing someone deeply in physical, psychological, emotional, and behavioral ways because that person is significant in one's life. Private disclosure, on the other hand, concerns the *process* of telling and reflects the *content* of private information about others and us. However, besides intimacy, there are many reasons people tell their personal information. Individuals may wish to relieve a burden, gain control, enjoy self-expression, or possibly develop intimacy, yet, the goal is not always intimacy.

### Supposition 2: Privacy Boundaries

CPM theory uses the metaphor of boundaries to illustrate the lines between being public and private. Within the boundary, people keep private information (Petronio, Ellermers, Giles, & Gallois, 1998). However, because we are social beings, we also reveal private matters to others. In this theory, privacy is defined as the feeling that one has the right to own private information, either personally or collectively; consequently, boundaries mark ownership lines for individuals. Personal boundaries are those that manage private information about the self, while collectively held boundaries represent many different sorts of privacy boundary types (see Figure 1.2).

Collectively held privacy boundaries are such because the information is not solely about the self. However, they are differentiated according to the type of private information that is being regulated. Thus, for collectively held boundaries, the information may be private to a group, dyad, family, organization, or even a society as a whole. The collective selected becomes privy to the information that is about the group. Individuals can be responsible for personal as well as many different kinds of collective privacy boundaries.

Boundaries may be permeable or impregnable and are linked with other privacy boundaries. The lines of ownership may be ambiguous or clear. People work to strengthen their boundaries surrounding private information; they may also seek to attenuate the borders when they pursue intimacy. The boundaries may also become weakened by events outside the control of the owners. Thus, the boundary management may become turbulent when there is an invasion from outside sources or the management system does not work. Boundaries function to identify ownership of information leading to subsequent control over who knows about private matters.

There are *life span changes* for a person's privacy boundaries (Berardo, 1974) (see Figure 1.3). Very young children in U.S. society manage small privacy boundaries. Bok (1982) argues that "the ability to deal with secrecy is rooted in the child's growing consciousness of identity, and of being able to act, to intervene, to alter, to resist if need be" (p. 29). Being

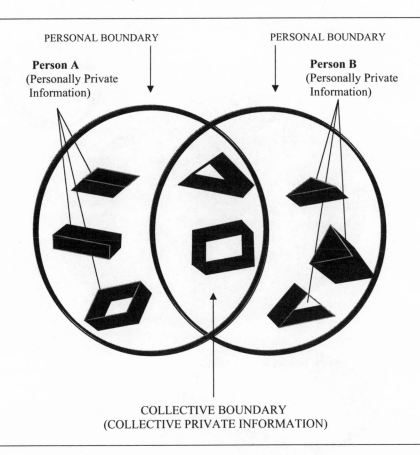

PERSONAL BOUNDARY                    PERSONAL BOUNDARY

**Person A**                              **Person B**
(Personally Private                     (Personally Private
Information)                            Information)

COLLECTIVE BOUNDARY
(COLLECTIVE PRIVATE INFORMATION)

**Figure 1.2**
Boundary Types: Personal and Collective

unable to differentiate between self and other at an early age and the cognitive complexity of a privacy management process makes it less likely that children are concerned about the maintenance of private information. However, families often begin to teach their children rudimentary forms of privacy rules when they express parameters for disclosure to others. Consequently, while a child is not necessarily concerned with privacy per se, family members begin to teach the child about privacy and ways to maintain it.

As children continue developing their separate identities, so too do they come to establish boundaries around information they consider personal. During the adolescent stage, one of the chief issues in the deindividuation process is the formation of privacy borders (Youniss & Smollar,

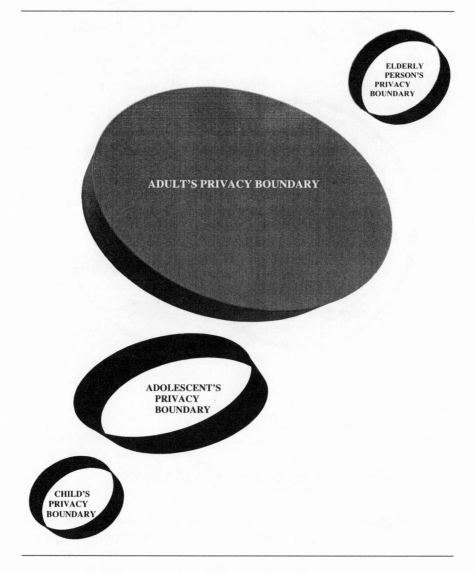

**Figure 1.3**
Boundary Life Span Changes

1985). As a result, the adolescent's boundaries expand to accommodate the increasing privacy needs that he or she develops. When individuals enter adulthood, their boundaries must increase so that they are able to control a great deal of private information about themselves and others.

Although privacy boundaries are large during adulthood, when individuals become more elderly, privacy often shrinks. Because of competing needs, such as issues of safety, for instance, privacy boundaries grow smaller as an older person requires someone to bathe him or her, take care of finances, or attend to health concerns (Petronio & Kovach, 1997). Thus, over a life span, privacy boundaries are modified to accommodate private information belonging to the individual.

### Supposition 3: Control and Ownership

There have been numerous discussions about the "right to privacy" in the United States. Schoeman (1984) argues that privacy is regarded as a *"claim, entitlement, or right* of an individual to determine what information about himself (or herself) may be communicated to others" (p. 3). We equate preserving privacy with maintaining personal dignity and autonomy and with safeguarding the self. "Although we live in a world of noisy self-confessions, privacy allows us to keep certain facts to ourselves if we so choose. The right to privacy, it seems, is what makes us civilized" (Alderman & Kennedy, 1995, p. ix).

Legally, people continue to grapple with the meaning of ownership rights (Alderman & Kennedy, 1995; Gavison, 1984). In spite of the legal controversies, when someone tries to take control over information that we believe is ours, we claim a violation of privacy (Schoeman, 1984). Ownership and control are important to each other. Because the information belongs to us, we want to determine who is privy to it and who is not. Through control, we may protect against unwanted exposure. "Control . . . is one way of setting the conditions which make up privacy or for determining the content of the private activity" (Laufer, Proshansky, & Wolfe, 1974, p. 13).

CPM argues that because people consider private information something they own, and over which they desire control, they both reveal and conceal the information. Individuals want to be in control because there are risks as to how this information is managed. Accordingly, people feel the right is theirs to determine what others know about them. Individuals feel violated when others (like credit card companies) find out something about them without their permission. It does not fit their calculus. People are not in control of something important that belongs to them—their information (Johnson, 1974). Sometimes people work hard to get back control by canceling subscriptions or changing doctors when influence over the information is compromised. Individuals want the information to stay within their domain—their privacy boundaries.

We manage control across two types of boundaries and exercise *levels of control* within each type of boundary. Since CPM contends that privacy boundaries are multiple in nature, we regulate ownership and concurrent control for both personal and collective boundaries. We have personal ownership of private information that is about the self and we expect the right to control the boundary regulating concealing and revealing. At the same time, we co-own private information that we have shared or has been shared with others. Collectively owned information is controlled mutually by those privy to it and those who are considered to be within the boundary. When we are told private information by others, we enter into a contract of responsibility to be co-owners of the information.

We are co-owners of many types of private information. For example, we not only control our personally owned private information, we also are given information that belongs jointly, and we even have private information that belongs to our whole family (Vangelisti, 1994). There may be private information belonging to a corporation where we are employed or to groups of which we are members. Consequently, on many levels, we often co-own information with others. In each case, we erect boundaries around the private information to mark the lines of ownership and control.

Hence, control that maintains ownership rights is important for both personal boundaries and for collectively held boundaries. While control helps preserve ownership, the need for it also suggests that private information is not just a possession. Instead, embedded in the notion of owning private information is the potential for vulnerability. The choice to share the information or keep it often hinges on a risk-benefit ratio for those involved. We know that revealing exposes us to a certain amount of vulnerability, but so does concealing. Thus, the possibility of risk heightens the significance of control issues for privacy management. We feel the need to control our risk-benefit ratio by determining how much vulnerability we are willing to experience. Because of the possible liabilities found within ownership and co-ownership of private information, we engage in boundary control for personal and collectively held boundaries.

However, we exercise varying levels of control (see Figure 1.4). For example, when our boundaries are thick and we do not allow much accessibility, we maintain high levels of control over the private information. Individuals also may employ moderate control where they would have somewhat thinner boundaries. In addition, people may have very thin boundaries resulting in less control and more openness. Nevertheless, control and issues of ownership are salient in privacy management.

### Supposition 4: Rule-Based Management System

The management system provides a structure for understanding the way that private information is handled. Because CPM argues that boundary

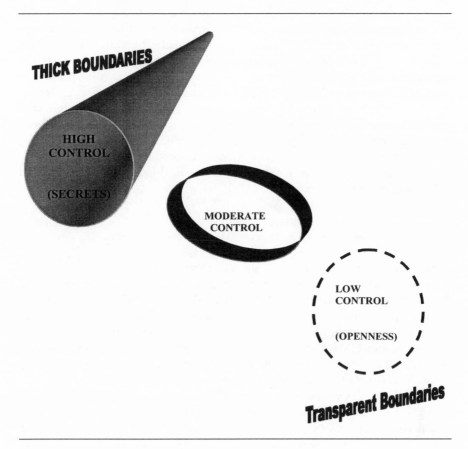

**Figure 1.4**
Levels of Control: Privacy Boundaries

regulation occurs on two interrelated levels, personal management and collective systems, we need to examine the way the elements and assumptions work for personal and collective boundaries. Thus, when we control access on a personal level, managing private information that belongs to us, the information is singularly owned.

Collective management systems represent times when we are co-owners of private information. Once a disclosure is made to someone, whether the recipient is a willing partner or not, he or she is expected to take on a certain level of responsibility for managing the information revealed (Petronio, 2000a). CPM proposes that initial disclosures set into motion a need for boundary coordination because there is an expected guardianship of the information often assumed by both the discloser and recipient.

The rule management system depends on three management processes. The first process is that of privacy rule foundations representing the way the rules develop and their properties. The second is the process of boundary coordination. This process reflects how privacy is regulated through rules when people are engaged in managing collective boundaries. Third, boundary turbulence signifies the assumption that coordination does not always function in a synchronized way. Consequently, there are times when people are unable, for a variety of reasons, to work together so that they have a smooth coordination process. Boundary turbulence illustrates when boundary coordination goes astray and rules become asynchronized.

### Supposition 5: Privacy Management Dialectics

In general, "dialectics" refer to the assumption that in social life, people experience tensions between opposites and contradictions. Though some have questioned whether CPM is dialectical, the basic thesis of the theory is grounded in the unity of dialectics including disclosure-privacy, concealing-revealing, public-private, openness-closedness, and autonomy-connectedness (Baxter & Montgomery, 1996). The following discussion illustrates the way CPM is both consistent with and different from other dialectical approaches explaining disclosure events.

The dialectical tension considered in the theory of Communication Privacy Management concentrates on the forces pulling between and with the needs of being both private through concealing and public through revealing. There is a clear simultaneity of actions toward and away from disclosing and remaining private. The pull between and with private behaviors and public disclosures is not an easy equation. Revelations make information public. The degree of publicness depends on a number of issues, such as how many people are privy to the information, how much is disclosed, and who receives the information. Nevertheless, once a person discloses private information, it becomes a little less private and more public. Most of the existing research on self-disclosure only considers the revelation dimension of the equation without taking into account what a person is giving up when he or she does disclose.

Considering the other side of the equation, we may measure our degree of privacy only in comparison to how public we are with others. For example, celebrities may not have given much thought to privacy until their new status thrusts them into the public arena. Once there, celebrities come to realize that having control over private information is important to maintaining their persona. Finding themselves in the limelight, they no longer are able to take a break from presenting or managing their image, even in the most secluded areas of their lives. The more public they are, the more narrowly they come to define their privacy. However, they are also more protective of the privacy they still own. These dialectical forces are critical to understanding how people manage their public and private lives. The dialectical underpinning for CPM has a number of dimensions in common with leading dialectical perspectives. However there are aspects of the CPM theory that deviate and extend current thinking about dialectics in communication.

Those advocating a dialectical perspective for disclosure have focused their energies on understanding openness or disclosure in relationship to the opposing force of closedness or privacy. Several scholars lead the way. Altman (1974, 1993; Altman, Vinsel, & Brown, 1981), Baxter (1993, 1994, 1988, 1990; Baxter & Simon, 1993; Baxter & Widenmann, 1993; Baxter & Wilmot, 1984), Montgomery (Baxter & Montgomery, 1996; Montgomery & Baxter, 1998), and Rawlins (1983, 1991, 1992) are among those who have both theorized and conducted research on dialectics, particularly in the context of relationships.

## Contradictions

Although CPM is considered dialectical by Petronio, the particular dialectical perspective taken within the theory is similar to and different from the positions held by Baxter and Montgomery (1996; Montgomery & Baxter, 1998) and Altman (1975; Altman, Vinsel, & Brown, 1981). Using the four shared assumptions of dialectical perspectives proposed by Baxter and Montgomery (1996) (e.g., contradictions, dialectical change, praxis, and totality), we can see the way a dialectical position is defined in CPM theory. For most dialectical theorists, the discussion of dialectics centers on a dialogue about contradictions (Altman et al., 1981; Baxter & Montgomery, 1996; Rawlins, 1992). Baxter and Montgomery (1996) state that contradictions are "the dynamic interplay between unified oppositions" (p. 8) reflecting two types of opposites, logical and functional. Logical opposites are defined as X and not X. Functional opposites, on the other hand, are identified as "X and Y, where both X and Y are distinct features that function in incompatible ways such that each negates the other" (Baxter & Montgomery, 1996, p. 8).

As with Altman's boundary regulation theory, Petronio argues that CPM adopts the functional approach rather than the logical approach to opposites. Thus, CPM does not claim that the type of contradiction considered is that which is private and not private. Instead, CPM suggests that privacy and disclosure are opposites having distinct features from one another that function in incompatible ways. Disclosure is not privacy and privacy does not represent the act of disclosure. Nevertheless, the two concepts reflect polar opposites.

The unity of opposites is another aspect of contradiction that is defined in two ways. One, the unity of identity suggests that each opposition "presupposes the existence of the other for its very meaning" (Baxter & Montgomery, 1996, p. 9). CPM adopts this perspective by arguing that disclosure is meaningful only in relationship to privacy. In other words, disclosing implies that we are giving up some measure of privacy. However, disclosure cannot occur if there exists no private information that can be told to others. Correspondingly, CPM also accepts the contention that there is interactive unity for privacy-disclosure. Thus, privacy is a necessary condition that one protects or gives up through disclosure. In addition, CPM offers multiple oppositions to privacy. Hence, not only is privacy-disclosure considered, but also the related opposites of revealing and concealing, public-private, autonomy-connectedness, privacy-deception, and openness-closedness are illustrated in this volume.

Some confusion about the legitimacy of CPM as a dialectical theory is grounded in the way Baxter and Montgomery frame CPM as dualistic rather than dialectical. Hence, they assert that CPM treats the oppositional forces of privacy and disclosure as static and independent of one another, coexisting in a parallel form, rather than treating it as dynamic. By comparison, Baxter and Montgomery propose that treating disclosure as dialectical should "emphasize how parties manage the simultaneous exigency for both disclosure and privacy in their relationships and, especially, how the 'both/and' ness of disclosure and privacy is patterned through their interplay across the temporal course of the relationship" (Baxter & Montgomery, 1996, p. 10).

CPM theory is framed as a dialectical management system that takes into account the simultaneous regulation of privacy in light of the disclosure of private information (Petronio, 1991). Although the reason for suggesting that CPM is dualistic is not completely clear, one possible clue is found in the focus on the notion of equilibrium and balance in the earlier versions of the theory. Altman, et al. (1981) offer an alternative to the definition of unity given by Baxter and Montgomery. Thus, Altman and his colleagues point out that, in addition to complementarity and integration, the strength and balance of opposites should be considered.

Altman et al. offer two ways of thinking about strength and balance of opposites that shed light on CPM's use of balance. First, they point out that we could assume "polarities always partially intersect and that one or the other pole never becomes so strong that it completely contradicts its opposite" (Altman et al., 1981, p. 121). This idea is similar to the unity of identity proposed by Baxter and Montgomery, however, the related concern of Altman et al. in this regard extends the discussion to balance.

Hence, Altman and his colleagues point out that the psychological sense of homeostasis, equilibrium, and balance is inconsistent with the underlying thesis of dialectics. Yet, the interpretation of balance adopted by Altman et al. is in harmony with a dialectical perspective and is one that has been assumed by CPM theory from the beginning.

Thus, Altman et al. argue that balance should be defined in terms of relative strengths. In other words, they suggest that dialectical opposites shift in strength given the circumstances, individual needs, or variations that evolve out of interaction between people. They refer to this shifting process as adaptiveness, where no one opposite has ultimate dominance, but where there is movement in focus without giving up the significance of the dialectical relationship between the two opposites.

Perhaps another way to reflect on the idea of balance is to understand that "assessment" is an alternative word for balance. Considering the body of literature based on CPM, assessment as a replacement for balance fits effectively with the idea of boundary management. Thus, CPM theory has proposed that when we think about disclosure in relationship to privacy, we "assess" the maintenance of each before we opt to make some of our private information public while keeping other parts hidden away. In this way, we give relative strength to the part of the information we want disclosed publicly and relative strength to that part remaining out of view. However, without the tension between the two, we cannot determine the nature of the relative strengths for each in connection to the other.

Because CPM depends on this interpretation of balance, the theory is not aiming for equilibrium in the psychological sense. Instead, it argues for coordination with others that does not advocate an optimum balance between disclosure and privacy. As an alternative, the theory claims there are shifting forces with a range of privacy and disclosure that people handle by making judgments about the *degrees* of privacy and publicness they wish to experience in any given interaction. In other words, using boundary rules, people decide whether to give up some portion of one (disclosure or privacy) in order to have some part of the other (privacy or disclosure). Disclosing some private information does not mean giving up all privacy. Privacy still exists. Consequently, we cannot understand this connection without acknowledging the relative tensions of the two opposites in a kind of unity.

## Dialectical Change

When we consider dialectical change, Baxter and Montgomery argue two combinations of issues. First, they note that change may be based on efficient cause or formal cause. Efficient cause represents a linear antecedent-consequent relationship. Formal cause is a more patterned relationship among phenomena. Second, Baxter and Montgomery point out that change may be considered teleological (thesis-antithesis-synthesis) or is a spiraling change with no end state. On the first issue of change, CPM follows a formal cause perspective similar to Altman's transactional theory (his extension of his original boundary theory). On the second issue of change, CPM argues a combination of teleological and spiraling change. Though other dialectical theorists may argue that the definitions of each type of change model are incompatible, there is room for aspects of each to converge into an alternative way of examining change.

**Formal cause option.** Following the formal cause option, CPM theory proposes that it is more fruitful to consider the whole disclosure-privacy process, including the way patterns change in a disclosure event for *both* the person revealing and the confidant. CPM argues that without focusing on the mutual relationship between the sender and receiver, a complete understanding of the communicative exchange is not possible. Without considering the person revealing and the individual(s) listening to the private information, we are not able to fully appreciate the complexity of the event. In addition, we must consider how change takes place over time within and across multiple privacy boundaries—allowing for rule change over time, understanding the nature of boundary coordination, and examining change when the behaviors are unpredictable—to fully grasp the fluidity and complexity of change for each disclosure-privacy event. Thus, formal cause best reflects the way CPM defines change for revealing and concealing episodes because it considers the whole of the process.

Framing the model of dialectical change used in CPM falls outside of the distinct categories proposed by Baxter and Montgomery (1996). The dialectical model CPM follows is not as clear-cut, although it fits portions of both the teleological approach and the idea of spiraling change proposed by Baxter and Montgomery. In addition, aspects of the openness-closedness cycles suggested by Altman et al. contribute to the way change is treated in CPM.

**Teleological model.** CPM ascribes to a teleological model as individuals disclose, giving up a measure of privacy, thereby initiating a linkage where there is the formation of (at the least) a dyadic boundary. Once that dyadic boundary exists and the individuals are co-owners, the information becomes collectively controlled through negotiated rules about permeability for boundary maintenance. Thus, one pole (disclosure) becomes more dominant (thesis), which in turn sets in motion a change in the opposing pole (privacy) such that some private information is relinquished (antithesis). The synthesis occurs when that disclosive message moves from being personal in definition, transcending into a dyadic boundary.

The synthesis is indicated by co-ownership of the information and the necessity of formulating mutually agreed upon boundary rules to regulate the newly established dyadic boundary. However, CPM also allows for the continuation of tensions, even when a type of synthesis is achieved. Thus, although coordination represents a process that attempts to maintain the synthesis, CPM argues that there are times when coordination fails. As a result, boundary turbulence erupts when people are unable to abide by or agree on mutual rules for boundary regulation thereby disrupting synchronized coordination.

**Linear and spiraling change models.** Although Baxter and Montgomery appear to suggest that any one theory cannot ascribe to both a teleological model and a spiraling change model, dimensions of the spiraling change model also occur within CPM in both linear and cyclical ways. However, the cycle of change may be closer to the proposal of Altman et al. than Baxter and Montgomery. Consequently, linear change is illustrated by the way individuals manage their personal or collective boundaries using rules that permanently modify the nature of their boundaries or the ways they regulate them.

For example, as newly married couples determine mutually held privacy rules for their marital privacy boundaries, they are also laying the foundation for what will become a family boundary. When children are incorporated into this family structure, they are taught privacy rules the parents establish for family private information.

Eventually, those boundary rules for family private information may become more concrete, forming family orientations that regulate the family boundary. Thus, as rules become more stable, the resulting orientations are often noticed by statements such as: "in my family, we never talk about our parents' salaries to people outside." This movement from dyadic to family boundaries with concomitant rules illustrates how we might have linear change over time.

CPM also assumes a spiraling interplay of disclosure-privacy opposites. Thus, "boundary rule change" often operates within "a model of indeterminacy in which two opposing tendencies simply continue their ongoing interplay, although the meaning of the interplay is fluid" (Baxter & Montgomery, 1996, p. 12). Through rule change, boundary connections among and between people become linked and disengaged in a spiraling fashion. Boundaries come together and pull apart depending on the ebb and flow of private information being maintained. Through the examination of rule change, we see the fluidity of the patterns that constantly come into existence, change, or dissipate. For example, CPM theory proposes ways that rules change to accommodate entrance into existing boundaries and subsequent socialization to learn operating rules for the collectivity. In addition, there are triggered rules that respond to changes in disclosure expectations, reflecting the need for adjustments to old rules to fit a new circumstance (e.g., divorce). Further, rule change may become salient when current rules fail to meet disclosure-privacy needs and require a complete overhaul.

In a number of instances, boundary management means dealing with repeated and newly established patterns. These patterns require a dynamic mechanism (rule change) allowing for an ebb and flow of revealing-concealing in multiple circumstances across many boundary lines. Thus, changed rules may result in alterations of the way people cycle through periods of openness-closedness or represent variations on the degree of revealing-concealing.

## Totality

In general, totality refers to understanding phenomena in relation to other phenomena. Baxter and Montgomery propose two ways to consider totality, through the location of contradictions and interdependence among contradictions. They claim that dialectical tensions are located at the level of interpersonal relationships. This assertion moves the unit of emphasis (analysis) away from sole focus on the individual and into a relational arena. "Dialectical tension is thus jointly 'owned' by the relationship parties by the very fact of their union" (Baxter and Montgomery, 1996, p. 15). CPM theory is both consistent with and different from this definition of totality.

On one level, CPM theory locates contradictions squarely within relationships as Baxter and Montgomery propose. Thus, CPM argues that people co-own private information and coordinate their efforts to manage the degree of access others have to it. In addition, disclosures are made to others linking them relationally into a jointly "owned" privacy boundary. Totality takes place when revelations are made and privacy is shared.

However, CPM is different from the proposal of Baxter and Montgomery in two ways. First, CPM expands the idea of totality to accommodate multiple kinds of relationships. Thus, privacy boundaries may not only be interpersonal, as with intimate partners and friendship relationships, but they may also include groups of people such as families, work groups, organizations, and societal institutions. Anywhere people are linked through the sharing of private information constitutes a level of totality because everyone privy to this information is expected to enter into a bond that establishes rules for boundary regulation.

The coalescing factors are the sharing and management of private information on a collective level. The private information is jointly owned by all members within the privacy boundary. As such, they need to coordinate the development, usage, and regulation of boundary rules to manage the ebb and flow of co-owned private information to those outside the boundary.

Individuals, therefore, participate in collective ownership of many different privacy boundaries. For each, the process of synchronization is necessary in order to effectively control the tension between disclosing and concealing private information within the boundary. Thus, people within the boundaries must coordinate with others so that the rules are known and used according to agreed-upon ways. When this is accomplished, the boundary regulation process is synchronized and coordination takes place. However, CPM allows for the difficulty of achieving synchronicity and argues for instances of boundary turbulence. Asynchronicity or turbulence occurs when the rules for managing the tensions between privacy and disclosure somehow fail to be coordinated among the boundary members. Asynchronicity may occur for a variety of reasons. For instance, a confidant may not want to be linked into a boundary by knowing the disclosed information. People may presume the listener is interested only to find out that the recipient is unwilling to participate in boundary regulation.

The second way that CPM differs from the definition of totality given by Baxter and Montgomery is in allowing for a personal privacy boundary. The individual is given the right to maintain personally private information within CPM. In this way, CPM is closer to the position advocated by Altman in his boundary theory. The basic mechanisms that function to develop and change boundary rules for collectives are the same for individuals. CPM argues that one way collective boundaries are formulated is through linkages made when individuals decide to reveal personally private information.

When personal information is shared, it moves into a collective domain where the information is no longer under the sole control of the individual. Joint ownership, therefore, means relinquishing unilateral control. Thus, through the disclosure of personally private information, collective boundaries are established. CPM lets us understand the "self-disclosure" process on an individual level, gives a way to track the transformation of individual boundaries into multiple ones, and provides a means to comprehend decisions people make through rule usage to manage any number of privacy boundaries. Hence, at a fundamental level, Baxter and Montgomery argue that disclosure is a cocreation between people. Alternatively, CPM proposes that the disclosure of private information may be the province of the individual, but once it is "disclosed" the boundary shifts into a co-owned entity where the rules for boundary regulation must be cocreated.[2] Consequently, CPM affords individuals the right to own private information independent of others, yet it also shows what happens once people share this information with others.

**Interdependence.** Baxter and Montgomery also advocate the interdependence among contradictions. The knot of contradictions (principal and secondary) is evident in CPM theory. As discussed earlier, CPM argues that the privacy-disclosure dialectic is the principal tension. However, many secondary contradictions interface with privacy-disclosure. For instance, when people enjoy privacy, this condition also allows for autonomy. Yet, there is the opposition of disclosure where we find connectedness. In some circumstances, recipients are reluctant confidants (Petronio, 2000c). Being drawn into a privacy boundary unwillingly impacts the dialectics of autonomy-connectedness and freedom-responsibility. The knot of contradictions is also seen when new privacy boundaries are formed or old boundaries need modification; the adjustments people make effect stability and change.

**Internal and external contradictions.** In addition to principal and secondary contradictions, Baxter and Montgomery propose that the knot of contradictions also includes interplay between internal and external contradictions. Internal contradictions are representative of "within boundary" issues. Consistent with this distinction, CPM claims that when individuals are within dyadic, group, family, organizational, or societal privacy boundaries, there is a necessity to formulate "within group" regulation rules that control the access and protection of the private information. Once the rules are established, the collectives then must abide by the agreed-upon rules in making judgments about the flow within and outward to others. The within boundary activities revolve around rule maintenance (e. g., development of rules, rule adjustments, and sanctions for breaches of rules) that taps into many of the interfacing dialectics discussed earlier.

The external contradictions are represented by two types of "across boundary" activities. First, because we are social, people simultaneously engage in administering multiple privacy boundaries. The interface between managing personal, dyadic, group, family, organizational, and/or

---

2. CPM also proposes that there are times when disclosure is mutually shared giving the illusion of co-creation. Thus, the establishment of collective boundaries does not necessarily occur when only one person discloses. Instead, two people could theoretically enter into a conversation wherein they reciprocate disclosure co-creating a dyadic privacy boundary.

societal privacy boundaries means there are always external dialectical tensions outside of a particular privacy boundary. For example, while functioning with a marital relationship, the partners also want to maintain their own personal privacy boundaries to preserve autonomy. Within families, members must find ways to manage dyadic boundaries between siblings, for example, while also abiding by boundary rules established for the family boundary.

Because across boundary activities are often difficult to maintain, there are times when individuals make mistakes about the rules. The boundary turbulence that erupts may be a result of issues such as misunderstanding the rules, believing in different rules, applying rules from one boundary to another, and ignoring collectively held rules. Boundary turbulence speaks to the complexity of across boundary maintenance and to the complications often found with maintaining multiple dialectical tensions. As a side note, making boundary turbulence central to managing dialectical tensions sets CPM apart from other dialectical theories. The concept allows the researcher a way to examine the inconsistencies in regulating tensions and captures the extent to which turbulence becomes a change agent for the dialectical contradictions.

The second aspect of external contradictions reflected in CPM is across boundary lines. Not only do people regulate across boundaries, but the basic idea of rules controlling the permeability, linkage, and ownership of the boundary directly addresses the way that external contradictions are managed. The decision criteria of culture, gender, motivations, context, and the risk-benefit ratio proposed by CPM underscores the contributing factors for judgments about regulating privacy-disclosure. These factors feed into the development of boundary rules that manage the ebb and flow of privacy and disclosure to those outside the boundary. As Baxter and Montgomery (1996) point out, the internal and external contradictions "interrelate in dynamic ways" (p. 16). Consequently, the rules not only need to be coordinated among individuals within boundaries, but they also need to be coordinated across boundaries as well in order for the interface of the privacy-disclosure dialectic and its correlate dialectical tensions to be functional for people.

**Contextualization.** The last aspect of totality Baxter and Montgomery (1996) propose focuses on the "contextualization of dialectical interplay" (p. 17). CPM differs somewhat from Baxter, Montgomery, and Altman, in that, Petronio makes a distinction between the notion of context and that of "contextualization," or where the dialectical management is taking place. Context for Petronio represents one dimension effecting decisions about the tension between privacy and disclosure. Consequently, context is an influencing factor in developing or changing rules that regulate this tension.

Although context is important, it is only one of several dimensions essential for privacy management. For CPM, communication is the focal point while context is a player in effecting that communicate exchange.

However, Altman, Baxter, and Montgomery all ascribe to the significance of dialectics situated within relationships. Clearly, CPM also recognizes that the very nature of communicative interactions presumes some type of relational connection. Thus, the contextualization or how the dialectical tensions are situated for privacy management assumes that whenever private information is disclosed, a privacy boundary is formed around the participants. Consequently, the dialectical tensions are situated in the kind of boundary formulated; however, those boundary parameters are often marked by the relationship between people (e.g., marital, family, group).

### Praxis

Of all the dialectical characteristics, praxis has been the most widely addressed in CPM. Praxis reflects the notion that "people are at once actors and objects of their own actions" (Baxter & Montgomery, 1996, p. 13). Individuals are proactive and reactive simultaneously. To witness the outcome of praxis, we consider the practices used for disclosure episodes. Dindia (1998) argues that one way to see praxis in disclosure is through privacy regulation. Application of CPM to life circumstances has illustrated the practices of disclosure where people are both proactively making choices while reactively dealing with responses to those choices.

One example of praxis is seen with disclosure between marital couples. When couples are learning each other's communication styles, routines develop from decisions about privacy rules for both the disclosing spouse and receiving partner (Petronio, 1991). When partners use disclosure strategies that are ambiguous (e.g., hinting), for instance, receiving spouses must assess their choices for a response. Because the disclosure is implicit, receiving partners need to evaluate expectations in terms of responsibility and degree of autonomy desired.

In addition, the receiving partner often makes attributional searches to consider the reasons the spouse is hinting at some issue. Ultimately, the receiving spouse decides on a way to respond. Clearly, any response by the receiving partner triggers a reaction from the disclosing spouse. In this way, couples negotiate patterns of behavior that are used to coordinate the regulation of their emerging dyadic privacy boundaries. If the choices made seem compatible with expectations by both parties, a certain degree of fit occurs and predictable patterns of interaction emerge.

CPM has been applied to a number of investigations such as child sexual abuse (Petronio, Reeder, Hecht, & Mon't Ros-Mendoza, 1996), disclosure among individuals with HIV/AIDS (Greene & Serovich, 1996), and medical mistakes (Allman, 1995). In each case, the research identifies patterns of disclosure episodes found in privacy management for all parties involved in the dialectic of privacy-disclosure. The contribution that CPM makes is in giving a theoretical framework to understand the interface between individuals involved in a disclosure/privacy exchange. Thus, CPM allows researchers to consider not only an individual's "self-disclosure," but also the reactions of recipients and the counteractions of those initially setting the privacy-disclosure dialectic into a praxis pattern. The negotiation of rules, the choices to apply rules, the management of permeability, linkages, and ownership, and maintaining boundaries across and within, call for considering more than just the individual. The theory intersects the individual with the collective to gain a broader view of a specific communication phenomenon where people manage private information.

## PRIVACY RULE MANAGEMENT PROCESSES

CPM proposes that the degree of revealing and concealing is regulated through rule management processes. Thus, people use rules to regulate the degree of access to or protection of their private information. Privacy rules are used in all matter of managing revealing and concealing, for example, in determining who receives a disclosure, when, how much or how little, where the disclosure occurs, and how a person might conceal information. For instance, husbands might have rules for responding to their wives' questions about their appearance. Some men might answer every question with a polite response, perhaps saying, "Dear, you always look good in whatever you wear." Other men might gently offer an alternative suggestion or offer a brutally honest response. To capture the way privacy rules function overall, CPM identifies three rule management processes that include: (a) foundations of rules ranging from the way they are developed to the elements that make up their attributes, (b) their boundary coordination, and finally (c) their turbulent nature.

### Management Process 1: Privacy Rule Foundations

In general, the notion of rule foundations focuses on two main features, *development* and *attributes*. The first feature concentrates on the way that rules develop. Individuals use certain criteria such as cultural expectations, gender, motivation, context of the situation, and risk-benefit ratio to establish privacy rules. The second feature reflects the particular attributes of rules. There are two key dimensions: the way people acquire rules and the properties of these rules. Accordingly, for the first dimension, rules are acquired by learning preexisting rules or they are negotiated as people formulate new collective boundaries. For the second dimension, rules have four properties. First, they may stabilize, becoming routine for people. Second, rules may become so permanent that they form the basis for orientations to privacy. Third, rules may also change. Fourth, there are sanctions that people institute to control the use of rules.

### Privacy Rule Development

Rules are formulated based on decision criteria such as cultural expectations, gendered differences, motivations for revealing and concealing, the context of the situation, and the level of risk in revealing or concealing. Thus, there are five decision criteria used to develop privacy rules to manage our boundaries.

**Cultural criteria.** People are socialized into certain norms for privacy in their culture and those norms are basic to the way they conceive of privacy (DeCew, 1997). Thus, cultures may vary in the degree to which privacy plays a role in social life. For example, more individualistic cultures tend to value privacy, as illustrated by a German person's need for shutting doors to rooms in a home. However, almost every culture has some need for privacy (Altman, 1977; Schoeman, 1992). Consequently, each individual develops expectations for privacy, in part, by considering cultural values.

**Gendered criteria.** Though gender differences are being questioned in current research, there is evidence to suggest that men and women have different ways of defining privacy boundaries (Canary, Emmers-Sommer, & Faulkner, 1997; Petronio & Martin, 1986). Within a boundary system, men and women appear to have distinct sets of rules for judging how revealing and concealing should be regulated. Similar to cultural variations, men and women develop rule sets that are predicated on socialization and a unique view of privacy. This is not to say that they are precluded from coordinating those rule sets; however, men and women may initially come to an interaction with different visions of how privacy and disclosure work.

**Motivational criteria.** People also make judgments based on their particular motivations for privacy and disclosure. Some people are motivated to seek the opportunity to express their feelings, whereas others may have a greater need to mask their reactions to conversations (Jones & Archer, 1976). In addition, the same behavior may result from a variety of motivations: people seek control by disclosing certain information; however, they might likewise want self-clarification and disclosure to obtain it. Individuals may also be motivated to protect themselves from others. In all, goals and needs for regulating revelation and concealment form a basis for judgments about useful rules.

**Contextual criteria.** In addition to culture, gender, and motivation, the context of the situation may function as a critical element in formulating rules that regulate revealing and concealing. There are two elements of context, the social environment and the physical setting. The social environment includes contextual factors such as judging the appropriateness of raising a particular topic in a situation, changing circumstances, and the timing of revealing or concealing in a context. For example, when a person is newly divorced, he or she may need to talk about the experience to cope with his or her emotions. Not having been divorced before, the individual is challenged to establish new privacy rules to accommodate the change in his or her circumstance. Hence, the social environment influences rule development.

From the research by Altman and his colleagues (e.g., Altman et al., 1981), we find significant evidence that the physical environment plays a substantial role in the way people define privacy. In addition to marking territory, personal space, and issues of crowding, physical surroundings impact both our nonverbal behavior and our choices about revealing and concealing private information. Hence, the nature of some settings influences the decision rule to disclose or protect privacy. For instance, the Zuni home is described as a sacred place and therefore private (Werner, Altman, & Oxley, 1985):

> It is a "living thing," is blessed and consecrated, is a location for communication with the spirit world . . . , is a place for religious observances, and is a setting within which occupants reside, live, eat, and raise children. (Werner et al., 1985, p. 20)

This environment invites revealing private information.

In another example, the physical setting played an important role for children and adolescents in decisions to reveal sexual abuse (Petronio et al., 1996). Selecting the setting where the children told about their sexual abuse was a significant dimension of controlling the riskiness and making the decision to reveal. Consequently, in settings where a trusted other was engaged in mundane tasks, such as when the child and a disclosure target were watching television, or within a home considered a "safe haven," the children revealed their abuse. Thus, both the physical setting and the social environment combine to represent the context of the situation, forming another decision criterion that can be used to develop rules for boundary regulation and privacy management.

**Risk-benefit ratio criteria.** Because control over ownership is a significant element in managing privacy boundaries, rules that are developed take into consideration the level of felt vulnerability and expected advantages from revealing or concealing. Consequently, individuals evaluate the risks and benefits for granting or denying access to privacy boundaries. For instance, individuals may anticipate more benefits than risks from revealing and calculate the extent to which disclosure is a positive option. Rules that reflect that choice are developed and implemented. On the other hand, if risks are high, privacy protection may result and rules are established to maintain a desired level of privacy.

Because there is a potential for vulnerability, the consequences of telling or not telling are essential in formulating the access and protection rules people use to manage their privacy boundary. Thus, a risk-benefit quotient contributes to establishing the rules that manage privacy boundaries and function as a decision criterion. As a whole, these decision criteria form the basis for rule making. They contribute to people's judgments about how to manage the balance of privacy and disclosure.

### Privacy Rule Attributes

Rule attributes represent two dimensions that include the way people *acquire* rules and rule *properties*. In general, individuals acquire preexisting rules through socialization or negotiate rules in situations that call for changes or establishment of new rules. Once individuals learn the rules, they often put *sanctions* into place, preserving the nature of agreed-upon boundary rules. Rules also have a number of properties that function in a variety of ways, from depending on routinized rules that are stable to those triggered in novel situations.

**Rule acquisition.** People learn preexisting rules or negotiate new rules so that they can create collectively held rules for a particular privacy boundary. Thus, while some rules are learned anew, others are taught, as people become part of an ongoing boundary. The main way that these preexisting rules are acquired is through a socialization process. For example, families teach their children, as they grow, the expectations that the members have for the way that privacy relevant to the family is regulated. In addition, in the process, families teach their children ways to manage personally private information.

Likewise, organizations and groups that are ongoing, teach new members the set of rules is used to regulate collectively held privacy. For some businesses, elaborate training programs are used to ensure that new members understand and follow privacy rules. For example, many companies with top-secret government contracts have programs in place to secure the dissemination of this information.

Given that collectives engage in socialization of pre-existing privacy rules, it is not surprising to find that they also work to guarantee that new members abide by the collectively endorsed rules. Consequently, the members engage in enacting sanctions to reinforce the importance of following the privacy rules for collective boundaries.

As people formulate new collective boundaries, they negotiate the rules that they use jointly to manage the privacy boundary. They may use explicitly stated rules that function as the initial foundation of the collective rule structure. Alternatively, they use implicitly suggested privacy rules that may be more ambiguous making it difficult for participants to reach a consensus. Regardless, there is a need to determine how the newly formed collective boundary is managed. Thus, a period of negotiation takes place to accomplish this goal.

**Rule properties.** Rule attributes also have certain properties that reflect the dynamic nature of privacy rules. Rules can grow and change, but they can also be a stable factor in guiding privacy judgments. Thus, CPM proposes that rules can become *routinized* and highly dependable when they work well for the person or collectivity over time. However, while the rules give stability for privacy judgments, they are also flexible so they can meet changing privacy needs. For instance, a husband and wife may routinely avoid discussing their sex lives with their young children. Yet, the routine may change as their children grow into adults.

In some instances, privacy rules may become so well ingrained through repeated use that they function as a type of privacy value or *orientation* (Karpel, 1980). For example, some families state that, as a whole, they do not talk about their financial worth in public. All the members of the collectivity understand that, in their family, they do not talk to outsiders about finances. Other families might say that their family places importance on openness among its members, whereas they never talk to outsiders about private matters. These rules become so entrenched in the way families think about privacy that they reflect more stable values for the group.

On the other hand, rules can change when an event or situation *triggers* the need to reformulate them. For example, when someone gets divorced, he or she is used to disclosure patterns following a particular course in the dissolving marriage. The rules must change as part of the redefinition of their relationship. The divorced couple has to adjust the frequency, amount, depth, and breadth of private disclosures each makes to the former spouse. If they follow the same pattern used when they were married, their disclosure interactions would be more dysfunctional than functional. Hence, rules may be triggered, become routinized, or develop into more long-lasting expectations for privacy.

Finally, rule usage may be controlled by sanctions put into place by boundary members. Once those in the collective boundary come to an agreement about the rules regulating boundary access or protection, individuals who do not abide by these endorsed rules may find that others impose penalties for the infractions.

### Management Process 2: Boundary Coordination Operations

The second management process centers on boundary coordination. An important aspect of coordination is accepting that boundaries around private information include both personal and collective borders. Besides the fact that each individual has a personal boundary to manage, private disclosures extend to information that is coconstructed or information over which we are given guardianship by someone else.

As a result, comprehending the way privacy rules regulate revealing and concealing often goes beyond personal matters that affect only the self. For example, a woman may disclose that she is getting married unbeknownst to her family. She makes it clear that she wants the confidant to keep the information private until she tells her parents. This example shows that when a person confides, the recipient is held responsible for the information and a set of expectations is communicated by the discloser. In this sense, the confidant becomes the co-owner of the information.

We become co-owners in many ways. Besides being directly told, we are drawn into a boundary when we are privy to information about a third party, when there is a mutual or reciprocal disclosure, and when we learn private information by accident. Regardless of how we come to know private information, private lives often extend beyond one's own experiences, thoughts, and feelings. We are invited in or pulled into another's boundary and asked to protect someone else's sacred information. Ironically, we do not always live in complete isolation; instead, our private lives often include the responsibility of holding other people's disclosures in confidence.

Hence, the information that characterizes private lives spans more than what belongs solely to one person. Therefore, the way people coordinate privacy rules also takes into account this multidimensional focus. People manage private information from other family members, significant relational partners, groups to which they belong, organizations for which they work, and their own personal information all at the same time. The challenge is to coordinate a set of rules that manages the boundary around this information that is satisfying to all parties

In order for coordination to take place, the rules need to be agreed upon so that there is synchronicity between and among the co-owners. In other words, agreement must be reached so that each co-owner will abide by an established set of rules. Sometimes the guardian (co-owner) complies, at other times it is difficult to abide by the rules, and there are also situations where rules are not discussed or acknowledged.

For instance, a doctor knows that a patient with the HIV virus is continually having sex with unsuspecting partners. She is privy to this information and bound by doctor-patient confidentiality. However, she determines that she must disclose the patient's status to protect others from the disease. In this sense, she "co-owns" the knowledge of the patient's behavior. In her role as guardian, she feels the best way to handle the situation is to reveal the information. In this case, she does not follow the rules set by the discloser, but she initiates a variation of her own.

We live in a complicated social world where we co-own the knowledge of private matters on many levels. Thus, we are answerable for balancing many types of private information. To do so, we need rules guiding us toward ways to manage not only our own privacy boundaries, but also those we share with our spouse or relational partner, with groups in which we have membership, with our family members, with our professional associates, and even with our community. We coordinate rules to address the tension of revealing and concealing on each level with others whom we hold accountable and with those who hold us accountable for shared private information.

Coordination also depends on three distinct ways that boundaries are managed. Hence, boundary members regulate private information through rules that moderate boundary *linkage*, boundary *ownership* rights, and boundary *permeability*.

## Boundary Linkage

Boundary linkages represent the connections that form boundary alliances. Linkages occur in many ways and how a linkage is made can potentially influence the level of commitment a person has to negotiate rules for privacy management. For example, someone may overhear private information on a plane from a stranger. Because that person is privy to the information, he or she may feel somewhat responsible for preserving the information. Although one might argue that person is technically linked because he or she knows the information, that person is not the intended target and therefore have less of an obligation to negotiate privacy rules for management. Including a third party in a disclosure may also mean that the link is less compelling than if that person is the designated target who is supposed to be incorporated into the privacy boundary.

People are linked into a privacy boundary based on many issues. For example, linkage for a target may depend on attraction (Sote & Good, 1974), status (L. Brooks, 1974), gender (Sollie & Fischer, 1985), or relationship to the target (Derlega, Metts, Petronio, & Margulis, 1993). In addition, linkage may also be determined by willingness to form connections because of personality characteristics. For example, people who are more Machiavellian tend to be less willing to form bonds with others (Brown & Guy, 1983), whereas those who have secure attachment styles tend to be more able to connect their boundaries with others (Mikulincer & Nachshon, 1991).

## Boundary Ownership

We live in a world where we co-own private information on many levels. When people share personal issues, they expect a certain level of respect for the significance of that information. However, once the information is revealed, coordination is necessary to identify the specific nature of boundary lines. How much *responsibility* is expected and how much leeway a confidant has in determining who else hears the information are matters of judgment and negotiation.

Boundary ownership refers to *rights and privileges* individuals perceive they have and others accord them *as co-owners*. There are three issues embedded within the notion of ownership. *First*, the way boundary lines are drawn around private information must be mutually clear. When the parameters are clear, the rules for access and protection are unambiguous. For example, if a spouse tells his or her partner that he or she has a gambling problem, the spouse may make it clear that the information should remain within the dyadically created boundary. The partner is not privileged to talk about this information to anyone else and understands the parameters of co-ownership. However, when the boundaries are unclear or fuzzy, the confidant or co-owner often does not recognize or understand the rights and responsibilities or rules for managing the boundary.

Thus, when information is co-owned, rules mark where and how the boundary lines are drawn. Often sanctions are imposed when the boundary lines are clearly drawn. If confidants breach these expectations, the discloser may punish them by locking them out of further revelation or even reprimanding them. However, identification of ownership or co-ownership is not always obvious. Thus, the lack of clarity may lead to conflict over ownership issues.

The *second* dimension of ownership suggests that it is not static. Boundary lines may be extended or contracted to meet privacy needs. For instance, in some cases, a person may disclose and, therefore, extend a personal boundary into a dyadic boundary. As co-owners, the two may determine that it is acceptable to move boundary lines to include family members. Thus, a boundary that was originally personal may broaden to become part of a family boundary around private information owned by the members. In this case, all privileged members become co-owners. If the rules for boundary regulation are clearly articulated and explicitly discussed, the boundary lines are unambiguous for the members.

The *third* dimension of ownership reflects the level of congruity in boundary definitions between co-owners. At times, the definition of boundary lines becomes contradictory. For example, one person might think the lines around certain private information link another person into a boundary and the other person does not define the boundary lines in the same way. This situation might be witnessed when one partner does not wish to disclose previous romantic relationships, whereas the other partner feels he or she should be given that information. In this case, the boundary lines around ownership of private information are different for each person and lack congruity and synchronicity.

Likewise, conflict may erupt because of the incongruity of border definitions for certain kinds of disclosures. Similarly, synchronicity may also be a problem when only one person believes that certain private information should be shared and co-owned. Telling too much information is yet another example. This represents forcing ownership and therefore confounds boundary synchronization. The confidant becomes an unwilling co-owner and compels individuals to manage private information they did not wish to know and for which they did not agree to accept any responsibility.

**Boundary Permeability**

People manage varying degrees of revealing and concealing. When boundary access rules are used, they may lead to a range of behaviors, from granting complete access of the private information to only partial disclosure. When boundary protection rules are enacted, individuals may restrict or conceal private information. Levels of boundary permeability therefore range from open access (thin boundaries) to closed access (thick boundaries).

CPM argues that when the boundaries are closed and protection rules prevail, the information within the borders is more likely to be considered secret. By definition, then, secrets are a highly restricted set of private information. On the other hand, when boundaries are opened and access rules prevail, the information is more likely to be fully revealed. By definition, open access means unrestricted disclosure.

Although we do have secrets and people may be very open, more typically, people regulate the permeability to varying degrees through an array of access and protection rules. For example, people may completely hide health concerns from others for a period of time, cautiously expose flaws they find in themselves to certain others, use discretion in commenting on another's behavior, or be completely open with one other person. In each case, the permeability, that is how much information is allowed to pass through the boundary, varies depending on the rules for access and protection.

### Collective Coordination Patterns

The rules that regulate boundary linkage, boundary ownership, and boundary permeability for private information not only function for a personal management system, but also play a role in collective systems. However, the way linkage, ownership, and permeability are regulated varies depending on the kind of collective boundary coordination pattern people use. CPM proposes at least three kinds of collective coordination patterns. They include collective coordination that is *inclusive* where person A knows more about person B's private information than person B knows about person A's.[3] This means that inclusive management involves coordination that can be predicated on a power differential in ownership and control over the private information. We also find *intersected* collective boundary coordination where two or more people share private information in equitable ways. The coordination system involves the way two people mutually co-own and control the shared private information. Person A and person B equally manage the jointly held information. However, the collective management only pertains to information that has been mutually shared. For individuals participating in these boundaries, each continues to have personal control over all private information they own exclusively by themselves. Last, there is *unified* collective boundary coordination representing a situation where all members of the boundary are responsible for the jointly held private information, such as within families.

As this discussion suggests, there is a clear interrelationship among boundary linkage, ownership, and permeability for all collective boundary management systems. Yet, considering them separately, within each type of system, allows us to examine the mechanisms that help formulate the coordination people enter into as they manage multiple levels of private information. The distinction between a personal management system and

---

3. Although collective boundary coordination may include more than two people, for ease of discussion, the examples focus on only a dyadic boundary.

collective ones also allows us to recognize that we attempt to maintain control over personally held private information and at the same time engage in managing private information with others.

## Management Process 3: Boundary Turbulence

Collectively owning private information necessitates coordinating rules so that the individuals involved do not experience clashes over expectations about privacy management. Because coordination is complex and occurs on multiple levels, people often encounter boundary turbulence. Turbulence erupts in many ways throughout the coordination process. For example, people may violate or misuse privacy rules, hampering the ability to synchronize when, where, how, and with whom private information might become publicly disclosed. Turbulence may also be experienced because people use different criteria to develop rules and perceive dissimilar levels of risk concerning revealing and concealing. Boundaries may become turbulent when the level of permeability is not coordinated or when people create linkages that violate ownership expectations. Boundary turbulence illustrates that boundary coordination is not always smooth and that boundary regulation is not a perfect system.

Nevertheless, when there is boundary turbulence, individuals attempt to correct the problem and integrate new information into the rule system so that adjustments may be made to achieve coordination. In this way, privacy management is like other open systems. This theory leaves room for self-correcting actions to take place in order for the system to evolve and remain functional. Thus, people change the rules to fit their needs, accommodating new situations and different requirements so that they can maintain a certain level of control over privacy boundaries in their lives.

Communication Privacy Management Theory equips us with a way to comprehend the calculus we use to handle the tension between revealing and concealing private information. Given the importance we place on this communicative activity, it is essential to know why we make certain choices. Underpinning this theoretical proposal is the fundamental belief that privacy and disclosure are dialectical tensions. Throughout the book, we find a detailed map of a system that allows us to understand how people manage the privacy-disclosure dialectic. CPM gives us a way to consider the logic people use to make judgments about their private information.

## ORGANIZATION OF THE BOOK

This book presents a coherent theoretical proposal that helps guide us through the terrain of private disclosures. Chapter 1 outlines the major points and assumptions of Communication Privacy Management Theory. Thus, it lays the groundwork for using the theory to understand how revealing and concealing work as a dialectic and the way people use rules to make decisions about being public and private.

The CPM theory stresses that it is necessary to consider communicative interactions between people to grasp private disclosures. This theory offers concepts and structures to help see the way people coordinate the forces that influence choices about privacy. The book is organized to illustrate the fundamental elements of the CPM theory outlined in chapter 1.

Chapter 2 turns to a discussion about the foundations of rules and the way they are developed. Given that rules are fundamental to understanding decision making for boundary control and privacy management, we need to examine the nature of privacy rules and the basis upon which they are developed. Individuals use five decision criteria that underpin judgments they make about which rules to use. This chapter explains the use of these criteria and their development. In addition, the chapter also explains the second dimension of rule foundations, rule attributes.

Because a primary consideration for CPM theory is communicative interactions, chapter 3 highlights the communal nature of privacy management. We learn how people coordinate their boundaries with others through linkages, permeability, and ownership. The collective character of privacy management forces the issue of the roles a confidant plays in revealing and concealing.

Past investigations into disclosure have underestimated the significance of others in the revealing and concealing equation. People either tell private information to or withhold that information from other individuals. Consequently, confidants are fundamental to private disclosures. CPM argues for the need to seriously consider how a confidant is changed by the experience of receiving a private disclosure and the way a confidant changes a disclosure episode.

Chapter 4 presents collective coordination patterns that have emerged to date from research. In addition, the chapter focuses on four kinds of privacy boundaries and discusses how people engage in coordination at each level. Thus, in this chapter we see that two types of dyadic privacy boundaries, relational and marital, share commonalities because people coordinate with just one other person. However, there are also differences because the nature of the relationship factors into the revealing and concealing equation. As more people are involved in group boundaries, the issue of managing both personal and dyadic privacy boundaries becomes clear, as does the idea of regulating "whole boundaries" surrounding private information common to all members. This more complex boundary coordination process is most obvious in families and organizations. Because of the intricacies of boundary coordination, especially when there are many people involved, the management system fails at times.

Chapter 5 offers a discussion on boundary turbulence that illustrates how boundary coordination breaks down and the way people try to restore synchronicity to the management process. For example, when people betray others, there is little room for adequate boundary coordination and smooth regulation of privacy rules. In fact, the rules have been violated, just as they are when people spy on each other. Although these are deliberate acts throwing coordination into turmoil, people also make mistakes that have a disruptive effect. Making errors in judgment about expectations for recipients, miscalculating disclosure timing, and bungling rules for appropriate topics all cause coordination problems.

People may also be perplexed about markers for boundary lines. Considering when deception is really privacy can be difficult because the people involved are at odds over boundary ownership. Pretending to own someone else's private information and making it public is one way to think about gossip, another problem area for boundary coordination. Individuals also may run into boundary definitional predicaments, such as misusing public space as private, thus interfering with boundary coordination.

Finally, turbulence erupts when individuals are faced with privacy dilemmas. These are situations where people are given private information as confidants, accidentally come across private matters, or snoop and discover private information that puts them in a bind. If they talk about it, someone might get hurt; if they keep it confidential, someone might get hurt. Either way, the information is like the metaphorical "hot potato."

Chapter 6 concludes with a discussion about how CPM theory has been used to understand everyday problems. Three issues are presented that represent research using the CPM theory. First, medical mistakes are analyzed by considering the way physicians manage the double burden of acknowledging their misjudgments and having to conceal the information for fear of reprisals. Next, the chapter explores how CPM is instrumental in learning about disclosure and privacy concerning HIV/AIDS status. The chapter concludes with a more in-depth discussion of the way CPM helps us to understand the logic children use to disclose or conceal sexual abuse.

Communication Privacy Management Theory has provided a frame to investigate many different kinds of private disclosures. The hope of this book is to expand the way people think about revealing and concealing, embracing the notion of rule management, boundary coordination, and restoration after turbulence. From this shift in thinking about private disclosures, people may begin to recognize that revealing and concealing are rarely individual events. Instead, the choice to engage someone by telling private matters spreads responsibility to them, and the decision to block others out has both positive and negative consequences for relationships.

# 2

# Rule Management Process 1

## *Privacy Rule Foundations*

Chapter 1 presented an overview of Communication Privacy Management, highlighting the fact that this theory depends on a rule-based management system. Thus, although boundaries provide a metaphorical structure, rules make the management process work. Accordingly, it is useful to examine the basis upon which rules are generated, developed, and the way they function to accomplish privacy management.

Pearce (1976; Pearce & Cronen, 1980) and his colleagues (e.g., Harris, 1980) have argued that rules play a significant part in communicative interactions. Their work has given research a way to regard specific interaction patterns and isolate sequences of talk. Like CPM, they argue, "patterns of communication are always conjointly produced by two or more actors" (Cronen, Chen, & Pearce, 1988, p. 75). Their Coordinated Management of Meaning rules analysis focuses on the way structure in the conversation generates talk and how talking reconstitutes or changes structure (Cronen et al., 1988).

As a concept, using rules is a meaningful way to understand different kinds of communicative interactions, including revealing and concealing. Rules are particularly valuable to the Communication Privacy Management theory of private disclosure because they tangibly show the way people regulate and therefore coordinate their privacy boundaries with others. Decisions that depend on rules are made about the permeability, linkages, and ownership of our privacy boundaries (Fisher, 1986). Rules allow us to see the patterned actions that people employ to make their decisions about regulating private disclosures. Therefore, knowing the way rules develop and function is fundamental to comprehending boundary coordination, boundary turbulence, and the larger privacy management process.

The nature of privacy rules is elemental to the rule management process that regulates private disclosures among and between people. There are two main features of privacy rule foundations. The first feature is *privacy rule development*. Second, *rule attributes* represent the way people acquire rules and rule properties (see Figure 2.1).

37

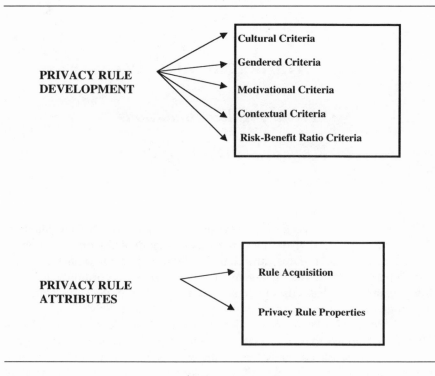

Figure 2.1
Privacy Rule Foundations

## PRIVACY RULE DEVELOPMENT

Rule development focuses on the way people come to know or establish privacy rules. For both personal boundaries and collective boundaries, there are times when individuals need to develop new rules, learn preexisting privacy rules, or negotiate rules that manage boundaries.

Through examining the establishment of new rules, we are able to understand an underlying process that contributes to all rule development. Even after rules are created, they often go through a process of change. At any point where rules become defined anew, people depend on privacy rule criteria to develop the rules used in regulating their privacy boundaries. Consequently, it is useful at this point to consider the criteria upon which privacy rules are developed.

There are fundamental criteria that underlie the way people establish privacy rules. CPM proposes that individuals depend on five criteria to generate privacy rules for access and protection of private information, including: (a) culture, (b) gender, (c) motivations, (d) context, and (e) risk-benefit ratio.

These criteria alternatively or in conjunction take the foreground thus influencing rule making, as the others remain in the background having less immediate influence over rule generation. However, each contributes to the fundamental production of rules people use to regulate their privacy boundaries.

Accordingly, each *culture* has privacy values that are the basis for judging levels of disclosure or privacy. As Hunter (1991) points out, "culture orders our expectations, makes sense of our lives, [and] gives us meaning" (p. 53). Through cultural expectations for privacy, people open or protect their boundaries to varying degrees. Culture represents one resource people use to develop rules for regulating their privacy boundaries.

*Gender* may also contribute to the production of rules for privacy management. Particularly if we think about gender as a basis for formulating norms idiosyncratic to men and women, gender differences may contribute to alternative rule structures that regulate boundaries for men and women. Consequently, men and women establish rules based on their own unique perspective of how to enact disclosure or maintain privacy.

*Motivations*, likewise, influence the establishment and enactment of rules to regulate boundaries around private information and the proclivity to disclose (Reis & Shaver, 1988). When a person has needs, such as a low tolerance for ambiguity, he or she may depend on rules that allow for gathering and disseminating private information to satisfy these needs.

Often reciprocity is seen as motivational because the decision to open privacy boundaries in response to disclosure is based on certain individual needs. Liking and attraction likewise motivate people to develop certain rules for boundary access or concealment (Chaikin & Derlega, 1974a). Consequently, the needs that individuals have impact the choices they make about establishing privacy rules for boundary regulation.

*Context* also has an impact on the types of rules that emerge. For example, when people encounter traumatic events, they often need to establish new privacy rules and depend on the expectations of the situation to determine the most useful rules to use. Experience with sudden earthquakes is one situation that calls for a very specific set of management rules that may be different from those ordinarily used by individuals. Under this circumstance, people may need to disclose private feelings to overcome the trauma of the situation. Thus, context often sets the stage for developing new rules that address the situational needs of the privacy regulation (Pennebaker, 1991).

*Risk-benefit ratio* is the fifth criteria individuals and collectives use. Individuals and co-owners calculate the risks and benefits of disclosing or remaining private. By determining the relative significance of a risk-benefit ratio for the dialectic of privacy-disclosure, rules are established reflecting an assessment about the conditions for revealing and concealing. However, neither privacy nor disclosure is ever without some measure of risk and benefit. Consequently, the risk-benefit ratio, while providing a foundation for rule development, also functions as an additional dialectical tension that influences privacy decisions through rules that are generated.

Culture, gender, motivations, context, and risk-benefit ratio together lay the foundation for the development of rules that people use to manage the boundaries that regulate the revealing and concealing of private information.

### Privacy Rule Development: Cultural Criteria

Cultural issues play an important role in determining rules for conduct (Cronen et al., 1988), especially decisions concerning disclosure of private information (Benn & Gaus, 1983). Cultural expectations inform individuals about the appropriate social behavior that ultimately controls boundary accessibility. At the base of these expectations lays the fundamental value of privacy influencing boundary rules.

Each culture has a degree to which privacy is important and develops ways to regulate that privacy (Altman, 1977). For example, in a 1993 poll, 47% of Americans in comparison to 35% of Canadians reported that they were very concerned with threats to their personal privacy ("Americans Guard Privacy," 1993). The value put on privacy is a critical factor in determining rules for regulating that privacy. As research shows, cultures vary in the way they treat privacy (Moore, 1984; Roberts & Gregor, 1971). Altman (1977) argues that privacy is generic to all cultures but that it "differs among cultures in terms of the behavioral mechanisms used to regulate desired levels of privacy" (p. 66). Thus, all societies have some degree of privacy, yet the rules for access or protection may vary greatly. As Altman further notes,

> the possible universality of privacy concerns the capability of a person or a group to regulate interaction with others, sometimes being open and sometimes being closed, depending upon circumstances. On the other hand, privacy regulation may be culturally unique in terms of the particular behavioral and psychological mechanisms used to regulate it. Thus, while the capability for privacy regulation may be culturally universal, the specific behaviors and techniques used to control interaction may be quite different from culture to culture. (p. 69)

The dialectical tensions between privacy and being public are evident in considering cultural expectations for revealing and concealing (Roberts & Gregor, 1971). Each culture values privacy differently and the values we place on privacy influence the rules we have for managing our privacy boundaries. Someone from a different culture may invade our privacy because he or she follows different rules. Undesired exposure of this kind often leads to boundary turbulence but also underscores cultural differences for privacy. There are many examples of cultural differences where privacy is concerned.

The Mehinacu in central Brazil provide such an example (Roberts & Gregor, 1971). "Many features of the design of the Mehinacu settlement and dwellings make social life highly observable and audible" (Roberts & Gregor, 1971, p. 205). In most areas of the village, the Mehinacu are highly visible and easily observed by other members of the tribe. Yet, these people developed certain boundary rules for managing privacy that allow a degree of autonomy from others. The Mehinacu practice ways to regulate social interaction where others follow routinized rules for privacy that are based on cultural expectations. For example, there are secret paths leading to remote places that people use to close their boundaries and retreat from other villagers. They also have a rule about discretion. Each villager is under an obligation to avoid exposing another's misconduct. Roberts and Gregor (1971) observe that:

> A good wife, the men say, is a woman who does not ask where her husband is going when he leaves the house in the late afternoon decorated with red paint and wearing his finest earrings. It is quite possible that he is planning to meet a partner for an extramarital affair, but a good wife will never press the point. Similarly, a courteous kinsman or comrade will not ask questions that might place an individual in an awkward position. These questions include serious inquiries about a man's possessions, his sexual intrigues, his knowledge of village witches, and somewhat surprisingly, even his plans for the next day. (p. 215)

As this example shows, for the Mehinacu culture, the collectivity maintains the boundaries around co-owned information and abides by rules set by the group that are influenced by the cultural norms for privacy.

Obviously, reducing exposure means more privacy and more boundary control. However, privacy values vary from culture to culture. In U. S. culture, people have expectations for privacy that are more moderate when compared to British and German cultures (Benn & Gaus, 1983; Spiro, 1971). Great Britain and Germany are less tolerant of exposure and have more sanctions against breaches of privacy. Nevertheless, in the United States, the desire for protection is great enough to assume "a right to privacy."

"The word 'privacy' does not appear in the United States Constitution. Yet, ask anyone and he or she will tell you that they have a fundamental right to privacy. They will also tell you that privacy is under siege"

(Alderman & Kennedy, 1995, p. ix). The right to privacy as we know it today in the United States is founded on the Fourth Amendment which protects our right to be free from unreasonable search and seizure (Alderman & Kennedy, 1995).

For people in the United States, the value of privacy has been taken a step beyond cultural expectations and centered in a legal domain that is geared to protect individuals from unwanted invasion. This legal protection codifies the assumptions about privacy initially determined by the importance U.S. culture placed on control over one's personal life. A number of state laws have been developed to cover invasion of privacy issues (Alderman & Kennedy, 1995). However, even the legal definitions of privacy are sometimes ambiguous (Warren & Brandeis, 1984). Nevertheless, the rules that turn into laws help identify the degree of accessibility for people in U.S. culture. The cultural factor in rule making for private disclosure sets the values used to determine rules for boundary access or protection. As cultures vary in the importance they place on regulating private information, the decision to reveal or conceal depends on these fundamental values. Clearly, the choice of granting accessibility or disclosing private information may be essential to the values of a culture.

## Privacy Rule Development: Gendered Criteria

For the most part, an argument can be made for the impact of gender on privacy rule development. Like culture, gender has the potential to influence the way men and women define the nature of their privacy. Some research suggests that men and women use different sets of criteria to define ownership of private information and the way it is controlled (Petronio, Martin, & Littlefield, 1984; Petronio & Martin, 1986). Consequently, women and men develop dissimilar rules for regulating privacy boundaries because they see revealing and concealing from different vantage points. Although there may be many cases where men and women use similar rules and times when they negotiate rules together, to understand the basis for gender as a criterion for rule making, we turn to the literature on gender differences in disclosure.

### Mediating and Moderating Gender

In an attempt to provide coherence to this area of inquiry, Rosenfeld, Civikly, and Herron (1979) note a number of issues that mediate an understanding of the findings on gender differences. The focus of the literature is primarily on revealing rather than concealing private information. Thus, we know more about the kinds of criteria women and men use to construct disclosure rules than we do about the ways that men and women retain their privacy. However, the criteria leading to disclosure tends to be equivocal at best regarding the amount of private information men and women reveal.

For example, several studies find that women disclose more than do men (Bath & Daly, 1972; Cash, 1975; Chelune, 1975a; Davis, 1978; Garai, 1970; Hyink, 1975; Kopfstein & Kopfstein, 1973; Ryckman, Sherman, & Burgess, 1973). Yet, other studies find that men and women disclose more equally (Annicchiarico, 1973; Certner, 1973; Hoffman-Graff, 1977; Kohen, 1975; Shapiro & Swensen, 1977).

To discern issues for developing privacy rules, several considerations may help identify the influence of gender. For example, Rosenfeld et al. (1979) suggest that intervening variables such as characteristics like attractiveness (Cash, 1975; Sote & Good, 1974), status (Brooks, 1974; Colwill & Perlman, 1977; Lord & Velicer, 1975), age (Littlefield, 1974; Sinha, 1972; West, 1970), family setting (Alsbrook, 1976; Blaker, 1974; Burke, Weir, & Harrison, 1976), the content of disclosure (Hyink, 1975; Mulcahy, 1973), and avoidance of disclosure (Burke et al., 1976; Egan, 1970; Rosenfeld, 1979) contribute to gender differences found in the literature. Based on a meta-analysis, Dindia and Allen (1992) identify moderator variables that may account for some of the inconsistencies and add to our understanding of boundary rule making.

Dindia and Allen (1992) point out that the sex of the target, the relationship to the target, and measures of disclosure are issues that confound gender and disclosure of private information. They find that women disclose more than men do to other women and same-sex partners. Women also seem to disclose somewhat more than do men to opposite-sex partners. However, women do not disclose any more than men do to male partners. Sex differences in disclosure tend to be greater in same-sex interactions than in opposite-sex interactions (Dindia & Allen, 1992). Further, women seem to disclose more to other women but not more than men do to other men.

In addition, Dindia and Allen (1992) discuss the discloser's relationship to the target. They report that,

> relationship to the target did not, by itself, moderate the effect of sex on self-disclosure. Sex differences in self-disclosure to strangers were not significantly different from sex differences in self-disclosure in relationships (i.e., self-disclosure to a friend, parent, or spouse). (p. 114)

However, the way disclosure is measured does contribute to an understanding of the differences.

Using categories developed by Chelune (1979), Dindia and Allen considered disclosure measured from self-report, observer ratings, recipient ratings, and objective metrics. They found the largest effect size for observer and recipient ratings as opposed to self-report and objective metrics. Thus, they note that observers report that women partners disclose more than men partners do; however, they caution the readers about the spurious nature of this finding (Dindia, 2000).

Nevertheless, they argue that this inflation in observer ratings may result because observers are dependent on sex-role norms that affect expectations about the appropriateness of women disclosing more than men. Depending on these expectations may lead to the perception that individuals are more frequent recipients of disclosure from women than they are from men. Perhaps one of the main implications of gender for privacy rule making may be the reliance on expectations about private disclosures.

**Sex-roles.** As Hill and Stull (1987) submit, sex-role attitudes (Chelune, 1975b, 1976; Cline & Musolf, 1985; Derlega, Winstead, Wong, & Hunter, 1985; Grigsby & Weatherley, 1983; O'Neill, Fein, Velit, & Frank, 1976; Pearson, 1980; Rubin, Hill, Peplau, & Dunkel-Schetter, 1980; Winstead, Derlega, & Wong, 1984), sex-role identity (Derlega, Durham, Gockel, & Sholis, 1981; Snell, Belk, Hawkins, 1986), and sex-role norms (Derlega & Chaikin, 1975; Rosenfeld, 1979) have all been considered influential factors in determining gender differences in disclosure. Sex-role attitudes are those behaviors considered appropriate for women and men concerning disclosure. Sex-role identity refers to "self-description in terms of personality traits originally thought to be 'masculine' or 'feminine'" (Hill & Stull, 1987, p. 87). However, other discussions of sex-role identity focus on notions of instrumentality and expressiveness (Hill & Stull, 1987). Sex-role norms refer to expectations of appropriate self-disclosure.

Further, the concept of sex-role attitude is most closely aligned with Jourard's (1971) early discussion on sex differences. He argues that in comparison to women,

> the male role requires men to appear tough, objective, striving, achieving, unsentimental, and emotionally inexpressive. . . . The male's self-structure will not allow men to acknowledge or to disclose the entire breadth and depth of his inner experience to himself or to others. (p. 35)

Jourard suggests that role expectations for men appear to inhibit their ability to disclose. Hill and Stull (1987) make an interesting point in their discussion. They suggest that consistent with Jourard's early proposal,

> most of the theorizing about gender differences in self-disclo-
> sure has focused on the inhibiting effects of male-role pre-

scriptions, yet the two measures of sex-role attitudes that have been used in research focus primarily on female-role prescriptions. (p.87)

*Sex-role identity.* Hill and Stull (1987) also mention sex-role identity as a possible answer to the riddle of gender and disclosure, and consequently the impact on privacy rule making. They point out that this research line is very complex. Sex-role identity, as a perspective, emphasizes an orientation to masculinity and femininity that considers them to be separate dimensions. The most consistently used measure of this perspective is the Bem Sex Role Inventory (Bem, 1974, 1977, 1979, 1981). In addition to the anchors of masculinity and femininity, Bem posits that androgyny (i.e., an adjusted difference between a person's femininity and masculinity scores) is also an additional dimension of sex-role identity. Bem also indicates that individuals may score as sex-typed or sex-reversed. Spence, Helmreich, and Stapp (1975) have a similar measure called the Personal Attributes Questionnaire.

There are a number of findings supporting a sex-role identity approach to gender and disclosure. For example, Derlega, Durham, Gockel, and Sholis (1981) argue that understanding sex typing of disclosure topics is important because it may impact how both women and men reveal. They find that men more than women are willing to disclose about personal information that is perceived to be masculine in nature. On the other hand, women tend to be more willing to reveal personal information that reflects a more feminine role. Derlega et al. maintain that men in the United States are socialized to value achievement, competition, and success, whereas women are socialized to value emotionality and sensitivity. These values developed by men and women contribute to decisions about privacy rules for the privacy-disclosure tension.

Snell, Belk, and Hawkins (1986) similarly investigate male and female willingness to disclose about masculine-instrumental and feminine-expressive dimensions. Unlike Derlega et al. (1981), these authors find somewhat different results. They conclude that men, more than women, seem willing to discuss personal information about their feminine-expressive traits with both female friends and intimate partners. Men also are more willing to disclose about their masculine-instrumental side to male friends. Women, on the other hand, are more willing to reveal personal information about their feminine-expressive traits to male friends and personal information about masculine-instrumental traits to women friends.

Given these results, Snell et al. (1986) propose that researchers should explore gender-role conformity as an underlying factor affecting the differences in rules that men and women have about private disclosures. They suggest a promising explanation lies in applying self-presentation to understand these tendencies. Snell et al. (1986) state that men, for instance, may have been more concerned than women with presenting an image of themselves as highly competent, instrumental individuals to male friends, but more concerned with presenting themselves as feminine-expressive to female friends and to their partner-spouse. Women in contrast, may have been more concerned than men with presenting an image of themselves as highly understanding and considerate individuals to male friends, but more concerned with presenting themselves as instrumental and self-assertive to their female friends. (p. 264)

Alternatively, this outcome may also be a result of the finding that men hold more rigid gender roles than women. Snell et al. report that both men and women presented a more traditional gender-role identity to men than they did to women. Perhaps both men and women sense that their female relational partners will be more understanding of their nontraditional characteristics than their male relational partners will be.

The role of self-presentation also speaks to underlying sex-role norms and the development of privacy rules. Hill and Stull (1987) emphasize differing expectations that set the stage for appropriate disclosure for men and women. Men and women focus on diverse issues in managing their self-presentation thereby impacting the choices that they make for disclosure to others.

Socialization from earliest childhood experiences into sex-appropriate role behaviors may also explain choices for private disclosure. Thus, there appears to be some strength to considering gender as an influencing factor in developing privacy rules. For example, as boys and girls learn that they should communicate according to differential rules, peers and adults alike may reinforce their choices for disclosure episodes. In addition, Derlega and Chaikin (1976) offer that,

> besides the role of early child experiences in the development of self-disclosure patterns, cultural norms operate in adulthood to maintain sex-linked differences in self-disclosure. After self-disclosure behaviors are acquired, their maintenance depends on continued reinforcement, which is achieved by expectations of reward or punishment for culturally acceptable behaviors. (p. 376)

Not only do observers depend on expectations to evaluate the appropriateness of revealing, disclosers may also use the same type of assumptions in deciding when to talk about private information (Chaikin & Derlega, 1974b; Chelune, 1976; Cunningham, 1981; Feldstein, 1979).

In many ways, the notion of expectations appears to be the most persuasive argument to understand how gender functions as an underlying structure for privacy rule making. The reoccurring theme of expectations permeates many different explanations of disclosure by men and women. Some have argued that men and women compose two different communication cultures within a national culture like the United States (Derlega, Metts, Petronio, & Margulis, 1993; Maltz & Borker, 1982; Petronio, Martin, & Littlefield, 1984; Petronio & Martin, 1986; Tannen, 1990). Socialization in different "gender cultures" may explain why men and women typically do not use the same criteria to disclose. Maltz and Borker (1982) contend that rules for engaging in and interpreting friendly conversations are based on gendered cultural differences:

> We argue that American men and women come from different sociolinguistic subcultures [communication cultures], having learned to do different things with words in a conversation, so that when they attempt to carry on conversations with one another, even if both parties are attempting to treat one another as equals, cultural miscommunication results. (pp. 199–200)

Tannen (1990) depends on this thesis in the position she articulates about gender differences and communication across the sexes. Maltz and Borker (1982) point out that since conversation is a negotiated activity, "systematic problems develop in communication when speakers of different speech cultures interact and that these problems are the result of differences in systems of conversational inference and cues for signaling speech acts and speaker's intent" (p. 201). Thus, gender socialization forms a set of cultural expectations that serve as the basis for disclosure rules.

*Gendered expectations.* In many studies, the criteria of gendered cultural expectations are often embedded in assumptions about the research. For example, Shaffer, Smith, and Tomarelli (1982) report a serendipitous finding that is contrary to assumptions made about gender and disclosure. When examining disclosure with new acquaintances, male participants anticipating future interactions with their partners disclosed more intimate information than did female participants. Although a modeling explanation is offered, the degree to which differential socialization may account for their findings is emphasized as an explanation. In other words, men and women may use dissimilar criteria to develop different rules for determining disclosure.

Shaffer and Ogden (1986) replicated this study and found that the expectation of future interactions with a new acquaintance is an important moderator of disclosure. This expectation has an impact on self-presentational strategies used by men and women. Shaffer and Ogden emphasize the importance of socialization, particularly when examining the way self-presentational expectations differ for men and women. As these studies suggest, a unique communication culture may be responsible, in part, for socializing men and women differently when it comes to the development of boundary rules for disclosure.

Also suggestive is the research by Petronio et al. (1984) and Petronio and Martin (1986). Early research by these authors proposes that individuals use *prerequisite conditions* and *anticipated ramifications* as determinants of criteria used to judge willingness to disclose. Thus, prerequisite conditions refer to criteria that must be met before men and women would be likely to disclose. Anticipated ramifications are the outcomes expected or estimated by the individuals prior to disclosure. "We suggest that prerequisite conditions and anticipated ramifications function as boundary regulators [rules] aiding in the adjustment process" (Petronio et al., 1984, p. 268). Thus, these findings suggest that men and women use different criteria based on gendered cultures. Their assessment of prerequisite conditions and anticipated ramifications for disclosure are explained by a cultural group view. The results show that women placed a higher importance on sender and receiver characteristics than men. Before women will disclose they need to feel certain that the target will be discreet, trustworthy, sincere, liked, respectful, a good listener, warm, and open in return.

Although the findings for men approached significance (therefore were not reported), they hinted at the possibility that men depend on the appropriateness of the situation (Petronio et al., 1984). In other words, men may find that the situation has to be right before they will disclose information. For example, suppose a wife and husband go shopping together at a mall. The wife wants to talk about the need for her husband to be more romantic. She determines that shopping is the best time to bring up this topic for conversation. When she starts to convey her feelings about needing more romance and explains how this would help their sex life, the husband becomes increasingly uncomfortable.

For the wife, the situation is much less relevant than whether she feels untroubled and relaxed about bringing up the topic with her husband. The fact that she likes and respects her husband and that he is generally receptive to her disclosures is more important than where she discloses. The husband is more mindful of the circumstances and cannot believe that his wife is revealing such intimate details when others could overhear them. The situation for him seems to override other considerations in this example. Thus, we might presume that men more than women emphasize the situation and that women stress sender/receiver characteristics more so than do men. These basic criteria for disclosure may be the catalyst for presuming that men and women do not understand each other's disclosure patterns.

The type of information revealed may also be predicated on gendered cultural expectations for men and women (Fisher, 1986). Men and women appear to be working from different sets of gendered cultural expectations for disclosure (Derlega et al., 1993; Maltz & Borker, 1982; Petronio et al., 1984; Petronio & Martin, 1986). Although there are cultural commonalties in the dominant cultural group, men and women rely on different orientations to disclose. Hence, men and women may open their boundaries using distinct criteria that underpin boundary rule making for disclosure, meeting a gender-specific set of expectations. Instead of focusing on the amount of disclosure, finding the criteria may uncover an overall pattern for rules man and women use to disclose private information.

### Privacy Rule Development: Motivational Criteria

Motivational factors may also contribute to rule making for privacy management (Taylor, 1979). When people are judging whether to open boundaries or keep them closed, their rules may be predicated on their needs surrounding private disclosures. Taylor (1979) argues that the expectations of rewards or costs are motivating to reveal or conceal private information. Attraction and liking are also motivating, as is reciprocity. From a perspective that highlights the relationship between private self-consciousness and disclosure, Davis and Franzoi (1987) point out that there are three hypotheses that represent a motivational basis for disclosure. They include (a) an expressive need hypothesis, (b) a self-knowledge need hypothesis, and (c) a self-defense need hypothesis, and influence the way that boundary rules change.

The *expressive need* hypothesis submits that the act of disclosure to others is itself rewarding and therefore fulfills an individual's need to express feelings and thoughts to others (Davis & Franzoi, 1987; Derlega & Grzelak, 1979). However, it is possible that individuals will also be motivated to reveal because they wish to know more about themselves (Davis & Franzoi, 1987). Seeking *self-knowledge* through disclosure is an alternative reason for revealing to others. *Self-defense*, when individuals feel the potential risk is too great they avoid engaging in self-disclosure, is a third hypothesis. In these ways, developing privacy rules may be influenced by the needs people have for disclosing private information to others.

Related to these motivational issues, Rosenfeld (1979) finds that when men do not want to open their boundaries, they avoid disclosure because they fear losing control. Women avoid disclosure because they have a need to prevent personal hurt and problems in their relationships. These reasons may all be considered types of self-defense, illustrating an explanation for tightening boundary access and protecting private information because of individual needs. Disclosure reciprocity may also motivate a response leading to revealing private information.

A more general tendency hinging on control concerns motivations for topic avoidance in close relationships. People are stimulated to guard their

personal privacy boundaries either to protect the development of a relationship or de-escalate a relationship (Afifi & Guerrero, 2000). Topic
avoidance is one way that individuals guard their privacy. As a result, when
the motivation to enhance a relationship exists, people may refrain from
disclosing issues that hamper the development of intimacy. Individuals may
be prompted to develop rules that regulate discussing certain topics because
they fear bringing up unpleasant issues or disclosing disagreeable points
could possibly halt the intensification of a close relationship. Alternatively,
individuals may also be motivated to abstain from raising topics because
they want to halt the development of a close relationship. In both cases, the
strategy of topic avoidance is the same, but the motivation for controlling
privacy boundaries is very different.

## Reciprocity

Disclosure researchers have long been interested in the nature of reciprocity,
or the "dyadic effect" (e.g., Altman, 1975; Bradac, Hosman, & Tardy, 1978;
Hendrick, 1987; Jourard, 1971). From Jourard's earliest introduction of this
phenomenon, the concept of reciprocity has received a great deal of attention.
Although there have been persuasive arguments refuting the power of disclosure reciprocity (Dindia, 1982, 2000), some have described this concept as one
of the best-established and most reliable predictors of disclosure (McAllister
& Bregman, 1985; Miller & Kenny, 1986). As such, this may function as a
motivating factor in regulating boundaries and establishing rules.

The notion of disclosure reciprocity is predicated on the social
exchange theories of Homans (1950, 1956, 1961) and Thibaut and Kelley
(1959) and on Gouldner's (1960) "norm of reciprocity." Simply put,
Jourard (1971) states that

> In an ordinary social relationship, disclosure is a reciprocal phe-
> nomenon. Participants disclose their thoughts, feelings, and
> actions to others and receive disclosure in return. I called this rec-
> iprocity the "dyadic effect": disclosure begets disclosure. (p. 66)

There appears to be an assumed symmetry in the disclosure exchange.
However, underlying this reciprocal action is the motivation to increase
rewards and decrease costs for disclosers. People tend to react positively
and, therefore, are more willing to disclose in return (Taylor, 1979). Yet,
being privileged to receive disclosure is presumably regulated by feelings of
obligation or a certain level of indebtedness for being selected as a recipient (Taylor, 1979; Walster, Berschied, & Walster, 1973). In turn, revealing
similarly to the discloser, thereby enhancing the benefits for both parties,
relieves this indebtedness.

**Reciprocity outcomes.** There have been a number of studies linking the reciprocity effect with outcomes. For example, mutual disclosure is often defined as an index of positive mental health and is considered an influential factor in the development of relationships (Jourard, 1971). There tends to be more reciprocity earlier in relationships when the interactants are less familiar with each other as opposed to in spousal relationships, supporting the ideas proposed in Social Penetration Theory (Altman, 1973; Altman & Taylor, 1973; Morton, 1978). The acquaintance process is characterized by an increase in intimacy of information that depends on a reciprocity effect. However, reciprocity appears to decline as the relationship advances (Morton, 1978).

There have also been a number of conditions where reciprocity varies. For instance, highly intimate disclosures tend to elicit significantly more positive disclosures than moderately intimate revelations (Hecht, Shepard, & Hall, 1979). Highly intimate information elicits reciprocal disclosures regardless of whether the information leads to disliking the discloser (Derlega, Harris, & Chaikin, 1973). Thus, the privacy of information revealed appears to be a consideration in how individuals define decisions to reveal suggesting that how private the information is may impact a person's motivations to respond.

**Personal characteristics.** Personal characteristics also have been found to moderate reciprocal disclosure (Harden, 1986). For instance, disclosure flexibility may be a factor in determining willingness to disclose (Chelune, 1979). Flexibility refers to the capacity of a person to modulate his or her propensity to disclose according to interpersonal and situational demands (Chelune, 1979). Chelune (1979) states that

> Individuals with low self-disclosure flexibility—that is, consistency in disclosure levels across situations—are more likely to show trait-like relationships between global indices of self-disclosure and other personality measures. (p. 6)

Disclosure flexibility is similar to self-monitoring (Harden, 1986; Snyder, 1979). Considering levels of monitoring, high self-monitors tend to depend on cues in the environment or from the social situation for information about appropriate behavior, whereas low self-monitors tend to be more internally directed. Based on Rubin's (1975) alternative explanation for disclosure reciprocity, researchers have investigated the utility of self-monitoring or flexibility and its relationship to disclosure.

Rubin (1973, 1975) argues that, rather than a social exchange model, modeling might be another way to understand reciprocity and, in particular, to account for some laboratory results. He states that under the pressures of an experiment, participants "accede to the demand characteristics of the experiment" (Rubin, 1973, p. 164) when confederates cue the participants by disclosing and expecting disclosure in return. The confederates model the behavior and participants reciprocate the behavior of the confederates because they determine that disclosure is considered the appropriate response.

Although there is some evidence contradicting Rubin's (1973) proposal, research (particularly that on self-monitoring) applies Rubin's argument (Taylor, 1979). For example, enacting self-monitoring behavior may increase the susceptibility to reciprocity patterns because of experimental demands (Ludwig, Franco, & Malloy, 1986). In some experimental research, high self-monitors were found to be more likely than low self-monitors to reciprocate disclosure and to do so by matching intimacy, emotionality, and descriptive content (Shaffer, Smith, & Tomarelli, 1982). Consequently, Rubin's thesis appears to have some merit concerning the relationship between self-monitoring and reciprocity of disclosure. Nevertheless, Dindia (1982) debates a more fundamental aspect of this research literature.

**Questioning reciprocity.** In an insightful review, Dindia (1982) disputes the soundness of disclosure reciprocity research citing the inconsistencies between conceptual and operational definitions as a basic flaw. She points out that reciprocity has been conceptually defined as "mutually contingent self-disclosure" (Dindia, 1982, p. 506), that is, disclosure begets disclosure. However, operationally, reciprocity has been defined in a number of ways "including a positive relationship between, or a similarity in, A and B's self-disclosure and a positive effect of A's self-disclosure on B's self-disclosure" (Dindia, 1982, p. 506).

Her assessment covers studies on reciprocity implementing both experimental and nonexperimental designs. Using a sequential analysis, Dindia tests whether one person's disclosure has a subsequent impact on reciprocal revealing. She finds that subsequent self-disclosure may be related but is not necessarily reciprocal. Dindia (1988) applies a rigorous comparison in another study using several statistical tests of disclosure reciprocity. In this study of 30 dyadic conversations between strangers, she again uncovers little evidence of disclosure reciprocity.

Dindia (1988) explains the problems found in the reciprocity literature. She notes that reciprocity might be recast considering the possibility that this type of disclosure does not occur in a turn-by-turn sequence. There may be a lag time where other nondisclosive information is communicated before reciprocal disclosure takes place. Related to this is the importance of determining the appropriate unit of analysis that constitutes a reciprocal exchange.

Dindia (1988) refers to a discussion by Roloff and Campion (1985) on responses to a linguistic or nonverbal cue. They argue that interactants may "chunk" incoming information in various ways, perhaps using more macro units to judge responses to information than the researchers might depend on in their analysis (Roloff & Campion, 1985). Dindia suggests that how interactants "chunk" disclosive information may vary with each researcher's definition of the units or the way that people consider a turn sequence.

Dindia (1988) points out that the operational definitions used in reciprocity research may not adequately measure the nature of the concept. If researchers consider an immediate response as the only way to define reciprocity, that definition changes the way the concept is understood. In addition, Dindia highlights the fact that there may be a difference in topic reciprocity and self-disclosure reciprocity. Depending upon how reciprocal disclosure is defined, researchers may find that individuals are motivated by topic continuity rather than responding with disclosure (Dindia, 2000).

Given that reciprocity is not a unitary concept, in that it is more multidimensional than often operationalized, the motivation for rule making may vary depending on the way that people consider responding to private disclosure. Thus, rules may be contingent on the need to keep conversations going to illustrate respect for the other person's willingness to reveal. Rules may also depend on the way people "chunk" the incoming information.

For instance, punctuating an interaction gives an illustration of this idea (Watzlawick, Beavin, & Jackson, 1967). The example of a husband stating that he withdraws because his wife nags and his wife saying that she nags because he withdraws shows that each has a different way of chunking. There is a foundation for reciprocal disclosure rules embedded in this punctuated interaction for the husband and wife.

Attention to lag time between reciprocal responses is also warranted. Some people may have a need to wait to respond. They may not be ready to disclose their feelings, although others have revealed. Their boundary rule for granting access may depend on a more deliberate consideration of the information before responding. Thus, quickly replying in kind may not be consistent with their disclosure needs in general. They may wait for days or weeks before circling back to the initial disclosure made by another.

For instance, a sister may tell her brother that in two months she is going to elope with a man she just met. The brother may wish to weigh his response or just let his sister "talk" out how she feels without letting her know his own feelings. The brother may not want to risk an argument or show his disapproval when his sister first confides. However, he may circle back to their conversation at a future date to see how his sister is coping with her decision and disclose his views when he feels safer doing so. As these discussions illustrate, individuals' privacy rules vary according to the extent they are motivated by a need to reply. This concept is also seen in *competitive disclosures.*

**Competitive disclosures.** Competitive disclosures reflect a concept not yet systematically studied, nevertheless experienced in many situations. When people talk to each other, one person may try to gain an advantage over the other by increasing the intensity, humor, or tragedy of the private information. When it comes to reciprocal disclosure, some people may try to top the level of privacy, the magnitude of intensity, or the amount of information revealed as a response. For example, in revealing "painful disclosures" such as private information about medical problems, older people reciprocate with each other more often than occurs with younger interactants (Giles, Coupland, Coupland, Williams, & Nussbaum, 1992). In reciprocating these painful disclosures, it is likely that the older individuals may be waging a competition by trying to illustrate that their problems are more severe, important, cost more, or are more devastating than someone else's. Older people may not be the only ones to enact competitive disclosure.

Adults of all ages may exchange private disclosures reciprocally to show up someone's revelation. Competitive disclosures may take place when someone is talking about his or her divorce, telling about difficulties growing up, or talking about medical problems. For example, in a conversation recently, two individuals started talking about their childhood. One said that he was so poor that he only had one shirt and pair of pants to wear to school. The other person listened and then stated that he and his family lived in a basement when he was growing up—that was how poor they were. Both represent disclosures; however, the response to the first turn seemed to escalate the severity of destitution.

Although not all conversations like this one may actually be motivated by competitive needs, there are instances where people feel compelled to exaggerate their disclosures to satisfy this need. Whether the private disclosure is reciprocally competitive or aiming at another response to hearing private disclosures, the motivation to reciprocate establishes the grounds for privacy rules.

### Liking and Attraction

Liking and attraction function as motivational factors empirically and theoretically linked to private disclosures and are instrumental in determining boundary rules. They function as criteria to develop rules important to granting access or providing protection of private information. For example, if a person likes another, he or she may be more willing to disclose private information.

There is a long history of examining liking and attraction as they relate to disclosure. In all, the research highlights the foundation this motivating force provides to develop privacy rules. For example, the relationship that physical attraction has to disclosure underscores the way that the level of attractiveness changes the rules used to grant or deny boundary access.

Thus, attractive men, as compared to unattractive males, disclose more frequently about themselves (Cash & Soloway, 1975). Level of attraction contributes to the likelihood that boundary access is granted and influences rules about disclosure frequency. Interestingly, when men perceive that women think they are attractive, they tend to decrease their disclosure about themselves. Perhaps the men are cautious because they do not want to tamper with the women's positive evaluations.

Furthermore, people disclose more to those who are liked, but revealing may be influenced by the nature of their relationship. For example, Collins and Miller (1994) report a significant positive effect of liking on disclosure in ongoing relationships but a weaker effect in initial relationships with strangers in laboratory settings (Jourard, 1971; Lynn, 1978; Taylor, 1979; Worthy, Gary, & Kahn, 1969). However, they caution, "it does not necessarily follow that liking always leads to disclosure or that disclosure is always preceded by liking" (Collins & Miller, 1994, p. 469).

**Attraction following disclosure.** In addition to attraction and liking as a condition existing before disclosure, there is a tendency for people to have positive feelings about their confidants after revealing (Collins & Miller, 1994). This relationship may contribute to assessing the merit of confiding and performing the role of confidant. The disclosure-liking link influences rule making because people judge the rewards of openness and the impressions of others as confidants. Liking also plays a role in the recipient's reactions. Although liking and attraction contribute to the way people establish privacy rules, there are some cautions suggested by Collins and Miller (1994). They provide a more systematic investigation of the disclosure-liking connection that isolates some of the apparent difficulties.

Collins and Miller (1994) offer a meta-analysis of the lineage between liking and disclosure, focusing on three of the more obvious connections. They examine: (a) whether people like others who disclose to them more than those who do not, (b) whether people disclose to those they initially like, and (c) whether people like others when they have received disclosure. The research indicates that people tend to like others who tell them private information (Archer & Berg, 1978; Brewer & Mittelman, 1980; Chaikin, Derlega, Bayma, & Shaw, 1975; Halverson & Shore, 1969; Kleinke, 1979).

Yet, the degree of the relationship varies significantly across studies, perhaps due to the researchers' methodological perspective. For example, self-report questionnaires typically involve people in ongoing relationships, while laboratory studies uses acquaintance or impression-formation tasks. Collins and Miller (1994) state, "it is clear that the relationship between the discloser and the recipient, and the nature of their interaction, will play an important role in determining the impact of disclosure on liking" (p. 465). They also point out those social norms evident for disclosures between men and women, which speak to the possibility of a gender difference in the disclosure-liking equation.

In studying the gender dimension of the disclosure-liking relationship, the impact of the disclosure on the recipient may be an important factor (Collins & Miller, 1994). However, the kind of outcome may depend on appropriateness of the disclosure, the way a recipient responds during the disclosure, and the quantity of the information disclosed as well as the perceived quality, content, interactants' gender, and whether the recipient feels positively toward the recipient. In addition to design issues and gender factors, the operationalization of the disclosure concept also accounts for variations.

**Loneliness and ambiguity.** There are other types of motivational forces that effect the way people decide rules for disclosure, for example, the level of loneliness a person feels (Berg & Peplau, 1982; Chelune, Sultan, & Williams, 1980; Derlega & Margulis, 1982; Franzoi & Davis, 1985; Horowitz, French, & Anderson, 1982; Solano, Batten, & Parish, 1982; Stokes, 1985). When people feel lonely, they are less likely to engage in disclosure activities and open their boundaries to others (Jones, Freemon, & Goswick, 1981). Their decision criteria are dominated by the extent to which they feel capable of moving from tight protection of privacy to a more moderate level that might allow periods of disclosure to others.

A low tolerance for ambiguity may also function to regulate privacy access and establish rules for how the boundaries are controlled. Those with a low-tolerance level may need more information and be motivated to grant more access through disclosure. In this way, the need to know and be known drives the desire to control boundary access. The rules people with a low tolerance for ambiguity develop also speak to the level of information-seeking individuals enact (Afifi & Guerrero, 2000). When the need to reduce uncertainty is high, people develop rules that allow for excessive soliciting of private information from others. Conversely, individuals with a high tolerance may use privacy rules that not only aim to protect their information, but that of others as well.

Boundaries slide open or closed to varying degrees depending on the cultural considerations, gender, and motivations. Culture, gender, and motivations serve as constants in rule making for privacy boundaries. However, certain life events may occur that disrupt the influence of these criteria for rule making either temporarily or on a long-term basis.

### Privacy Rule Development: Contextual Criteria

Context is an issue that influences the way privacy rules are established and changed. In this discussion of context, several life events are selected out of many possible situations to highlight the way rules emerge and are modified to meet the immediate needs of the circumstance. Life events may be categorized into three large groups of situations, including *traumatic events*, *therapeutic situations*, and *life circumstances*.

These events do not represent mutually exclusive categories. Clearly, traumatic events may lead to experiences with therapeutic situations. Likewise, life circumstances may also result in a need for therapy. For each, however, people modify or alter the way they typically reveal and conceal private information. Sometimes the change in private disclosures is dramatic. In other circumstances, small, temporary adjustments in the rules are made to manage privacy boundaries.

*Traumatic events* are situations where people cope with disruptive situations that may change their lives forever. Often these events come up suddenly and without warning. They require people to endure unpleasant, highly stressful circumstances that are not easy to tackle.

*Therapeutic situations* reflect circumstances where people talk to a therapist, counselor, psychologist, or clinician to contend with situations that are out of their control. During these encounters, revealing and concealing private information often takes on new patterns to reach the goals of therapy. However, therapeutic situations are not solely related to the client. There are issues in privacy management patterns for the both the client and therapist. Therapists have many demands on their ability to manage their privacy boundaries in coordination with their clients. The rules for revealing and concealing, at times, may become blurred.

*Life circumstances* represent situations that may be less stressful than traumatic events. Nevertheless, they often require changes in the way people control their privacy boundaries. Privacy rules may temporarily need to be changed to cope with the demands of these situations or they may become permanently changed. For example, life circumstances reflect times when significant relationships terminate or when people lose their jobs, become disabled, or become parents.

### Traumatic Events

Traumatic or distressful events are physically and psychologically unhealthy (Pennebaker, 1989). However, we know that disclosure during distressing times contributes to improved physical and mental health (Funabiki, Bologna, Pepping, & Fitzgerald, 1980; Jourard, 1971; Parker &

Brown, 1982; Pennebaker, 1990, 1995; Perls, 1969; Rippere, 1977; Tardy, 2000). People who are unable or unwilling to reveal when experiencing troubles are more likely to develop both physical and psychological problems (Cooper, 1984; Locke & Colligan, 1986). However, people willing to disclose are more likely to survive as compared to those who keep their feelings a secret (Derogatis, Abeloff, & Melisaratos, 1979; Locke & Colligan, 1986). Coates and Winston (1987) report that highly stressed housewives (Brown & Harris, 1978), widows (Vachon, Rogers, Lyall, Lancee, Sheldon, & Freeman, 1982), and rape victims (Atkeson, Calhoun, Resnick, & Ellis, 1982; Meyer & Taylor, 1986) who discuss their problems with others seem to be much less likely to show symptoms of serious depression.

When people experience traumatic events that increase their level of stress dramatically, one clear way to cope is through disclosure. However, for disclosure to take place during traumatic events such as enduring incest, losing a loved one, or learning one has a catastrophic illness, changes in the way people regulate privacy boundaries may be necessary. The shift in circumstance, therefore, may trigger a different set of rules to meet the demands of the situation. People in these distressed situations may reveal in ways that, for them, are atypical or idiosyncratic, but necessary to cope with the stress (Carpenter, 1987; Coates & Winston, 1987; Coyne, 1976a, 1976b; Funabiki, Bologna, Pepping, & Fitzgerald, 1980; Lorentz & Cobbs, 1953; McDaniel, Stiles, & McGaughey, 1981; Parker & Brown, 1982; Persons & Marks, 1970; Rippere, 1977; Silver & Wortman, 1980; Weitraub, 1981). Stiles (1987) posits that,

> a person in psychological distress finds it difficult to view events objectively or from others' perspectives; instead, he or she is preoccupied with internal states and meanings. This preoccupation tends to be represented in speech: distressed people talk [more] about their distress. (p. 261)

Stiles presents a *fever model* of disclosure that captures the situational dimension of rule making. For people in psychological distress, catharsis and self-understanding become the predominant goals and, therefore, function as critical guidelines for rules to open boundaries. Stiles likens catharsis to a "talking cure" that relieves a burden people feel when they are distressed. He suggests that the benefit of catharsis is related more to the "depth and extent of the disclosure itself and especially to the intensity of accompanying affect than to any specific quality of the other's response" (Stiles, 1987, p. 263).

Self-understanding also results from disclosure when one is distressed. In his model, Stiles (1987) points out that a level of homeostasis can be achieved. In other words, distress leads to disclosure, which in turn relieves one's burden, adjusting the amount of troubled feelings one is able to maintain. The fever model (which describes the "I have to talk to somebody" situation) functions as a regulatory mechanism for maintaining the homeostasis between distress feelings and boundary control. These situations affect rule making because people need to relieve their burden and adapt or revamp existing rules to fit their current need to talk.

Although disclosure may feel extremely necessary when experiencing distress, there are situations where disclosure may initially be more problematic than advantageous. Only after a person has survived a trauma is she or he able to relieve the pressure of the situation by revealing. Two circumstances illustrate this condition. They include sexual abuse and surviving the Holocaust.

**Sexual abuse.** Given the benefits of disclosing close in time to the distressing situation, it is clear why incest survivors find it so troubling to keep the conspiracy of silence. Yet, for incest victims, disclosure creates its own difficulties (Herman, 1981). The perpetrator often imposes the restriction of secrecy. The threats range from those that are insidious to brutal promises of additional harm (Frawley, 1990). Although Frawley (1990) suggests that disclosure of incest to a "validating, believing other" (p. 251) is critical in the healing process, disclosure in this circumstance is complex.

As Courtois (1988) indicates, disclosure by children experiencing incest is both "longed for and feared. Victims long for someone to notice and to assist them but fear disbelief, blame, and disavowal instead" (p. 326). The paradoxical character of disclosure for those experiencing incest often leaves them unable to discern the best course of action. Even when they confide in friends or family members, intervention is not guaranteed (Herman, 1981). Herman (1981) advises that,

> disclosure disrupts whatever fragile equilibrium has been maintained, jeopardizes the functioning of all family members, increases the likelihood of violent and desperate behavior and places everyone, but particularly the . . . [person experiencing abuse], at risk for retaliation. (p. 131)

Disclosure may not always be as disruptive as Herman (1981) implies. Nevertheless, family members may feel that having the information leak out is risky for all involved. Consequently, often when incest survivors tell their families as adults, they may be asked to keep the veil of silence. For example, Ray (1996) identifies cases where the abused person told her family after she was an adult. She states:

> My parents believed me. But, they made it very clear they didn't want me to tell anyone else, not even my brother or sister. (Denise, abused by her uncle)

My mother tried to get me to promise I wouldn't tell anyone else, not even my father. What she didn't know was that she was about the last person I told. (Suzanne, abused by her brother) (p. 282)

Thus, the privacy rules stipulated by the family members are such that others may not know about the survivors' experiences, even when they are adults. The disclosure of this private information may be made, but cannot be exposed to an audience beyond the immediate family members.

Although not all families respond in the same way, most typically, a disclosure paradox exists for incest survivors. As Ray (1996) points out, revealing sexual abuse as an adult or child may lead to stigmatizing by others. Nevertheless, much has been made of the ability for adulthood disclosures to take place. The survivor of incest who is able to reveal the experience tends to receive a more positive response and, consequently, is able to purge the troubling memories of the traumatic event (Courtois, 1988). As this discussion illustrates, the exigency of the situation may prevail in determining the kind of privacy rules people develop.

The same is true for children's reports of sexual abuse. In chapter 6, we find examples of how children manage privacy boundaries regarding sexual abuse. Children use a number of privacy rules to disclose the abuse. Sometimes the privacy rules that sexually abused children use call for testing out old rules, such as telling their mothers, and instituting new rules when their mothers failed to help them overcome the abuse. Thus, we can see how the context functions as the basis on which boundary rules are often determined.

**Holocaust survivors.** *Survivor disclosure* is also seen in research with Holocaust victims. As Gordon (1990) points out, "those who survived the Holocaust endured a systematic attempt to strip them of every fiber of their humanity" (p. 228). The role of disclosure for survivors, Gordon notes, symbolizes their experience through verbalizing the events, thereby providing a representation of their encounters. Disclosure also serves as an acknowledgment of the events they endured (Pennebaker, Barger, & Tiebout, 1989).

As survivors, and not unlike those who experienced incest, the process of disclosure has to be learned anew. Given that during their internment, Holocaust survivors were forced into acute depersonalization (Bettelheim, 1960) and altered ways of interacting with others, they had little choice but to accept the depersonalization that moves one to apathy and, finally, emotional numbing (Gordon, 1990). Human contact, especially to reveal the imposed traumas, necessitates an education process to learn how to trust others again and to provide nutriment to repair their damaged sense of self so disclosure can occur (Rapaport, 1958).

Interestingly, Gordon points out that after World War II, survivors faced negative reactions to their initial attempts at disclosing about the atrocities they experienced. Danieli (1984) states that these attitudes disconfirming the survivors' encounters in the concentration camps led to a conspiracy of silence about the Holocaust. "Feeling betrayed by the inability of their relatives to share their sense of loss, grief, and rage, survivors felt even more isolated" (Gordon, 1990, p. 231). This scenario is similar to that of incest survivors on the dimension of the silence conspiracy.

Gordon (1990) posits that through the willingness of Holocaust survivors' children to listen, some of these individuals have been able to purge the events about which they kept silent for many years. However, some children have not been able to listen, and some parents have not wished to burden them with these disclosures. Based on their Holocaust survivors research, Pennebaker, Barger, and Tiebout (1989) advise that often parents do not want to burden their children with the knowledge they had about their experiences. Since they find the experience so very difficult to cope with, they did not want to encumber their children.

Thus, for the survivors these researchers studied, many had not disclosed much of the circumstances they endured in the Nazi concentration camps. Yet, Pennebaker et al. (1989) found that encouragement to disclose, even after such a long period, often resulted in improved health long after their revelations.

Although the research is in short supply, there may be similar health outcomes for individuals who are HIV positive when they are encouraged to disclose (Greene, 2000; Spencer, 1991; Spencer & Derlega, 1995; Yep, 2000). The relationship between revealing and health benefits for people experiencing situation-induced trauma seems very promising (see chapter 6 for further discussion). Thus, as this discussion illustrates, privacy rules for traumatic situations may be different from those used in daily life. The choice to talk to friends about a feeling may not rely on the same type of decision rules for opening privacy boundaries and confessing.

### Therapeutic Events

Much has been written about the role of disclosure and therapy (e.g., Cherbosque, 1987; Dawson, Schirmer, & Beck, 1984; Derlega, Margulis, & Winstead, 1987; Doster & Nesbitt, 1979; Hendrick, 1987; Palombo, 1987; Plasky & Lorion, 1984; Simonson, 1976; Stricker & Fisher, 1990). Doster and Nesbitt (1979) argue that there are four different models characterizing the disclosure-therapy relationship. They include a fulfillment model, an ambiguity reduction model, an interactional model, and a social learning model.

In the fulfillment model, disclosure is viewed as a process whereby individuals become known to others and come to understand others. Through disclosure, the individual may be able to reach personal and interpersonal potential. The therapeutic situation presumably leads to helping the client reach the goal of self-actualization. Therapists adopting this approach are expected to be neutral and nonjudgmental recipients of disclosive information and to be open to the client (Culbert, 1967; Rogers, 1961). As Doster and Nesbitt (1979) suggest, this model emphasizes the therapist's self-disclosure more so than other orientations.

However, advocating mutual disclosure has lead to debates about ramifications for the therapists as well as the clients. For example, Lane and Hull (1990) advise that disclosure by the therapist should not interfere with or intrude on the client's progress. When the disclosure of the therapist dominates the discussion rather than allowing the client to work through the relevant issues, the use of disclosure by a therapist hampers the goals of therapy. Basecu (1990) concurs with this view, noting that inappropriate self-disclosure by the therapist seems the least useful, while some spontaneous revelations might be helpful if implemented in a responsible fashion. Palombo (1987) also points out that spontaneous self-disclosure in the therapeutic situation may be more healthy than reversing the role and placing the client in a position of providing support for the therapist.

The ambiguity reduction model is based on the assumption that individuals coming into therapy need to learn role-appropriate behavior. To reduce ambiguity, disclosure is identified as a suitable behavior to facilitate the desired therapeutic outcomes. Doster and Nesbitt (1979) maintain that there are many overlaps between this model of therapy with regard to disclosure and that of the social learning model. For both approaches, modeling (as a form of teaching the client appropriate behaviors), instructions, rehearsals, and feedback all help the client learn ways of functioning in society.

The interactional model, on the other hand, emphasizes the process of communication between client and therapist, including both verbal and nonverbal aspects of the process. The theorizing by Watzlawick et al. (1967) represents this orientation. Analyzing metacommunicative aspects of interaction, double binds, paradoxes, and so forth captures the emphasis placed in this perspective.

The distinctions offered by Doster and Nesbitt (1979) are somewhat helpful in understanding the constraints for therapeutic disclosure. This particular type of situation calls for the therapist to manipulate the privacy management of the client to the client's advantage. Depending on the approach adopted by the therapist, he or she must also manage personal borders to achieve the goal of disclosure for the client. In addition, the therapist must be mindful of the impact private revelations might have on the client. Thus, rule making takes into account the goals for both the client and therapist from each vantage point.

The rule-making factors obviously change with the different therapeutic orientations. For example, with the social learning or ambiguity reduction approaches, the client reproduces the expected behaviors identified by the therapist. The client, therefore, acts on the assumed rules for boundary access the therapist has taught him or her. In the fulfillment model, the client is encouraged to reveal, implying that the rules for this type of therapy involve unrestrained disclosure to become actualized and reach a full potential. In each case, the way privacy is controlled in the therapeutic situation is contingent on the approach advocated by the therapist.

## Life Circumstances

Although we have discussed extremely distressing situations, other events occur where privacy rule changing is unique to particular life circumstances. Some of these events may be stressful, but not necessarily at the same level as found in the category of traumatic events. Many situations fall into this category. To give a flavor of the way life circumstances are foundational to rule making and rule changing, life experiences such as relational disengagement and divorce, and how people with disabilities manage disclosure, are considered. These reflect examples of life events that influence privacy management. As these instances show, situational factors contribute to the rule making that guides boundary regulation.

**Relational disengagement.** In order to understand privacy management that occurs during relational disengagement, Baxter (1987) argues that termination is best represented by three stages. For each stage, there are concomitant disclosure patterns. The stages include, *private decision making*, *decision implementation*, and *public presentation*. Private decision making refers to the period when an individual privately contemplates feelings of dissatisfaction with a relational partner. For this stage, partners considering termination might use "disclosive directness" (p. 161) to seek out information about the other. This may involve interrogating another, thereby soliciting disclosive information.

Decision implementation involves the stage where the disengager actively engages in distancing from the partner. One way that this occurs is through developing rules that restrict the amount of private information that is disclosed. Baxter (1987) suggests that the type of disclosure patterns observed during this phase, such as avoiding private revelations, may cue the termination recipient of the change in status. The privacy boundaries become more tightly controlled where they were once open, allowing much more access. The change of access, therefore, signals the status shift.

Public presentation is enacted in order to fully accomplish disengagement; hence, the new status of the relationship becomes officially public and acknowledged by others at this stage (Baxter, 1987). Disclosure by both parties is typically directed to others about the unbonding process. The privacy management rules turn from focusing on the partner to closing him or her out. When there is disclosure about the relationship, it is more likely to be made to friends and family members than to the partner. This shift in rules is part of making the termination public.

Baxter (1979), in her study on disclosure as a relationship disengagement strategy, found that people withdrawing tend to avoid direct confrontation about the state of the relationship. A more indirect approach may be typical of those wishing to disengage (Baxter, 1979). However, as Baxter notes, "the fact that self-disclosure differences only accounted for approximately 14 percent of the variance perhaps suggests that changes in self-disclosure play a relatively minor role in one's total repertoire of disengagement strategies" (p. 220). Knapp and Vangelisti (1991) argue that disengagement and divorce take place in stages. Similarly, Baxter's (1979) research taps the earlier points where partners withhold emotions and repress anger or hurt, using instead more ambiguous forms of conveying feelings such as increased interruptions, contradicting the partner, and competitiveness (Bohannan, 1970).

The factors leading to decisions about boundary openness may change as the couple moves closer to termination, as Baxter's (1987) typology suggests. In addition, researchers have maintained that partners act differently depending upon whether they initiate the termination or are the recipients (Hill, Rubin, & Peplau, 1976; Price & McKenry, 1988). Consequently, the differences in privacy regulation and rules for disclosure may well vary depending on the role each person plays in the separation. In addition to divorce and disengagement, other situations call for rule adjustments and rule making.

**Disabilities.** Living with a disability everyday poses unique challenges for privacy management (Braithwaite, 1991). The discussion here is framed around situations where people have worked past the trauma of learning they have a disability and focuses on the everyday circumstances that people encounter. Braithwaite argues that people with physical disabilities face a number of challenges in relational initiation because of social stigmas, particularly when interacting with persons who have no physical disabilities.

Braithwaite reports that while people with disabilities expect questions about their situation early in a conversation with a new acquaintance or stranger, they use certain criteria to respond. She notes that the persons in her study who have disabilities do not disclose randomly, but, instead, are strategic in their responses. Thus, the decision rules include whether the person perceives the disclosure as appropriate to the relationship, whether the disclosure request is appropriate to the context and topic being discussed, whether the request is motivated by a healthy or morbid curiosity, and whether the person feels comfortable or in the mood to disclose.

In addition, there is also some attempt to delay revealing in order to establish the person as an individual first and reduce the emphasis on the disability. On occasions where the person with a disability determines that the questions ask for too much boundary openness, other strategies are enacted. For example, when people without disabilities asked inappropriate questions, the person who has a disability might change the topic, ignore the question, withdraw from the situation, or ask the offending person to leave. The person may also resort to approaches that are more direct by telling someone the information is none of his or her business.

Generally, the disclosures result from requests for information; however, participants in this study initiated openness when the interaction partner seemed uncomfortable (Braithwaite, 1991). Hence, privacy access was given in circumstances when the other seemed uneasy. Braithwaite notes "while communicating the desired impression of self to the other, controlling private information also influences how disabled persons see themselves" (p. 268).

As these discussions illustrate, culture, gender, and motivations contribute to the development of privacy rules that manage the way people give or deny access to private information. The context also has an impact on the formulation of privacy rules, both in the initial establishment of rules and in the changes that people make to manage their privacy boundaries. In this way, these criteria affect the foundation of rules for boundary management. In addition to these criteria, people also calculate the risks and benefits of revealing and concealing to develop privacy rules.

### Privacy Rule Development: Risk-Benefit Ratio Criteria

One reason we find it necessary to control our privacy boundaries is because we need to balance the risks and gains of revealing private information. Consequently, estimating the risks and benefits of revealing or concealing functions as important criteria to develop rules.

Clearly, the work by Pennebaker (1990, 1995) illustrates that disclosure for those in high stress situations is important and advantageous to their physical health. He cogently argues that inhibitions pose a health threat to many. Through numerous empirical tests, Pennebaker and his colleagues identify the benefits of disclosure when there have been traumatic sexual experiences in childhood (Pennebaker, 1990). He and his colleagues have also provided ample evidence that disclosure is instrumental in providing a health benefit for those dealing with the death of a spouse and for those living with HIV/AIDS (Pennebaker, 1995). For other traumas, such as experiencing earthquakes, other natural disasters, divorce, death of a child, or medical problems, research shows the advantage of revealing private thoughts (Tardy, 2000). Confessions under these circumstances help alleviate pain and open the doors for healing.

Yet, the willingness to tell is frequently measured against the feeling of risk a person perceives in opening privacy boundaries (Petronio, 2000a). For example, talking about divorce may be cathartic; however, it is risky if a person wants to establish a new relationship with the recipient of the disclosure. One of the reasons we erect a boundary around private information is because of risk. Although there are potential gains in telling information, as a dialectic, there is a simultaneous pull to consider the risks. We calculate the positive aspects of disclosures in relationship to the inherent vulnerabilities of making them public (Derlega & Grzelak, 1979; Pennebaker, 1995).

## Disclosure-Privacy Benefits

Attractive gains, especially for disclosure, such as the ones that Derlega and Grzelak (1979) identify, weigh against the perils of revealing. Consider *expression* as one reason to reveal. By telling others something private, we may be more able to cope with the information. If a person close to us died suddenly, we might want to express our grief by talking about our feelings. However, articulating our emotions about the situation may not take place if we think it would expose a weakness. *Self-clarification* is another reason to disclose. Through revealing private thoughts, we may be able to understand their meaning. Verbalizing our private feelings lets us formulate how we might come to think about issues important to us (Frank & Frank, 1991). The willingness to reveal, though, may depend on how fragile disclosure might make us feel.

*Social validation* may also be an outcome of disclosing. Telling others how we feel might lead them to reinforce our views or values. Yet, although we might receive confirmation of beliefs and their importance to others, we may also have them disconfirmed. *Relationship development* may be another positive outcome of disclosing. We may enhance the nature of our significant relationships with others by revealing private information (Derlega et al., 1993). However, although disclosure could maintain the intimacy between partners and work to increase the intensity of their desire to be in the relationship, it might also hamper its growth.

*Social control* over the situation may result from disclosing private information (Petronio, 1982). By telling friends or partners how we feel about an issue, we might have the power to influence the way they consider a topic. Nevertheless, the gains may diminish if our partners or friends think we are trying to manipulate them. These gains may be goals we anticipate from disclosure.

As we see, even when there are positive goals for disclosure, they are tempered by the dialectical considerations of the risks for revealing or concealing. Sometimes people may become vulnerable when they keep information from others and at other times, they may take a measure of risks when they disclose. Risks, depending on the kind, may not completely stop us from disclosing or from keeping the information tightly guarded. Yet, the risk-benefit ratio functions as one factor in developing rules as a basis for the decision to disclose or remain private. In a general sense, risks of revealing and concealing have at least two aspects: (a) the level of risk and (b) the types of risks associated with revealing and concealing.

### Disclosure-Privacy Risks

By definition, private information is important to us because it relates to "our conceptions of ourselves and to our relationships with others . . . the information matters deeply" (Schoeman, 1984, p. 406) to us. Not all of our private information has the same level of significance, although we may still consider it private. Private information changes in degrees of risk based on perceived repercussions for revealing and concealing (Greene, 2000; Petronio, 1991; Yep, 2000).

**Risk levels.** Some privacy-disclosure episodes might be defined as highly risky for some, but not risky for others. Consequently, the privacy-disclosure episode may fluctuate along a continuum from very risky to moderate and low levels of risk. The more risky the episode is considered, the greater the tendency for people to develop privacy rules that keep the privacy boundaries closed. High-risk episodes mean thicker and more tightly held boundaries with high needs for control, whereas low-risk episodes mean thinner boundary walls where individuals construct privacy rules allowing for more openness, and less need for control. For moderately risky episodes, the boundaries are of medium thickness and the privacy rules permit fluctuations from moderate-high to moderate-low.

*High-risk episodes* often revolve around encounters that may cause shame, threat, or severe embarrassment. An example of a high-risk incident is seen when we define something as a "secret" (Bok, 1982). Secrets illustrate that high-risk episodes may be problematic in both revealing and concealing. There are many kinds of secrets (Imber-Black, 1993). For instance, AIDS/HIV status or being an insemination donor are but two we see in our society today. These secrets highlight the risks of telling. Shame may reinforce the protective nature of this private information, justifying attempts to protect it from others (Schneider, 1992).

Secrets might also include knowledge or an experience whose value would diminish in the telling. For example, if you won a large sum of money in the lottery, telling others may create headaches and hassles. By keeping the information secret, you preserve the positive side of winning for you alone.

Secrets are most risky because they have the potential to result in a high level of vulnerability if known by others (Warren & Laslett, 1977). Consequently, people are more likely to protect secrets. As Bok (1982) states,

> to keep a secret from someone . . . is to block information about it or evidence of it from reaching that person, and to do so intentionally; to prevent him [or her] from learning it, and thus, from possessing it, making use of it or revealing it. (p. 5)

People keep secret information because there is a "fear of the real or imagined repercussions the hidden information would bring with exposure" (Lane & Wegner, 1995, p. 237). Sometimes keeping a secret makes the person feel guilty (Karpel, 1980). Guilt feelings may emerge for secrets because, although there is a right to privacy, there is not an equivalent right to secrecy (Warren & Laslett, 1977). Secrecy has a more negative connotation perhaps due to the restricted nature of the information and the kinds of things people generally keep secret. The implication is that a person "hides" something that otherwise would discredit him or her. However, it seems that the intent to hide the information is viewed as problematic even though telling would result in a negative outcome for the secret holder and perhaps even the confidant.

Nevertheless, research argues that keeping secrets, as opposed to telling, may have consequences for the secret holder (Kelly & McKillop, 1996; Lane & Wegner, 1995). Harboring secrets about a traumatic experience such as physical violence toward a child or sexual abuse may lead to a paradox (Harber & Pennebaker, 1992; Imber-Black, 1993). There are both physical and psychological symptoms associated with bearing the traumatic hardship alone (Kelly & McKillop, 1996). On the other hand, revealing secrets involves risks. Thus, secrets above all other types of private information pose the largest burden for us.

Secrets, though posing a high risk, also serve important functions (Vangelisti, 1994; Vangelisti & Caughlin, 1997). In several studies investigating family secrets, the findings suggest that family secrets tend to be viewed negatively (Vangelisti, 1994). Interestingly, "when people perceived

their family secrets served certain functions [i.e., avoided negative evaluations, maintained privacy, defended themselves], they reported being less
likely to reveal those secrets to outsiders" (Vangelisti & Caughlin, 1997, p.
694). In addition, the quality of the family relationship tends to affect
whether a member is willing to reveal or protect information seen as secret
to the whole family. Thus, both function and relational quality have import
for the way secrets are treated in families.

*Moderate-risk episodes* tend to revolve around events, attitudes, values, and experiences that people find uncomfortable, troublesome, or
aggravating for others to know. However, the perceived ramifications are
less daunting than they are for secrets. For example, a person's salary, failure in a class, being denied tenure, or a past relationship may be private
experiences. If discovered, the information at this level of risk may result in
moderate feelings of humiliation, uneasiness, wariness, and, perhaps, anxiety. Individuals recognize a clear outcome that may have some influence
on them or their significant relationships.

However, their discomfiture is less intense than with high-risk
episodes. Likewise, protecting moderately risky information, for example,
may have consequences of a modest nature. Because it is not traumatic,
people may find it easier to keep private. In fact, benefits may arise from
the ability to insulate the information from others. For example, if you are
successful in your career, you might not want your subordinates to know
that you do not have a college degree.

Privacy-disclosure episodes with *low risk levels* tend to reflect situations such as telling or keeping "white lies" or conflicting opinions about
an issue. The perceived risk is not high; however, individuals are mindful
of how they will disclose the information. The consequences for protecting
or disclosing the information may be beneficial or negligible.

**Risk types.** Along with the level of risks, potential disclosers consider the
types of risks we may project or discern if others know our private information. There are many possibilities; however, the following risks are
among the more obvious. Although they are presented as independent categories, it is likely that they are not mutually exclusive. In addition, it is
also likely that there is an interface between level and type of risk. Hence,
for each type, the level of risk may be high, moderate, or low.

*Security risks* represent instances where people cautiously disclose
because telling might shift power away from them, jeopardize their personal safety, or jeopardize the safety of others. For example, people might
perceive risk if they thought they could lose their job by disclosing a theft
in their business. Those individuals who are HIV positive often judge the
hazard of telling their health status to others based on a safety risk they
perceive (Greene & Serovich, 1998; Yep, 2000). They may have their

homes taken away or others may harass them if they disclose. Likewise, people may judge safety risks for their loved ones before they disclose private information. A mother might be careful not to tell others that her daughter is pregnant for fear of negative repercussions. In all these ways, safety risks play a part in the disclosure equation.

*Stigma risks* are another type of risk that we may take into account when we judge whether to reveal or conceal private information. These risks are specific to the individual's inner self or self-identity. By disclosing, we might perceive that others could discredit us. For example, if you reveal that you hate all of your colleagues at work, this disclosure could lead to a negative outcome. Others may interpret such a statement as an uncomplimentary insight into your attitudes about your job. Disclosing an unpopular opinion or a religious belief that is different from that held by those to whom you reveal may also be a stigma risk. Being cast in a disparaging light by others is a risk from the disclosure.

Stigma risks are based, therefore, on the assumption that others might negatively evaluate behaviors or opinions of an individual. In this way, they underscore at least one function of maintaining secrets in families that Vangelisti (1994) found in her research. When a person predicts negative evaluations by others, it is more likely that he or she will not risk revealing to those outside the family as a whole and may not even risk telling family members at all.

*Face risks* are more generic in nature. We may anticipate situations where our disclosures cause us embarrassment, embarrass others in our group, or serve as threats to face. We are likely to anticipate the need for a defense if private information becomes public. For example, revealing we once failed a test or caused discomfort to others is embarrassing. Perhaps telling about a situation where individuals were in a compromising situation might renew the risk of reliving the embarrassment. Self-defense is a function or motivator for keeping information private (Petronio & Martin, 1986;Vangelisti, 1994).

Therefore, when the face risk is great, a person may not want to reveal personal information. Sometimes individuals may be able to predict the reactions of others to their private information (Cupach & Metts, 1994). In this situation, people might enact preventive facework (Cupach & Metts, 1994). On the other hand, they may not be able to project a reaction and, therefore, will need to reclaim face as a corrective action after the fact (Cupach & Metts, 1994). Because loss of face is a possible risk for disclosure, people often factor the ramifications into a disclosure decision.

*Relational risks* for revealing private information may come in many forms. For instance, telling your partner about something he or she did that you did not like may pose a threat to the relationship. As disclosures, complaining about lack of support from a spouse, accusing a partner of loving someone else, or telling your partner that he or she makes you feel unhappy have a level of relational risk if revealed. Although bonding may be a function of keeping something private, revealing may provoke exactly the opposite response, for example, when a relational transgression is revealed. As Cupach and Metts (1994) point out, there are levels of severity. When the transgression is severe, its disclosure rocks "the very foundation of the relationship culture—the collection of rules, values, attitudes, and beliefs from which the relationship-specific identity is derived" (Cupach & Metts, 1994, p. 56). Even when the transgression is less severe, relational issues are still in need of repair.

Complaints may also be disclosed and result in relational risks that the individual weighs against the benefits of telling. Sometimes complaints are more difficult to judge because they may be emotional disclosures that need airing (Shimanoff, 1985, 1987). However, the risks are often sufficient to cause peril in the relationship. Thus, there may be a need to judge whether to reveal the information based on the advantages of telling.

*Role risks* are those that have the potential to jeopardize our standing if we disclose private information. If a supervisor discloses personal information about his marital relationship to a subordinate, asks for advice, and the disclosure episode is viewed as inappropriate by the subordinate, the supervisor's role definition may be compromised. Being taken into a supervisor's confidence and asked to give advice tends to shift the definition of roles in a way that undermines the expectations for each position.

Because the gains of disclosure are often important to our well-being, we seek a way to minimize the potential risks of vulnerabilities. Private information is something that we believe belongs to us. As such, control plays an important role in granting or denying accessibility to boundaries around private information. Sometimes the risk is of a minor nature, and sometimes it is more substantial. We like to minimize risk and to maximize control over private information because we feel we have the right to govern the amount of vulnerability we experience (Petronio, 1991).

Rule development, therefore depends on these criteria to change or construct new rules. The decisions people make about rules to use often blend these five criteria in a way that builds a repertoire of options for people to use as they manage their private disclosures with others.

## PRIVACY RULE ATTRIBUTES

Privacy rules have two key dimensions; the way people *acquire* rules and rule *properties*. Hence, the way people acquire rules is through socialization of preexisting rules or by negotiating rules as new collective boundaries are formed. The rule properties include the fact that rules may become stable over time, develop into privacy orientations, or change. In addition, sanctions may be used by those in collective boundaries to ensure consistent use of agreed upon rules.

As we have seen, rules are developed based on certain criteria; however, people may learn preexisting rules and negotiate new rules with others as privacy boundaries are formed or changed. In addition, privacy rules have the possibility of ranging from stable entities to ones that change because of boundary needs. Thus, given that privacy management is a dynamic process, privacy rules necessarily reflect the embedded dialectic of stability and change. Understanding stability and change for privacy rules means considering the fluctuation between remaining routinized over periods or changing (triggered) to meet new privacy demands.

## Rule Acquisition

As noted, learning the rules takes many forms including socialization and negotiation.

### Socialization of Preexisting Rules

Although rule development is fundamental to privacy management, people do not continuously generate new privacy rules. Instead, individuals may enter preexisting privacy boundaries. They are often expected to learn ongoing rules already established by other co-owners of the information. Thus, when people become members of groups, families, or organizations where they are told collectively held private information as a definition of their membership, they are also expected to learn the rules that manage the information.

Thus, joining a collective boundary often results in learning to be coresponsible for existing private information that others in the group already know. When collective boundaries are joined or adopted by a new member, he or she becomes actively involved in learning the existing rules. This socialization process helps new members understand the expectations as to how they are to regulate this new boundary.

Although there are many good illustrations, two examples of how people learn pre-existing boundary rules are examined. First, we look at how young children learn family rules for managing privacy. Second, we consider the way people learn rules for organizationally held private information.

**Family rule socialization.** At a very young age, children learn the rudimentary aspects of privacy and with that comes the instruction of boundary rules (Wolfe & Laufer, 1974). Interestingly, infants and babies tend not to be accorded much privacy in U.S. culture. Witness the mothers changing their children's diapers in public places and the acceptable practice of very young children swimming naked in public pools. In part, the lack of concern for privacy with very young children is because they are not cognitively aware of such privacy needs. Their awareness does not evolve until they are out of the egocentric stage of development (Wolfe, 1978; Wolfe & Laufer, 1974).

Consequently, young children have very small, perhaps even nonexistent privacy boundaries they manage. However, as children move out of the egocentric stage, they begin to recognize that they can own objects and information that are separate from others and belong only to them (Wolfe & Laufer, 1974). Not until children understand that they may choose aloneness and become comfortable with this choice do they begin to recognize the dual need for separation and connectedness. Further,

> the developmental task and accomplishment of learning to function independently adds a critical aspect to the relationship between the self and privacy—the awareness of volition: the ability to choose aloneness (either physical or psychological) when capable of functioning in aloneness. The choice of aloneness, then, becomes a statement of the autonomy of the self. (Wolfe & Laufer, 1974, p. 34)

At this stage, children begin to develop their own personal boundaries and rules structure. Wolfe and Laufer (1974) found that having a definition of privacy tended to be a function of age. Thus, they note that 53.3% of the 5-year-olds in their study were unable to define privacy, whereas approximately 94% of the 7-year-olds could define the concept of privacy. Further, children from the ages of seven upward cited four major meanings of privacy. They included: (a) controlling access to information, (b) being alone, (c) no one bothering me, and (d) controlling access to spaces and places (Wolfe & Laufer).

Children appear not to have a clear sense of the complexities found in the notion of privacy until they are able to understand the concept of autonomy. Interestingly, observational evidence suggests that although privacy is not recognized by young children, they are socialized into family privacy rules by members at a young age.

For example, during a visit to a friend's house, a 3-year-old boy entertained my husband and me while his parents prepared dinner. He told us about his day. We listened for a while, but grew tired and stopped paying attention. This little boy was perceptive and recognized that our attention had wandered. To grab the floor, he looked us in the eye and stated, "My mom and dad sleep naked." We were immediately at his command; however, his parents also heard his disclosure. His father came rushing out of the kitchen and whisked him away up the stairs to his bedroom. On the way, the father stated repeatedly, "We don't tell company things like that, it should be kept private." The father was articulating a rule for how the child should treat information that is considered private for that family. The child had understood some part of the family rule because he repeatedly stated, "But Daddy, they are your friends."

The socialization of privacy rules is also seen with the regulation of space in the home. Parents begin to teach their children that certain places in the home are off limits and private to the mother and father (Parke & Sawin, 1979).

> Regulation of space in the service of privacy can be viewed as not only reflecting child-rearing practices but also spatial regulation, per se, can be conceptualized as a technique for control of social interaction among household members. . . . [Thus] physical space regulation can . . . serve both as a socialization tactic as well as a mirror of socialization practices. (Parke & Sawin, 1979, p. 88).

Regulating space, like all socialization practices for different kinds of privacy, reflects the fact that while the child's privacy boundary is small, older family members have more advanced privacy needs and larger boundaries to maintain. Thus, children seem to learn about privacy more from the needs of others than from their own immediate privacy concerns.

As children enter adolescence, they develop a greater need for autonomy, best observed in their increasing desire to have privacy (Petronio, 1994). Most clearly, during adolescence, children begin to develop their own set of privacy rules that may differ from those their parents taught them. During this stage, the children's boundary begins to increase significantly in size. Adolescents have more information, space, and possessions to control and actively work to increase their ownership during this phase.

Youniss and Smollar (1985) point out that the adolescent's main job is to develop a separate identity apart from his or her family and that the clearest sign of separation for adolescents is "limited contact with parents and possession of private lives apart from the family" (p. 77). In this way, adolescents are able to develop their personal set of privacy rules that pertain to their own world. Often the sense of control they are gaining is reinforced because they become reporters of their own extrafamilial activities. "They have, then, the power to control information that they give to their parents about themselves" (Youniss & Smollar, 1985, p. 77). They control and actively work to increase their ownership during this phase.

The socialization process continues in adolescence when the parents grant their children the freedom to enjoy their privacy. However, this freedom typically comes with the caveat that they follow certain parental expectations for appropriate behavior (Youniss & Smollar, 1985). The children learn that having personal privacy involves responsibility to others. Thus, they come to see that privacy is not a unitary concept but is dialectical with being a member of the family and enjoying social connections.

**Organizational rule socialization.** In most situations where people come into a preexisting group such as an organization, the rules are already established. This is not to say that rules might not change because of the person entering the group. However, part of learning about the organization is being taught privacy rules. Often organizations have rules about how they want their employees to regulate revealing proprietary information (Petronio & Chayer, 1988).

Nonetheless, how employees learn the rules may vary. Consequently, some organizations teach their employees these rules as they enter the organization and others expect their employees somehow to learn rules for disclosing information considered private to the organization. For example, in many corporations and government agencies there are strict rules for disclosure, such as those found in the Food and Drug Administration.

> The FDA asserts that present secrecy policies prevent it from satisfactorily answering its critics, limiting public confidence in its judgments and causing deep resentment among FDA staff, who cannot reveal data that would help rebut public attacks against their decisions. (McGarity & Shapiro, 1980, p. 838)

In this example, the privacy rules are clearly identified. In other cases, the expectations for disclosure of proprietary information may not be as evident. Thus, how people learn to regulate privacy boundaries seems critical to a smooth transition into the company.

A study conducted in a multinational corporation that has numerous government contracts found that mediated versus nonmediated message modes tended to predict the degree of certainty an employee felt in learning the rules for disclosure of proprietary information (Petronio & Chayer, 1988). Thus, these employees felt more certain about the rules for disclosure when they were written rather than oral. In addition, the more helpful the articulation of the rules was perceived to be, the more certain the employee was about the expectations of the corporation. These employees also indicated that the more helpful the mediated modes were perceived to be, the more satisfied they were with the way they learned the privacy rules.

When it came to specific confidants, employees indicated that nonmediated message modes, such as storytelling from other employees about the rules, increased the degree to which subordinates felt it was appropriate to disclose private organizational information to family members.

Thus, word of mouth seemed to be a more reliable source for learning some rules, like those concerning family members, and not others, such as talking to supervisors. In today's corporations, teaching employees how to determine which information to tell family members and what is taboo may be complicated.

Many companies hire individuals who are in relationships with partners who work for the competition or work at different levels in the same corporation. Keeping information confidential from those with whom we have a personal relationship may not be possible. On the other hand, the free transfer of that information may lead to grave problems for the organization. For example, a spouse of an employee in a multinational company told the CEO at a holiday party that he should have never fired one of her husband's colleagues. The CEO felt it was a breach of confidence for her husband to tell her about the firing or at least he should have instructed her not to make a public announcement of the event.

Though this example illustrates the difficulty in teaching employees organizational privacy rules, corporations also have a problem with insisting that employees keep propriety information from their partners. Policing is next to impossible, and mandating that corporations prohibit the flow of propriety information to family members is neither practical nor possible. Nevertheless, one executive mentioned that he thought the biggest breach in the privacy boundary often came from family members. Thus, the method of learning rules for boundary maintenance and the propensity for learning the rules is a challenge to organizations socializing their members into privacy expectations. Recognizing that we manage not only our personal boundaries but collective ones as well, we need to determine the best way to coordinate this management process.

### Negotiated Privacy Rules

Rule acquisition also reflects the process of negotiating privacy rules. Because CPM argues that boundaries are coordinated, privacy rules often emerge out of an interaction with others. As a collaborative venture, those coordinating boundaries mutually determine the rules that will regulate the collective privacy boundaries.

There are numerous ways that negotiations take place. For example, when people disclose their personal information, they frequently stipulate rules for others to follow. As they expand their boundaries around the information into collectively held entities, they also identify privacy rules they expect others to follow. For example, a person may say, "don't tell Jim about this." These are *disclosure warnings* that set the parameters of who may know and who is prohibited from knowing

(Petronio & Bantz, 1991). Because the information becomes co-owned, those individuals who make a disclosure may feel compelled to engage others in a pact to control further dissemination beyond the newly constructed dyadic boundary. However, the confidant may or may not comply with those rules. There are also times when the confidant requests additional clarification about third-party rules. For example, a confidant may inquire whether his or her spouse can be included in the boundary or excluded from knowing.

As negotiations proceed, people work through several sequences of conversational turns trying to arrive at a reasonable set of rules for protecting or accessing the private information that is revealed. This exercise also may include a reciprocal disclosure by the confidant whereby the initial discloser is then given additional rules to follow by the confidant-turned-discloser. In all, the dyad establishes privacy rules that evolve out of their conversation and that are used to determine how the private information is accessed or protected.

There may be a number of different ways that individuals accomplish negotiating privacy rules for access or protection of information (Petronio, 1991). Privacy rules may be articulated *explicitly* or *implicitly* by a discloser. Since the discloser is the original owner of the information, he or she often feels a right to determine the set of rules that should be used in third-party disclosures.

**Explicitly stated rules.** These occur when the discloser states these rules in a direct and unencumbered way (Petronio, 1991). The expectations for the way a confidant is to treat the information are unambiguous. There are numerous examples; one of the more obvious is the *disclosure warning* just mentioned (initially defined as prior restraint phrases; see Petronio & Bantz, 1991). These warnings are issued prior to telling the private information to identify the parameters for telling or keeping the information. Statements such as, "Don't tell anyone, but" and "Before I tell you this, I don't want it to go any further," clearly send a signal about the seriousness of the disclosure and indicate rules that should be used in future disclosures (Petronio & Bantz, 1991).

Disclosure warnings mark the information and identify the limits of third-party disclosure (Petronio & Bantz, 1991). Examining close friendships of senders and receivers, this research shows that a majority of both disclosers and recipients expect receivers to pass disclosures along, regardless of how private the information. This is true despite the use of such warnings. The recipients appear to live up to these expectations, especially with moderately and highly private information. The good news is that receivers who are given disclosure warnings tend to tell only trusted friends and family members. Gender is also found to be a factor in who abides by the warning. Apparently, men tend to believe that these warnings have some import, while women do not trust that the warnings work to keep private information within their desired parameters.

Disclosure warnings serve a strategic function for disclosure by marking the significance of the information and implying the status of the recipient (M. H. Davis & Franzoi, 1987; Stiles, 1987). These phrases may also be useful in tracking targets of disclosure (e.g., "Don't tell Mom this," or "Don't tell John this") by suggesting networks among recipients of disclosed information.

In addition to third-party targets, disclosure warnings may also specify a *time parameter* in which the private information is to be kept confidential; for instance, "I would appreciate your keeping this information secret for the next couple of days until I have a chance to tell my husband." Sometimes people also focus on which information may be communicated to others; for instance, "Only tell your mother that I was going to the doctor, not that I am pregnant." The utility of this linguistic strategy is yet unexplored. However, the importance of the disclosure may be discerned by examining these warnings.

**Implicitly stated rules.** These occur when the strategies tend to be more ambiguous and, therefore, the rules are less clearly articulated (Petronio, 1991). The lack of clarity may be beneficial to the discloser or may lead to problems. For example, if the discloser only *hints* at a rule for how to access or protect the private information, the confidant may not really understand the way he or she should treat privacy management. This uncertainty may result in misunderstandings and hurt feelings when the rule is not applied in the way the discloser envisioned.

On the other hand, an *implicit* strategy such as *hinting* has proved useful for sexually abused children when they use this option to test the way confidants might feel about the content of their disclosures (see chapter 6). There are numerous implicit strategies to communicate rules. Hinting is just one type. Individuals may also use *prompts*, getting the confidant to actually articulate a rule. For instance, a friend might say to a confidant, "Hum, how do you think we should deal with this information?"

As these examples illustrate, the original owner of the private information, who is choosing to share it with a confidant, attempts to convey some rule structure to guide the way privacy boundaries should be comanaged. However, there is also the possibility that nothing will be said or that the rules disclosers have in mind are so intrinsic to their assumptions that they do not articulate them. In this case, the rules may not be known until they are inadvertently breached. Once that happens, the turbulence that erupts often requires the discloser and confidant to adjust the old rules or negotiate the rules anew.

There are many other ways that people negotiate privacy rules when collective boundaries are formed. In chapter 4, we will see a number of examples of different strategies that people use to determine collectively held private rules.

## Rule Properties

Rule properties represent the qualities of privacy rules that describe their nature. Four properties typify privacy rules, including routinization, orientation, change, and sanctions.

### Routinized Rules

Interestingly, individuals may become so accustomed to the privacy rules they use that these rules serve as the basis for *routine actions*. Many interactions involving disclosure or concealment of private information follow a habitual pattern and the rules become routinized as they are used repeatedly to manage privacy boundaries. For example, as a matter of practice, some people may not talk about their finances. This routine practice may exist because at some point these individuals encountered a situation that prompted them to construct such a rule. Over time, this rule is evoked frequently and applied to all circumstances where discussions of finances take place.

Preestablished, routinized privacy rules often have a basis in negotiated rules. Yet, once formulated, these rules become patterned actions that people depend on to communicate with others about this issue over time. The routinized rules become integrated into typical patterns use for privacy management. When these routinized rules become so ingrained, the long-term repeated use often leads to an even more stable form of concretized orientations to privacy.

While routinized privacy rules are stable, by comparison, concretized orientation rules are unbending. To highlight the change in form, concretized rules may be considered *privacy rule orientations* (or values). The meaning of privacy orientation captures the substantive change in the rule structure that has a significant amount of stability. Orientation rules signal an ingrained value toward privacy and disclosure (see the section on family privacy orientations in chapter 4). Hence, orientations come about because people have consistently used the privacy rules across generations or for such a long time that they have become permanent privacy values. For example, families often develop privacy rule orientations over time. Family members might construct all their rules to reflect their value of openness and reinforce this orientation for all family members. Thus, each member is expected to tell any problems or issues he or she faces to other family members.

On the other hand, other families might have restricted orientation rules about disclosure and be more private. For these families, the members construct rules that limit the disclosure to one another, insisting that each member should solve his or her own problems without talking about them to other family members. Routinized rules and rule orientations toward privacy are examples of durable practices that are necessary because it is difficult for people to keep rule making at a conscious level every day. By depending on ingrained ways of choosing to reveal or conceal, people are not burdened with constructing plans or developing decision options every time they want to open their privacy boundaries. Some of the decisions are therefore routine or part of their privacy values stemming from already existing rules for privacy regulation.

**Triggered Rules**

Although privacy rules may be routine or reflect an established value, there are times when they do not accommodate a particular situation and change is necessary. In the discussion of boundary turbulence in chapter 5, we will see many circumstances that invite adjustments, modifications, or complete overhauls of privacy rules. Because privacy management does not function effectively when there is boundary turbulence, it is necessary to change or adjust the privacy rules so that synchronization can be attained and boundary coordination can be restored.

Thus, boundary turbulence may result because there are unpredictable events that call for establishing new rules or that alter routine rules for conduct. This may also occur when there are novel situations that we have not encountered before. Consequently, an unpredictable situation, a change in our lives that is unplanned, or a novel event may *trigger* a new rule or modification in our existing privacy rules.

Everyday interactions bring about many examples of rule change. For instance, a crisis, such as divorce, might require us to cultivate a new set of rules to determine how much we disclose to our former partner. A novel, yet planned situation (e.g., traveling to another country for the first time) may evoke the need for new rules or alter existing rules for boundary access to private information. When people get married, not only do both partners have existing rules that they have developed for personal information, but also, both have learned rules from their families about ways to treat private information that might be different from their new partner's family rules.

Some research indicates that because partners come from certain family rule orientations they often need to adjust their rules for privacy to fit the new situation (Petronio, 2000a). Talking about salaries, disclosing personal details about a spouse to a parent, and revealing personal habits often require rule changes when a person marries. In addition, information that had been considered personally private soon becomes dyadic in ways that the couple may not have expected, triggering the need for new rules. In all, there are a number of ways that the need for new rules can be triggered when relational status changes or some other situation intervenes calling for more functional privacy rules.

**Privacy Rule Sanctions**

If the rules have been articulated, all of the co-owners of the private information are held responsible for abiding by the established privacy rules. Sanctions may be imposed if co-owners do not follow the agreed-upon rules for privacy management. In other words, once the privacy rules have been negotiated, learned, or developed, everyone considered a co-owner of the information is held accountable.

Those who breach the privacy rules may be reprimanded, shut out of further disclosures, given partial information in the future, or warned about their violation. Sanctions are used to fortify the use of rules (Shibutani, 1986). Sanctions may be positive or negative. Positive sanctions, such as praising or rewarding, show approval of those who comply with the established rules in the collective boundary. Negative sanctions such as embarrassment or humiliation also function to reinforce the use of privacy rules.

Sanctions, positive or negative, are imposed to exercise some power and control over the way the private information is regulated (Shibutani, 1986). Sanctions are geared to reduce the sense of autonomy in decision making about who should know and how the information should be managed. They reinforce the fact that the private information is communal.

Because the private information belongs to everyone in the group, no one person has the right to make independent decisions about revealing and concealing. Thus, sanctions are used to strengthen the rules that have been agreed upon by the group. When members do not follow the expectations, the group members, individually or collectively, communicate the fact that a breach has occurred. These sanctions are necessary because the private information, if disclosed inappropriately, could result in vulnerabilities for all members of the group.

The sanctions also help identify rules that might have been only implied by the collective. For example, groups members may be so accustomed to how they regulate private information that they socialize a new member only through example. If the new member does not understand the parameters of the rules, he or she might use different ones to decide whether to reveal, how much to tell, or who to tell. When that group member is sanctioned by the others, the implicit rule becomes more apparent.

For example, remember the scene in the film *Ordinary People* (1980) where Calvin, Beth's husband, tells friends at a party that their son, Conrad, is seeing a psychiatrist. Beth is furious at her husband for making that private information public. However, Calvin does not understand why she is so angry. She explains in the car that he violated a privacy rule applied to their family boundary by revealing this fact to their friends in such a public manner. She tells him that he should know better. Beth is articulating a rule that was implicit regarding the way in which their collective boundary around private information concerning their family should be regulated.

Certainly there are many cases where management rules for collective boundaries are left ambiguous and as such, an individual's behavior is open for interpretation. Consequently, through sanctions such as the one Beth imposed, the group member violating the rule comes to understand the expectations of the other members. Thus, sanctions help identify and reinforce the way groups regulate collective privacy boundaries. Although there is room for change and renegotiation, they serve a useful purpose in making the collective privacy rules more accessible to members.

## CONCLUSION

To set the stage for understanding privacy management, this chapter has discussed the nature of privacy rules and their development to manage boundaries. As chapter 2 shows, the rules that evolve from the formation of collective boundaries may be negotiated or triggered, or people may be socialized into them. Further, the rules may become routinized and individuals within the boundaries may work to maintain the utility of the rules through sanctions. We have considered the way that people acquire privacy rules, rule attributions, and rule sanctions. A number of criteria are used to develop the rules people depend on to manage their privacy, such as culture, gender, motivations, context, and risk-benefit ratios.

As this chapter shows, when there are alternative ways of defining privacy rights based on cultural expectations, people use a different lens to judge revealing and concealing. Gender perspectives also affect the rule development process. Men and women often see expectations for privacy in dissimilar ways, and they formulate rules that are sometimes in opposition to each other. This makes heterosexual disclosure interactions potentially difficult.

Motivations also contribute to the foundation of rule production because the needs we have direct our choices about privacy. If we are lonely, if we feel embarrassed, if we have certain personality characteristics, or if we are of a certain age, our needs translate into another factor that guides rule making. We also take into account situational issues in determining the rules we use to control our privacy boundaries. Traumatic events, therapeutic situations, and life circumstances may call for completely different criteria than ordinary everyday interactions. Thus, privacy rules need to be altered to fit the requirements of the situation.

Rule making is also predicated on taking into account levels of risk and benefits. Some episodes are more risky than others are. As a result, we establish or adjust our privacy rules to fit the expected outcomes of revealing or concealing. In addition, we also take into account the types of risks we may face when managing our privacy boundaries. All of these criteria form the structural bases for the rule production that leads to regulating privacy boundaries. We depend on these criteria to judge what kind of rules should be in effect. However, the structural foundation of rules is only the beginning of understanding how privacy boundaries are managed.

This chapter explains that people not only make up their own rules, but also, because they must coordinate with others when they co-own private information, they are socialized to learn the preexisting rules of the boundaries they join. To get a sense of this idea, the chapter discusses family rule socialization and rule socialization found in organizations. People also acquire privacy rules by negotiating them when new joint boundaries emerge. There are both implicit and explicit strategies that people use to negotiate privacy rules managing boundaries. In this way, co-owners coordinate the way they will care for the collective privacy boundary.

Finally, while rules may be developed and have certain attributes that define them, for the coordination process to be successful, rule sanctions are imposed to collectively control how the boundaries are managed by the members. To completely appreciate the nature of privacy boundaries and a rule-management system, we need to consider how boundary coordination works. We do that in chapter 4 by exploring the concept of boundary coordination that reflects the interface between expanding the disclosure process beyond the self and examining the way rules manage both personal and collective boundaries.

Although self-disclosure has always focused on the individual, the actual disclosure process is one where private information about the self becomes the shared responsibility of both the discloser and the recipient. Intriguingly, the very nature of disclosing means changing the character of a boundary structure from personal to dyadic, dyadic to group or collective, and all the further permutations that are possible. This idea modifies thinking about disclosure as only a personal issue or within a personal boundary, to a collective boundary where one or more people are accountable for granting or denying access to collectively held private information.

# 3

# Rule Management Process 2

## *Boundary Coordination Operations*

The theory of Communication Privacy Management is about communicative interactions specific to private information. As such, communication to others or protection from others of private information plays a significant role. Thus, when people weigh whether to reveal or conceal private information, they often consider their knowledge about possible confidants. Because the information has the potential to render an individual vulnerable, considering the other when sending or keeping messages about private issues is critical. Thus, any theory about private disclosures must necessarily take into account how two or more people communicate. A core aspect of CPM, therefore, is the proposal that people manage multiple boundaries through privacy coordination. By framing the revealing and concealing process this way, we are able to detect the patterned actions of people as they manage many different kinds of private information on countless levels.

We not only have personal boundaries where we manage information about the self, but we also have collective boundary structures where we regulate many different kinds of private information with other people. To function within and among these collective boundaries, individuals use a coordination process. Given that people may be managing dyadic boundaries (sharing private information belonging to two people in a relationship), private group boundaries, private family boundaries, and a multitude of other types of collective privacy boundaries, issue of synchronization within and among boundaries becomes important.

Consequently, it is not enough to simply consider the self in revealing and concealing; we need to think about the larger disclosure picture. Chapter 4 offers an in-depth exploration of collective boundary types that individuals manage every day. In this chapter, we are concerned with an explication of personal versus collective boundaries, and the rule management operations used for both personal and collective boundaries to coordinate with others. Finally, because the recipient or confidant is so central to coordination, a discussion of the co-owner or confidant's role is presented.

The personal boundary is where individuals house their own private information. For CPM, the personal boundary takes into account many of the issues that have been considered in the discussions on *self*-disclosure (Derlega et al., 1993). However, CPM theory provides a systematic approach to understand disclosure about the self by focusing on the process of privacy management. In addition, the theory frames the content of information about the self as private. These two dimensions contribute significantly to broadening the scope of disclosure. The theory suggests that people use a rule system based on the decision criteria discussed in chapter 2 to manage revealing and concealing about the self.

CPM theory also expands the current thinking about disclosure to argue that, in addition to personal privacy boundaries, individuals also manage collective boundaries. The process used to manage both self-disclosure (personal boundary) and collectively owned private information is similar, but more complex as others share in the boundary responsibility. With self-disclosure, we personally determine who, what, when, and where private information is revealed because we own it (Cline, 1982; Derlega et al., 1993). We feel a need to control a boundary around personally private information about the self because of potential vulnerabilities. We develop personal rules for privacy management.

As we formulate collective boundaries and develop corresponding rules to manage them, we add to the number of boundaries that we regulate in everyday life. Consequently, CPM proposes that our disclosure process is not as simple as focusing solely on the self. Instead, we actually are involved in a much more comprehensive management system that regulates revealing and concealing on a number of levels.

For instance, think about the fact that in our families we are co-owners of private information that belongs to the family as a whole (Karpel, 1980). Everyone in the family might know about the parents' salaries, but no one is supposed to tell anyone outside the family. This information belongs to all the members, yet is restricted from nonfamily members. Thus, there is a family privacy boundary around the salary information signaling that all members have a shared stake in maintaining the boundary.

However, each person in that family also has information about himself or herself that is not necessarily accessible to other family members. This private information is personal, though one may choose to reveal it to another family member. Although disclosing, by definition, makes the receiver a co-owner, the discloser may still feel that he or she is the primary titleholder of the information. Thus, the fact that people tell their private information does not mean they completely relinquish personal privacy boundaries. The revelation may be about only one of many private issues or only part of a story.

Consequently, the personal boundary continues to mark private information about the self that has not been revealed. Likely, the discloser may continue to define the revealed information as belonging to him or her even though someone has been privy to it. Yet, the revelation links someone else into a budding new dyadic boundary because the information has been shared. In this way, personal boundaries expand into collective boundaries. Once a collective boundary is formed, there is an expectation of coresponsibility for the shared information.

Collectively owned private information transcends the individual level. Each member is only part of the larger whole and rules are jointly established to protect these boundaries (Collett, 1977; Fisher, 1986; Harré, 1977; Harris & Cronen, 1979; Putnam & Stohl, 1990; Petronio, 1991; Petronio & Kovach, 1997; Robinson, 1977; Shimanoff, 1987). Consequently, co-ownership of private information often reflects one vehicle individuals use to bond together in relationships. The boundaries function as a relational anchor for people in dyads, families, groups, and organizations. The managed care of these boundaries gives individuals an agency by which to maintain many kinds of relationships.

Viewing collective boundaries in this fashion helps us see why people associate disclosure with intimacy. Although intimacy is fundamentally different from disclosure, as suggested in chapter 1, disclosure contributes to the progression of relational intimacy through building a shared set of private information where there is an expectation of mutual reciprocal responsibility. However, co-ownership may not always be positive in nature. Just as likely are situations where ownership ties might be painful or embarrassing to the recipient. People might disclose information that could potentially be harmful to others. The confidant might be restricted in whom he or she can subsequently reveal to, resulting in negative outcomes for the relationship.

Considering these characteristics underscores the issue of responsibility that is so fundamental to being a co-owner of revealing and concealing. Although it is perhaps easier to see how hearing someone's confession triggers a sense of responsibility, not hearing a disclosure, yet suspecting that something is being protected, might also lead to a heightened level of responsibility. For example, suspecting that a teenage daughter is having trouble coming to terms with her budding sexuality, but not being privy to her thoughts, might heighten a sense of responsibility. This situation might prompt a person to solicit the private information. Regardless of how we come by the private information, once we are privy to it we are transformed into a co-owner, which means having some accountability for how it is managed. To manage our boundaries, whether collective or personal, we depend on rule management processes.

## COORDINATION OPERATIONS

Although the management of personal boundaries also depends on these rule management processes, when boundaries become collective, the processes are more complicated. Three management operations are used to coordinate privacy boundaries. First, boundaries are coordinated by rules that allow for *linkages* joining or converting one boundary type into another. Second, boundaries are coordinated through rules that allow degrees of *permeability* to regulate access to and protection of the information. Third, boundaries are coordinated through rules that stipulate *boundary ownership*, identifying those who have responsibility for the information and isolating the borders (parameters) of a personal or collective boundary. No claim is made that these component parts are mutually exclusive. In fact, they function in conjunction with each other to form the coordination process. Boundary linkage has import for permeability, and both influence the level of boundary ownership.

### Boundary Linkages

The way collective privacy boundaries are linked often depends on "disclosed" personally private information. The confidant becomes coresponsible for maintaining boundary regulation because telling may make both the discloser and confidant vulnerable. This vulnerability possibly differs for the discloser and confidant. For example, while the risk of telling for the individual may mean that the confidant tells others inappropriately, the confidant's degree of liability may depend on keeping a secret to avoid relational problems. Therefore, access to or protection of the once personally private information becomes a joint venture when a personal boundary is linked to form a collective boundary (see Figure 3.1).

### Linking from Personal Private Boundaries

From the earliest investigations of disclosure, the self has been at the core of its definition (Jourard, 1971). Chelune (1979) points out that

> the concept of self-disclosure has its roots in the existential and phenomenological philosophy of Husserl, Heidegger, Sartre, Buber, and Merleau-Ponty. To *disclose* means to show, to make known, or to reveal. "*Self*-disclosure is the act of making yourself manifest, showing yourself so others can perceive you" (Jourard, 1971, p. 19). (p. 2)

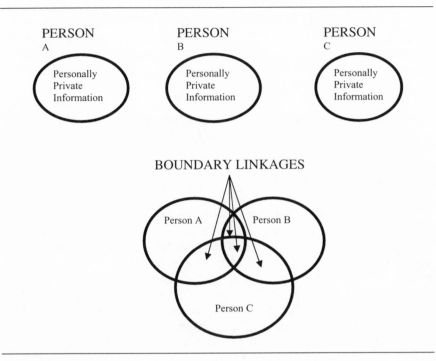

**Figure 3.1**
Boundary Linkages: Coordination Operations

Jourard was interested in how to measure the "real-self." He believed that revealing the real self leads to a healthy personality. He suggested, "everything and everybody in the world discloses themselves by one means or another as long as they exist" (Jourard, 1971, p. 19). For him, the more people talk about themselves, the more they discover their inner selves. Thus, Jourard emphasized the revealing process, as did those who followed (e.g., Berg & Derlega, 1987; Chelune, 1979; Dindia, 1994; Pearce & Sharp, 1973).

Although Jourard (1971) emphasized the process that people use to talk about themselves, CPM argues that the big picture is better understood when we look at the process of revealing and the management of many kinds of private information. As mentioned in chapter 1, when turning to the notion of private information we are able to broaden the concept of disclosure. We own and are responsible for different types of private information, not just that about ourselves. This shift is consistent with literature suggesting that disclosure may be an activity that involves more than the self (Altman, Vinsel, & Brown, 1981; Derlega & Chaikin, 1976; Parks, 1995; Petronio, 1991, 2000a, 2000b; Petronio & Kovach, 1997).

Once a disclosure is made, all who know are able to give others the information, even though it may still be seen largely as the property of the discloser. Thus, each co-owner may not have equal feelings of responsibility, but there is potential for disclosure by any party. Because of this prospect, either the parties negotiate privacy rules, or the person entering a group is taught the rules. To understand collective boundaries, we need to consider first the way they are formed and then the way they are managed or coordinated through rules.

## Boundary Linking Processes

Collective boundaries are linked in two ways; they may be *transformed* or *appropriated*. Sometimes both processes contribute to the development of collective boundaries; however, it is more likely that one or the other takes place. A boundary is *transformed* from a personal to a collective when someone self-discloses to a confidant. As one person reveals to another, the other individual becomes party to the information. Because there are often expectations that the confidant will treat the information with care and respect, the recipient shares in the responsibility of the information. Hence, a personal boundary grows into a collectively managed border.

Second, people join groups, families, or organizations where there exists private information that the members already shared and that is co-owned within a collective boundary. New people acquire this information through disclosure and accommodate it as part of their membership. In other words, preexisting private information needs to be *appropriated* by the new member who enters the group. Membership is often reflected by knowing private information and, thus, the new initiate becomes equally responsible for managing the revealing and concealing.

For example, organizations may consider certain information proprietary to a company, composing an organizational boundary. The organizational boundary is built around private information belonging to the company and is collectively held by the members. There may be risks if the information is revealed, and, therefore, it is managed by the organization as a whole. Secret contracts, products developed by the company, and terminations of colleagues are several examples of information that may be private to an organization.

## Nature of Boundary Linkages

The nature of linkages includes two major issues. First, boundary connections or conversions may be proportional, depending on the amount of contributions people make to the development of the boundary sphere. Second, the links may vary based on the strength or weakness of the ties that bond the privacy boundaries and the people in them.

**Proportional contributions.** The linkage that takes place may not reflect an equal contribution or, necessarily, any input from the new party or parties. People form or join boundaries differentially. For example, one person may have "donated" more of his or her personally private information that establishes the basis for the collective boundary than did others. In nursing homes, older people give up a great deal of their privacy, shrinking their personal boundaries, but expanding dyadic boundaries between their caregivers and themselves. The caregivers, on the other hand, do not give over their private information in return. Consequently, the collective boundary between the older person and caregiver is lopsided, based more heavily on the information belonging to the older person (Petronio & Kovach, 1997).

Disproportionate contributions may result from many different circumstances, such as role requirements like those of the nursing staff in an eldercare home. According to role expectations, the nurse's role limits how much he or she needs to tell, whereas the patient must reveal a great deal of very private matters to increase the success of care (Petronio & Kovach, 1997).

**Strength of ties.** The strength of the ties between people in the collective boundary influences the level of control they have over each other. People with weak ties, such as strangers, are likely to be less compliant in using existing rules than those already in the group. They may also feel less obligated to preserving the private information. Considering the weak ties of strangers for collective boundary control brings into question the phenomenon of the stranger on the train, plane, or bus. In other words, the fact that people are willing to open their personal boundaries to strangers because they are not in the disclosers' social network is useful. Yet, the stranger has no obligations. The bad news is that the stranger has no reason to comply with any implicit or explicit privacy rules that the discloser might attempt to negotiate. Further, the discloser does not know to whom the stranger might tell his or her private information. Thus, it is difficult in this circumstance to regulate further telling (third-party disclosure) of the private information because the weak ties reduce the commitment of responsibility.

On the other hand, when there are strong ties, like in a family, the prospects of coordinating the rules is greater because of the obligation each has to the other. Strong ties may assure a greater likelihood that the collective boundary members will cooperate with each other to determine boundary permeability. Thus, proportional contributions and strength of ties reflect a general sense of the way linkages might be considered. However, given that private rules are used to create the boundaries, the way they are used to link boundaries is fundamental to the coordination process.


## Linkage Rules

There are many *linkage rules* that people use to create a collective boundary. Because transformations and appropriations both depend on revealing private information to others, it is useful to examine some possible linkage rules that people use to understand the conditions under which collective boundaries might be formed. These rules take into account the foundational criteria mentioned earlier and the risk-benefit ratios people calculate.

The choice to open boundaries through disclosure, thereby initiating a collective boundary, depends on certain kinds of linkage rules, whether they are established through transformation or appropriation. People use many different types of rules. For our discussion here, we will focus on four consistently employed rules used to link boundaries. They include (a) rules about confidants, (b) rules about timing, and (c) rules about topic.

**Linking through confidant selection.** The disclosure literature is rich with many aspects of confidant selection. Several characteristics emerge within the research investigating to whom information is revealed. These characteristics include: attraction, status, age, gender, and relationship to the target individual. However, as in much of the disclosure research, the discussion of target characteristics is typically framed within a discussion of gender differences. Thus, this review reflects this trend as well.

Several authors (Cash, 1975; Rosenfeld et al., 1979; Sote & Good, 1974) note that the perceived attractiveness of a target affects willingness to disclose. However, there appears to be a tendency for attractiveness to be related to women's, but not men's, disclosure (Cash, 1975; Rosenfeld et al., 1979). Cash (1975), for example, found that individuals disclose more to an attractive same-sex partner and report engaging in less negative disclosure to an attractive opposite-sex partner. In addition, other research supports the contention that target attractiveness relates only to females' disclosure (Kohen, 1975; Sote & Good, 1974). Thus, linkage for women seems to be dependent on issues of attractiveness; however, this is not true for men.

Besides the level of attractiveness, *gender* alone also tends to be important. As Rosenfeld et al. (1979) point out, some studies show that there are greater levels of disclosure to opposite-sex targets, giving a clue to differences in ways men and women go about linking their personal boundaries with others (Annicchiarico, 1973; Brooks, 1974; Hyink, 1975;

Inman, 1978). Komarovsky (1974) and Cash (1975) both find that men reveal more to women who are either intimate girlfriends or same-sex friends. Thus, findings suggest that if we consider level of disclosure a critical factor for boundary linkages, female same-sex and opposite-sex disclosures between men and women are typically higher, thereby increasing the probability of these types of boundary linkages.

*Frequency* is also a factor in linkage building. For example, Cash (1975) finds that both men and women disclose more frequently to women than to men. Although Sollie and Fischer (1985) report that females are more willing to disclose personally private information to male romantic partners, when no male romantic partner exists, female friends are the favored targets of disclosure. Clearly, male friends are the least likely targets to be selected by either men or women, hampering boundary linkages.

*Status* is a consideration in determining the target of disclosures that allow for establishing connections. In general, people seem more willing to disclose and seek boundary linkages to high-status males than low-status males (Brooks, 1974). High-status targets tend to be selected by males, whereas females select lower-status targets (Brooks, 1974). There are also differences in disclosing behavior predicated on the symmetrical or complementary status of the target (Norton, 1982). Disclosure to a target whose status is complementary to the disclosers' status (i.e., a "one-up" position) is perceived as being more risky than disclosures to a symmetrical target (i.e., a peer). Therefore, boundaries are more likely linked with people considered peers.

The influence of status is evident in research by Jourard (1971) and Morgan (1976), who found that fathers might be perceived to have high status in families, but that fathers tend to receive the least amount of disclosure as compared to mothers, same-sex friends, and opposite-sex friends, no matter the intimacy level of the topic. Although fathers are important in the family, they are least likely to be connected with other members' privacy boundaries. This can be problematic for them because it means that they are more likely to be shut out of important conversations regarding their family. Only if they have a liaison who keeps them connected can they "be in the know" about family members.

The same issue prevails with children's choices for boundary linkages. For example, Morgan (1976) finds that disclosure to parents (i.e., complementary targets) is generally low as compared to peers (i.e., symmetrical targets) because of the riskiness involved. Parents are sometimes only loosely linked to their children's boundaries, making it difficult to provide useful guidance for the children.

In Jourard's (1971) and Morgan's (1976) research, age is also a determinant for target choice. Several scholars note that, in particular, adolescents' choices for target of disclosure highlight some interesting aspects of the disclosure process (Cohn & Strassberg, 1983; Denholm-Carey & Chabassol, 1987; Garcia & Geisler, 1988; Papini et al., 1990; Rivenbark, 1971). For example, targets for girls are generally mothers and female friends, whereas for boys, targets are most generally mothers and male friends (Denholm-Carey & Chabassol, 1987; Garcia & Geisler, 1988; Papini et al., 1990; Rivenbark, 1971). Therefore, boundary linkages, with some exceptions such as with mothers and same-sex friends, vary for girls and boys during adolescence. These choices for linkages reinforce the problematic position of the father.

*Level of intimacy* also plays a critical part in linking others into the privacy boundary. The tendency to link with friends through disclosures rather than with strangers has been reported in several studies (Chaikin & Derlega, 1974a; Falk & Wagner, 1985; Jourard, 1971; Morton, 1978; Rickers-Ovsiankina, 1956). As Hill and Stull (1987) point out, however, these findings are qualified by gender differences. For example, Stokes, Fueher, and Childs (1981) found that target persons who are well known to the discloser have a greater impact on the amount of disclosure reported by females.

Yet, for males, the tendency for linkage is to report more willingness to disclose to strangers and acquaintances rather than to persons known on an intimate level. Further, the reluctance of men to make disclosures to intimate targets, and therefore build boundary connections, is not dependent upon the gender of the target (Hill & Stull, 1987).

**Timing of linkage.** Confidant considerations may also affect the timing of the access that converts personal boundaries into collective ones. Considering the *timing* of a disclosure is crucial to the understanding of the boundary linkage process (Archer & Burleson, 1980; Derlega et al., 1993; Jones & Gordon, 1972). Timing is typically conceptualized in two ways. First, timing is seen as *conversational responsiveness*, which refers to the immediacy or latency of responsiveness on the part of the recipient after receiving a disclosure (Berg, 1987; Miller & Berg, 1984), influencing the increase or decrease of attraction and liking (Davis & Holtgraves, 1984; Davis & Perkowitz, 1979). Thus, if one follows a disclosure with a response immediately, greater attraction and liking occurs and boundary linkage will take place. However, if one is unresponsive to the disclosure, attraction and liking decrease, and so will the probability of boundary connections (Davis & Holtgraves, 1984).

Second, timing is conceptualized as the appropriate and optimal time for the discloser to reveal information during a conversation. Consequently, the ability to link boundaries may be enhanced or hampered depending on the choice of disclosure timing. Telling private information before someone is ready to hear it may interfere with the possibility of forming useful linkages. This aspect of timing also relates to recipients in that they evaluate the appropriateness of the disclosure in terms of when it occurs within an interaction. As Derlega et al. (1993) note, this aspect of timing is particularly important when it involves negative information.

For example, in a study by Jones and Gordon (1972), the time when study participants disclosed was manipulated, either in an early or late segment of an audio-taped interview. Participants listened to taped segments of these interviews between a student and his or her academic advisor in which the student explained why he or she missed a semester of school. When negative information, for which the student was directly responsible (i.e., missing school because of cheating or plagiarism), was revealed, participants liked the student more if he or she volunteered the information earlier rather than later in the interview. However, participants liked students less for revealing negative information for which they were not responsible (i.e., missing school because of their parents' divorce) if done so earlier in the interview as opposed to later.

These findings suggest that reluctance to disclose negative information for which one is responsible may give the appearance of avoiding accountability. Thus, the confidant may perceive the discloser as less trustworthy and be unwilling to form boundary linkages. On the other hand, when individuals are reluctant to reveal negative information for which they are not the responsible party, they may be perceived as being honest or respecting ownership rather than avoiding culpability or simply trying to gain sympathy (Barrell & Jourard, 1976).

Archer and Burleson (1980), provide additional evidence concerning the timing of negative disclosures and its relationship to forming collective boundaries. In this study, confederates revealed negative information to participants either early or late within the conversation. As in Jones and Gordon's (1972) research, confederates were liked more for revealing the negative information for which they were responsible (in this case a girlfriend's pregnancy) if they did so early in the interview. Both of these studies focus on the optimal time to disclose negative information so that boundaries may be joined. In general, negative information, especially when the discloser is personally responsible, is best revealed earlier within the interaction to assure boundary associations.

**Linking through topic selection.** The literature on *topic* as a condition to link boundaries is relatively large. The topic of disclosure refers to the choice one makes in the kind of private information revealed to another individual that leads to a transformed or appropriated boundary connection. One of the most prolific lines of research concerns the effect gender has on topic choice and the overall content of disclosure (e.g., Aries & Johnson, 1983; Burke et al., 1976; Caldwell & Peplau, 1982; Chelune,

1976; Dolgin, Meyer, & Schwartz, 1991; Gilbert & Whiteneck, 1976; Haas, 1979; Komarovsky, 1967; Morgan, 1976; Petronio, Martin, & Littlefield, 1984; Rosenfeld, 1979; Rubin, 1974; Rubin et al., 1980). For example, Caldwell and Peplau (1982) find that women, in general, are twice as likely to discuss personal topics such as feelings and problems with same-sex friends as are men. Similarly, Aries and Johnson (1983) find that females are apt to talk about *sensitive* topics such as doubts, fears, intimate relationships, and personal and family problems with other women. Men, on the other hand, report discussing only sports more often than women do with same-sex friends. Overall, differences in the way that linkages are created tend to be based on the level of intimacy for topics of disclosure discussed within same-sex friendships.

However, it is important to note that within the initial stages of opposite-sex relationships, the level of intimacy of discussed topics differs for men and women. Hence, for men compared to women, topics that are more intimate are discussed (Davis, 1978; Derlega, Winstead, Wong, & Hunter, 1985; Derlega et al., 1993; Green & Sandos, 1983; Huston & Ashmore, 1986; Peplau, Rubin, & Hill, 1977). Along this same vein, Hacker (1981), in her study of sex differences in disclosure, finds that a higher percentage of men than women report feeling comfortable revealing both personal weaknesses and strengths in same-sex and cross-sex friendships. Interestingly, none of the men revealed only weaknesses and none of the women revealed only strengths. Finally, one third of the women within this study state that they reveal only weaknesses in friendships with men, whereas almost one third of the men reveal only strengths in friendships with women.

Although age has been examined within the literature, there seems to be very little age difference in topic selection or the content of disclosures in forming boundary connections. Research on adolescents' self-disclosure to both parents and friends shows that girls tend to disclose more personal information, whereas boys disclose more about their future careers, attitudes, and opinions (Denholm-Carey & Chabassol, 1987; Papini et al., 1990; Youniss & Smollar, 1985).

O'Neill, Fein, Velit, and Frank's (1976) study on sex differences in preadolescents' self-disclosure also reports similar findings. In terms of the content of disclosure, girls disclose more than do boys about potentially embarrassing events, what they worry about, what makes them sad, behaviors they are ashamed of, and whether they like the way they look. Thus, girls tend to disclose more about emotions, anxieties, and issues of dependence, all of which tend to be topics more acceptable for females than for males (Bardwick, 1971; Denholm-Carey & Chabassol, 1987; Papini, Farmer, Clark, Micka, & Barnett, 1990; Sarason et al., 1960; Youniss & Smollar, 1985).

**Personality characteristics.** The characteristics that people have influence the way boundary linkages are produced. For example, some scholars (Brown &

Guy, 1983; Dinger-Duhon & Brown, 1987) investigated the effects gender and Machiavellianism have on disclosure patterns. Machiavellianism is described as "the extent to which an individual (1) holds a cynical view of human nature and (2) has internalized manipulative personality traits" (Brown & Guy, 1983, p. 93). Brown and Guy find that high-Machiavellian males are low self-disclosers when compared to low-Machiavellian males, whereas females who score high on the Machiavellianism scale also tend to be high self-disclosers. Thus, high-Machiavellian females may use disclosure as an influence strategy to determine how the boundaries are linked. As a result, their choices affect which topics are disclosed (i.e., which topics will aid in the manipulation) in order to achieve the kind of boundary linkage they are after.

Interestingly, and contrary to Brown and Guy's (1983) research, Dinger-Duhon and Brown (1987) specifically examine the use of self-disclosure as an influence strategy and find that Machiavellian females do not use disclosure as an influence technique. Further, their findings fail to show that high-Machiavellian females disclose more when compared to low-Machiavellian females. High-Machiavellian males, on the other hand, were found to use self-disclosure in a "non-affiliative fashion," whereas low-Machiavellian males self-disclosed only when they felt it appropriate to do so. Thus, these findings contradict the notion that Machiavellian females use specific topics of disclosure to manipulate their partners and the kind of boundary connections they are seeking. In fact, Machiavellian males are more self-disclosing during an influence task (Dinger-Duhon & Brown, 1987). This indicates that males may indeed select topics that may be used strategically to influence the recipient and boundary linkage goals.

Mikulincer and Nachshon (1991) provide another example of how personality characteristics may affect disclosure patterns and privacy boundary linkages. These researchers classified Israeli students as belonging to either secure, avoidant, or ambivalent attachment groups and assessed their differences in relation to disclosure patterns. Mikulincer and Nachshon found that secure and ambivalent individuals, as compared to avoidant individuals, disclose information that is more intimate and are more attracted to high-disclosing partners than low-disclosing partners. These results seem to provide further evidence that secure individuals want, as an interaction goal, to become intimate and emotionally close to others and work to guarantee that they have boundary linkages with others (Shaver & Hazan, 1988). Hence, they are prone to reveal more descriptive and intimate information to others and are more likely to aim to create a collective boundary.

**Linkages through acquisition of private information.** Most of the previous discussion focuses on how individuals manage their personal or collective boundaries to connect with others by giving out information. There are

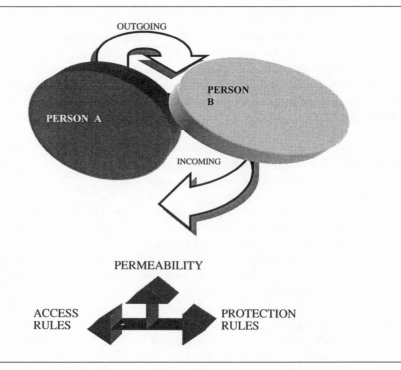

**Figure 3.2**
Boundary Permeability: Coordination Operation

also times when individuals seek out private information in order to establish boundary linkages or the boundaries are extended to incorporate more information that is private. There are many ways that boundary linkages are accomplished. For example, *probing* may be one way that people seek out another's private information to initiate a boundary connection. We often see therapists use this technique for learning about their clients (see chapter 4 for more details about this issue). In this way, they actively transform their clients' personal boundaries into a mutually shared information environment that therapists are coresponsible for as professionals.

*Asking direct or indirect questions* about private information informs individuals about the interest of others in the personal matters and is an attempt to encourage boundary linkage. Links may also be made through giving permission to disclose. For example, research with sexually abused children has found that they were more inclined to reveal about the abuse (and therefore link boundaries) when others told them about someone they knew who was abused (Petronio, Flores, & Hecht, 1997).

*Permission* is also a useful strategy when people make personal revelations and trigger feelings of reciprocity in others. Thus, when a person
wishes to discover private information belonging to someone else and
determines that direct questioning is not an effective strategy, the solicitor
guides the disclosure by depending on the norm of reciprocity. In order to
encourage (give permission to) the target to disclose the information, the
information-seeker first discloses something comparable hoping that the
target will be motivated to reciprocate with private information.

Linkages might also be extended to include additional private information through *information seeking*. The work by Baxter and Wilmot
(1984) offers an excellent example to illustrate ways that people might
accomplish linkages to include more private information though seeking
out information. For example, they may ask direct questions to discover
their partners' true feelings, ask someone else to get information (third-
party tests), hint (indirect-suggestion test), or do a public-presentational
test, an endurance test, a separation test, or a triangle test. These "secret
tests," as Baxter and Wilmot refer to them, are used by people already in
collective boundaries to link them further to others.

## Boundary Permeability

Permeability focuses on how opened or closed the collective boundaries are
once they are formed. Rules that control permeability are manifested in the
depth, breadth, and amount of private information that is revealed. Hence,
the notion of permeable boundaries considers the extent to which information goes out and the way that individuals in collective boundaries protect their private information. Most centrally then, how tightly or loosely
the privacy boundaries are held is a matter of permeability coordination
among the members (see Figure 3.2).

The boundary walls may be thick or thin, influencing the *access* to or
*protection* of private information. In this regard, we see that the individuals
within a privacy boundary may be in the dual roles of recipients or confidants and disclosers. Permeability takes into account the impact of receiving
disclosure and enacting the disclosing. When walls are thick, the boundaries
are tightly controlled, affecting the depth, breadth, and amount of private
information that is communicated. When the walls are thin, the boundaries
are loosely held and there is more permeable regarding these issues.

Coordinating collective boundary permeability depends on the degree
to which the members are able to achieve some measure of synchronicity in
determining how much access they permit. Part of the management process
relies on the ability of individual group members to negotiate an agreed-
upon level of permeability. Reaching that point hinges on how successful the

members are in cooperating with each other. To consider the issues members face as a collective, we first turn to a discussion of the way individuals respond to matters of access control for personal boundaries and its application to collective boundaries.

## Privacy Access Rules

Once boundaries are linked to form a collective sphere, the members need to develop ways to regulate access to the mutually owned private information internally. The goal for the group is to establish who, outside the boundary, can know the information, the amount of information they can know, when it is appropriate for them to know, and how they should be told. In this manner, the permeability of the boundary is controlled by the members. When the members negotiate these issues, they coordinate the way they manage the permeability of the boundary. However, as we find in the chapter on boundary turbulence (see chapter 5), there are times when the rules regulating permeability are not explicitly stated. Consequently, the coordination process is discordant and conflict might result.

Since all members have a measure of responsibility to manage entrée to the co-owned information, they need to agree on a set of access rules that establish the level of boundary openness. Determining access or protection rules for permeability incorporates the foundational criteria such as culture, motivations, gender, and situations. These rules also factor in risk-benefit considerations in their development. However, because we are talking about a number of people (i.e., two or more), the ability to negotiate rules is very complex. There are numerous issues to consider in rule negotiations for collectives beyond the foundational concerns mentioned earlier. We will only focus on a few of those factors in order to illustrate the complexity.

The depth, breadth, and amount of internal disclosures among collective boundary members may influence the way individuals manage private information that flows outward or boundary permeability. For example, collective boundaries may be opened up more to outsiders as additional topics are discussed and as they become more intimate (Altman & Taylor, 1973). When the range of topics, the degree of topic intimacy, and the length of time spent disclosing increase, so might the propensity for members to open the collective boundary to outsiders (Hill & Stull, 1987; Wheeless & Grotz, 1976).

Collective boundary walls may become more loosely held by the members when they talk more freely among themselves and when they talk more about intimate topics. In talking so openly within the boundary, the members may come to treat private information as second nature, forgetting that when it flows outwardly it has a potential to result in vulnerabilities for the group. Thus, talking so freely about group private information may reduce the perceived risk of information flow beyond the boundaries. Becoming comfortable with the information may influence judgments about collective levels of vulnerability.

*Depth* and *breadth* of disclosure also reflect the level of boundary permeability. For example, when considering men and women in situations where confidentiality is either assured or not, as in a counseling or therapy situation, a number of issues are salient for boundary coordination (McGuire, Graves, & Blau, 1985). Hence, rules for men suggest that they have more permeable boundaries than women in all conditions of assurance, but the differences are such that the depth of women's disclosures in the high-assured condition is less than the least amount disclosed by men in the low-assured condition. In collective boundary coordination then, men might opt for rules that contradict women's preferred approach for regulating access to collective boundaries. Men as compared to women in a counseling situation appear to have rules that advocate greater permeability in their privacy boundaries. In coordinating access rules, men and women might be at odds in their expectations for having the boundaries open to those outside.

Coordinated rules for boundary permeability may also depend on the nature or state of a *relationship*. For example, when relationships (i.e., dyadic boundaries) are in a depenetration process, as intimacy decreases, there is an indication that the breadth of disclosure decreases as well (Tolstedt & Stokes, 1984). However, these results do not suggest a curvilinear relationship. Tolstedt and Stokes are careful to note that once intimacy dissipates to a certain point, the breadth of disclosures do not continue to decline along with intimacy.

Tolstedt and Stokes (1984) also indicate that depth of disclosure is related to intimacy, but in an unexpected manner. Rather than decreasing as the intimacy of disclosures decreases, the depth of disclosure increases. When there is the least amount of relational intimacy present, there is a greater tendency for individuals to discuss positive personal topics, sharing judgments, evaluations, and positive feelings. This is explained by the fact that expressing negative feelings is riskier, thus, less socially acceptable than expressing positive feelings or opinions (Morton, 1978). Hence, it is suggested that these individuals continued to discuss personal topics as a way of avoiding negative disclosures about the relationship within the context of seeking help for their marital problems (Tolstedt & Stokes, 1984).

This is an interesting case because it illustrates the difficulties people face in collective privacy management when the boundaries are coming apart. The members are in the process of changing the rules because the information is moving back from collective to personal boundaries. The discussion of personally private information, instead of relationally relevant information, illustrates the state of this change.

**Privacy Protection Rules**

Although privacy access rules are important, so too are those rules that group members establish to protect private information by keeping it within the collective boundary. Again, there are many rules that people use to protect the information for which they are mutually responsible. One way protection has been discussed is within the notion of *discretion* (Bok, 1982). Bok (1982) defines discretion as an

> intuitive ability to discern what is and is not intrusive and injurious and to use this discernment in responding to the conflicts everyone experiences as insider and outsider. It is an acquired capacity to navigate in and between the worlds of personal and shared experience, coping with the moral questions about what is fair and unfair, truthful or deceptive, helpful or harmful. Inconceivable without an awareness of the boundaries surrounding people, discretion requires a sense for when to hold back in order not to bruise, and for when to reach out. (p. 41)

There are two points being made within Bok's definition. First, when there is a shared boundary, those inside need to protect the information collectively. Second, Bok casts the nature of discretion as a moral judgment. Judgment as a concept is clearly part of the argument CPM is making concerning a decision to tell or not tell private information. However, instead of the decision being a personal one, CPM suggests that people enter into a negotiation about rules for when, how, how much, to whom, and to what extent the shared private information is told to a third party. Sometimes the rules are not made explicit until a person breaches "an understanding"; then the group is called into making a collective judgment about which rules should prevail. In this way, the process appears less anchored in necessarily making a moral judgment and more dependent on group negotiation for the desired level of protection. Privacy protection rules reflect many strategies that people use to safeguard access to collectively held private information. The goal is to limit who knows the information; however, as these rules suggest, the level of protection varies with the kind of strategy used.

**Topic avoidance protection rules.** Boundaries may be protected using topic avoidance. There are situations where collectives decide that they are better served when they do not talk about a particular private topic in order to preserve the group boundaries (Afifi & Guerrero, 2000). The ability of the collective members to abide by an agreement to protect a topic may aid in reinforcing a group identity and overall impression management (Afifi & Guerrero, 1998; Afifi & Guerrero, 2000).

The group may negotiate using this protective rule because the members fear reprisal or anticipate negative outcomes if any one person discloses (Afifi & Guerrero, 2000). For example, a woman who used a donor egg to become pregnant shared her choice with several of her close relatives and, of course, her husband. They all agreed after talking as a collective that the boundaries around this information should be kept from everyone outside the group, including the child born from the donor egg (Stolberg, 1998, p. A1). Thus, the topic of the child's conception was restricted and protected by those within the boundary. Each had an obligation not to disclose the information to others. The need for protection was clearly understood because of the child involved.

Topic avoidance may come in all forms. For instance, Roloff and Ifert (2000) argue that complaints are often withheld from relational partners with various outcomes for the relationship. Withholding complaints may also influence the dyadic privacy boundary that the couple has established in both a positive and a negative way. Being protective of negative opinions of a partner's behavior (keeping the information within the personal boundary) may be positive because it reduces the opportunity for conflict (Roloff & Ifert, 2000). On the other hand, the negative side of protecting these opinions means that there are limited possibilities for changing undesirable behaviors. When the collective boundary goes beyond the personal level to the dyadic or a larger group, two or more individuals need to negotiate whether to make this information known outside the privacy boundary.

**Taboo topic protection rules.** We see many examples of privacy protection rules for collective boundaries. One of the more controversial protection rules is the "don't ask, don't tell" rule imposed by the U.S. military about sexual orientation (Garamone, 2000). This rule signals a taboo topic (Baxter & Wilmot, 1985). The Navy set up a collective boundary that disallowed revealing the sexual orientation of their personnel by using a protection rule. No one is to reveal. Ironically, the Navy protects itself from having to establish productive procedures for coping with an individual's personal sexual orientation and makes it off limits as a topic for anyone in the collective.

For collectives in general there are any numbers of taboo topics, which people regulate by generating boundary rules. In their research, Baxter and Wilmot (1985) identified six different kinds of topics that were off-limits for people in opposite-sex relationships. These include talking about the state of the relationship, extra-relationship activities, relationship norms for behavior in the relationship itself, prior relationships, conflict-inducing topics, and negatively valenced disclosures about the self. From these findings, we see that people reported individual protection rules for personal disclosures. It would be interesting to know the extent to which the partners negotiated these rules or assumed personal rules applied in a dyadic boundary. Thus, the interactive development of collective rules might be different from what individuals propose as topics that are off-limits for the relationship.

**Confidentiality protection rules.** One of the more central issues of privacy protection concerns the way members coordinate confidentiality. Given that each member has a fiduciary responsibility for the collective's private information, the way people negotiate terms of confidentiality is key to protecting the boundary. The notion of confidentiality is most often faced within the medical or health fields. However, by the very nature of our expectations and assumptions about private information, the concept is relevant to any case where two or more people are held accountable either implicitly or explicitly for the disposition of private information.

"Essentially, confidentiality is respect for people's secrets" (Gillion, as cited in Robinson, 1991, p. 279). Thus, "any relationship based on the revelation of such secrets is privileged for those into whose hands these secrets are given" (Robinson, 1991, p. 279). When we talk about medical patients, the burden is increased because of the implied contract that the doctor and patient have regarding private medical information. Many argue that the ability to provide adequate care is compromised if confidentiality is not "guaranteed" by the health care worker, particularly the physician (Friedland, 1994). Clearly, if not by law, by Hippocratic oath, the physician is bound by medical ethics to keep a patient's information private (Friedland, 1994).

Some studies show that for health care workers certain issues intervene in the practice of keeping confidences. For example, general practitioners in the Netherlands were found to be less likely to divulge information when they were younger, newer in their practice, female, and had a smaller number of patients (Lako & Lindenthal, 1991). Although physicians may institute a code of ethics about patients' rights, many other health care workers may not abide by the same protection rules.

For example, a newspaper account told the story of a man with AIDS who sued a drugstore because his children found out about his condition. A pharmacy clerk, handling the man's prescription, had told his son about the man's health status (Pardo, 1998). The pharmacy clerk's son attended the same school as the man's children and told them about their father. This example illustrates one of the issues with privacy protection. Though a physician may not have revealed the man's condition because she or he defined it as part of her or his responsibility to maintain protection, those not in the immediate collective boundary, however, may not feel as accountable or know the rules agreed upon by others inside the privacy boundary. Consequently, the pharmacy clerk in this example had weak ties to the boundary. This example illustrates that not only do permeability rules matter, but linkage to the boundary also affects the outcome of confidentiality.

Thus, protection rules that guide confidentiality are more likely to be enacted according to agreed-upon behaviors when there is an investment by those within the boundary. If people have little to lose, they may not feel compelled to keep confidences. In many types of privileged information the probability of keeping confidences is influenced by the degree to which people in the boundary recognize that knowing the information and telling it without regard for ramifications causes others and themselves to become vulnerable. In chapter 5 on boundary turbulence, we explore the consequences of boundary coordination when people do not abide by rules for protection.

## Boundary Ownership

Boundary ownership is the processes by which rules help determine the borders of the boundaries. We live in a world with multiple privacy boundaries where, at times, it is difficult to know when one boundary ends and another begins. Consequently, one of the goals of coordination is identifying and maintaining the borders of collective and personal boundaries (see Figure 3.3).

Defining personal borders around private information that we own seems like an easy task. For instance, I define personal information as mine, identifying my rules for access and protection. In this way, I work to maintain the parameters around that information according to my rules. The problem is that once I tell someone else, I shift the nature of those borders. I hold myself and at least one other person responsible for controlling disclosure to a third party. I may still consider the information mine because it has to do with me. Yet, disclosing makes the boundaries accommodate someone else, thereby allowing the once personal information to become dyadic. The issue is how borders of boundaries are defined.

## Border Definitions

So far, this book has argued that privacy borders do change; now we need to examine the circumstances that lead to boundary border definitions. There are two aspects of privacy border definitions: *first*, who legitimately owns the private information, and *second*, who has control. Although these dimensions are related to each other, they are not always

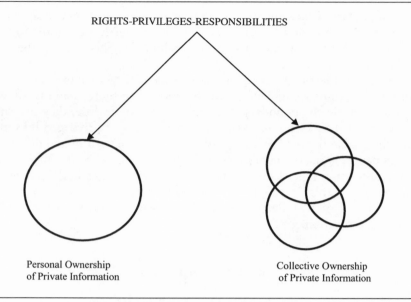

RIGHTS-PRIVILEGES-RESPONSIBILITIES

Personal Ownership
of Private Information

Collective Ownership
of Private Information

**Figure 3.3**
Boundary Ownership: Coordination Operation

necessary and sufficient conditions. Sometimes people who own the private information are not in complete control. Consequently, the borders shift to include individuals who are not chosen by the original owners to know the information.

We have already said that people own multiple boundaries surrounding different kinds of private information. Owning means the right to determine the borders of the boundaries surrounding the information. If it is mine, I have the right to keep it or give it to others. If I co-own the private information with others, we collectively determine who is in and out of that border. We experience a number of different types of ownership rights.

**Ownership rights.** In chapter 4, this book discusses the many kinds of boundaries surrounding ownership of private information. This section introduces the privacy borders that separate different kinds of boundary lines. Ownership reflects the understanding of individuals that the information is their responsibility and they will be held accountable for the way they handle it. In other words, the more people feel invested in the information, the more they claim ownership or co-ownership rights. Hence, loyalty to the discloser becomes one way that boundaries are clarified.

Claiming ownership rights also is empowering because it allows those individuals involved to build bonds with each other, united in managing the private information (Bok, 1982).

We have ownership claims on personally private information and that helps us determine the borders for something that is exclusive to ourselves. However, when we share that information with others, there may be two outcomes. One, we believe that the private information remains uniquely in our own to control. Two, we assume that others should share in that claim. Both may be true or neither may happen. In other words, if we believe that the borders are still defined as personal, we neglect to see the implications of sharing our information. Holding this claim may be the only thing we understand.

However, when we neglect to understand that someone else shares in the control, we lose the power to set parameters for rules to manage the information. If we recognize that we have made personal information communal, we are more able to stipulate or negotiate third-party disclosure rules and attempt more control over the newly formed dyadic boundary. Somewhat easier to define are the claims of a person who appropriates private information that is already considered collectively owned.

Entering a group that has established private information means that the members have already determined the borderlines for that which is held collectively. They socialize the new individual and thereby teach that person the rules for boundary management and the limits of the boundaries. The challenge for the new person is determining where his or her personal borders begin and end within the group. For example, when two people get married and the spouse vacations with his or her new in-laws, the situation calls for socialization into the spouse's family privacy boundary lines and merging his or her own personal privacy boundary limits.

Vacationing with new in-laws, Sally learned that the family talked, in public (around the public pool), about their financial dealings. She asked her husband whether this was typical of his family, to which he replied, "Yes." She stated that her rule was not to discuss something so private in public. When his family asked her how much she had lost in the stock market, she refused to answer. Sally drew her personal boundaries around financial information, marking it as private. However, she had to consider the fact that her husband's family marked financial information as private within the whole family and not within only a personal border.

As we articulate boundaries around other kinds of private information that we co-own, we work to manage ownership of the perimeters so that we do not experience boundary turbulence. The complexity is great because we are involved with many different kinds of boundaries. When we join groups in our families, in the organizations with which we affiliate,

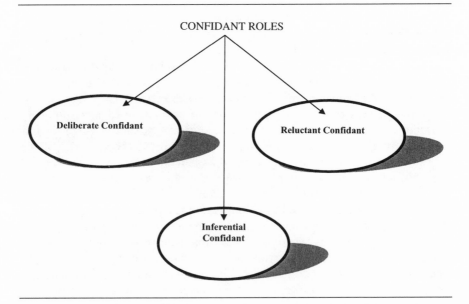

**Figure 3.4**
Boundary Co-Ownership: Roles

and in the communities of which we are a part, the boundary signposts need to be identified and managed. We also need to identify those borders to other people so they understand whether they have an invitation to join. To do this we use *boundary markers*.

**Privacy markers.** One way that people specify borders of privacy boundaries is through verbal and nonverbal codes. For example, verbal markers may be statements such as "I need to take a minute of your time," indicating that the person wants to establish a border (perhaps dyadic) separate from others. People might use the *disclosure warnings* also as a boundary marker by saying things such as, "Don't tell Dad this, but," "Only tell Jon and her husband this," "Keep this within the family," "It is best that we keep this information in the group," "We probably shouldn't tell Grandma this until we know more," "I have only told my very best friends this," "I am nervous about this getting out in the law firm, so let's keep it within these walls," and "This is for your ears only."

Nonverbally, people use a host of behaviors that mark the borderlines of a privacy interaction. For example, they use whispering to show the confidentiality of the information and limited exposure to others. People block others out of a conversation with their bodies to show the boundary lines.

Others lean inward when they want to convey that the exposure to their conversation is limited to the people with whom they are interacting. Individuals also huddle together forming a visual boundary in which they are revealing private information. We also close doors, stop disclosures abruptly, and change topics when those outside of the borders come too close to the interaction.

Some borderlines seem to be defined out of the nature of relationships that people have with each other. For example, people assume, for good reason, that spouses have a very clear perimeter around private information that they share with each other. For the most part, others respect the limits of not knowing their private information. This is also true for families. The more complicated aspects of families is within the larger family boundary (see chapter 4 for more details).

Thus, through relational definitions and from both verbal and nonverbal actions, people mark their privacy boundary lines to indicate when individuals are permitted inside and when they should remain outside. Most of us understand these markers well enough to judge them as signals for retreat rather than entrance. These markers are often necessary because boundaries are not always long-standing. Instead, they may be formed and reformulated, as they are needed by individuals.

## Boundary Co-Ownership: Private Disclosure Confidants

One of the more important issues in boundary coordination is the role of the confidant. Whether a person receives private information that already belongs to the group and is socialized into the rules or is a confidant from receiving a personal disclosure, the very nature of the coordination process depends on how the recipient treats the experience. The role a confidant plays (i.e., whether the person solicited the information or was an uninvolved bystander) and the influence that being a confidant has on the person who plays that role, impact the boundary coordination process and the rules regulating private disclosures (see Figure 3.4).

### Defining Confidant

Imagine that a young man is on a business trip. On the plane, he is sitting next to a middle-aged woman who starts a conversation with him. He is preoccupied with some personal problems, so he does not pay much attention to her. The woman is not discouraged, and she becomes even more personal in what she says. At some point, he feels obligated to reciprocate, and he

says something very general about himself. . . . It is now no
longer true that her actions influence only her own well-being.
She affects his mood and satisfaction about the trip too. (Derlega & Grzelak, 1979, p. 165)

Once disclosure takes place, the mutuality of the experience makes
an impression on both the sender and recipient. The role of confidant is a
significant position in the disclosure exchange. Research shows that people are typically selective when choosing the target of disclosure (e.g.,
Certner, 1973; Derlega et al., 1993; Rosenfeld et al., 1979). Less is known
about the consequences disclosure has for the recipients; however, they
play a critical role in the coordination process. Although Jourard (1971)
believed in the dyadic nature of disclosure, his focus emphasizes the disclosing person. Even so, Jourard's work flirted with the importance of the
recipient's role. Embedded in his basic assumptions was the suggestion
that revealing is the practice of sharing private information with others.
Focusing on the recipient or confidant affords a more complete description of the disclosure event.

Considering the role of confidant in boundary coordination raises
new questions about what it means to receive private information. Like the
person disclosing, the recipient also manages a privacy boundary. Once private information that belonged to the discloser is shared, the confidant
(either willingly or reluctantly) becomes an insider. Being selected as a target to receive private information may trigger a sense of responsibility in
the confidant. The discloser certainly has made assumptions about the
shared revelations. Miller and Berg (1984) argue that disclosive actions
instigate expectations for responsiveness in the receiver, who often feels
obligated to live up to those expectations. Yet, the type of responsiveness
and subsequent feelings of the recipient may vary depending upon whether
the person elicited disclosure or was selected by the discloser.

Barnlund (1962) argues that communicative acts carry a degree of
responsibility. For every interaction, the individual offering information
has some obligation to recognize the potential impact of this knowledge on
the recipient. This becomes more salient when the kind of information is of
a private nature and there is an expectation that the confidant will negotiate rules for revealing to a third party. For this reason, Rawlins (1983)
claims that for every disclosure event, a tolerance of vulnerability for the
discloser is managed in conjunction with the impact candor has on the confidant. Thus, revealing private information to someone has an effect on
both parties (Kelvin, 1977).

This discussion suggests several issues that arise from being a confidant. First, not all confidants experience the same ramifications. Second,
the critical variable that distinguishes among differential confidant burdens

is the kind of role a person plays. Third, some people may find that their personal resources are adequate for playing the confidant role because they are prepared to meet the demands. Others may have previous knowledge about a situation and understand that they are expected to develop good listening skills. Fourth, confidants may also be caught completely off guard and experience the most negative ramifications because they are the least prepared for the role. The nature of the consequences may depend on the type of confidant role a person enacts.

## Confidant Roles

Given the above discussion, we can conclude that there are three underlying dimensions to confidant roles. These include the degree to which a disclosure is (a) solicited or unsolicited, (b) expected or unexpected, (c) desired or undesired. As such, three different kinds of confidant roles emerge; there are: *deliberate confidants, inferential confidants*, and *reluctant confidants*. Depending on the role, the ramifications might change for the confidant (Petronio, 2000c).

The primary defining criterion for deliberate confidants is that the disclosure is solicited private information. There are many strategies used to obtain private information from individuals (Derlega, Margulis, & Winstead, 1987; Pennebaker, 1990; Stricker & Fisher, 1990). The most obvious example of individuals who enact this role is a therapist seeking to help people cope with life stresses (Doster & Nesbitt, 1979). In this case, the deliberate confidant may force the linkage with someone else, insisting on a certain degree of boundary permeability.

Confidants may also play an inferential role where there is potential for being a disclosure recipient. The primary defining criterion for inferential confidants is that the disclosure is expected because it is fundamental to the relational definition. The confidant has expectations of possibly functioning in this role; nevertheless, the information is not always sought out. Sometimes the confidant receives disclosures without asking, yet understands that this role is part of his or her relationship with the discloser. Other times, the inferential confidant does seek out private information, again according to the definition of the relationship with the discloser. Inferential confidants may push linkages and insist on boundary permeability. On the other hand, they might have their own boundaries compromised.

The prime example is found when considering marital couples. A spouse typically plays this inferential confidant role. When a partner needs to talk, the spouse recognizes that he or she is counted upon to listen and respond to the disclosure (Petronio, 1991). If a spouse appears to be troubled, the partner may solicit disclosure from him or her. In this way, there is a potential in this tacit role, by either soliciting or expecting to receive disclosure, to function as a confidant.

In contrast, the reluctant confidant role is enacted in cases where individuals do not expect to be recipients of disclosure and yet receive someone's private information. The disclosure they receive is undesired; this is the primary criterion defining the reluctant confidant role. The reluctant confidant does not seek out disclosive information, but receives it nevertheless. Being a confidant involuntarily means that the individual's boundaries have been linked either without consent or unwillingly. There are many instances where this kind of confidant role is experienced. For example, on a plane, an individual may begin to disclose to a person in the next seat without considering the possibility that he or she would prefer not to be involved. Not all reluctant confidants reject this imposed role; however, they do not desire being in the role. For each of the roles confidants play, the consequences are somewhat different depending on whether people actively seek disclosive information or they are expected to execute the confidant role.

Thus, finding oneself in the role of reluctant confidant may mean that one is completely unprepared to handle the consequences of a disclosure and have difficulty coordinating rules with the discloser. Given that the individual did not anticipate playing this role, the confidant may not feel equipped to be responsive in a productive way. In comparison, choosing to be a deliberate confidant may mean one is more able to accept the responsibilities or the burden of disclosed information.

Functioning as an inferential confidant also has some implications. For example, these trusted intimates might be expected to listen, yet they might find it difficult cope with the problems disclosed. Spouses or relational partners whose disclosures constantly remind the other about serious illnesses or inadequacies of the relationship may wear on the confidant (Cutrona, 1996). The impact of receiving private information, therefore, may vary according to the confidant role played in the disclosure equation. These confidant roles are important factors in the larger picture of a disclosure exchange. In addition, the experience and ability to respond may more generally influence the outcome for a confidant.

**Deliberate confidant.** When individuals wish to receive disclosure, they deliberately solicit private information from others. They may frequently depend on reciprocity as a strategy (Dindia, 1982). The most complete exploration of reciprocity is found in the writing on therapeutic relationships (Stricker & Fisher, 1990). However, as Simon (1990) notes, there appears to be no clear-cut consensus on the use of this strategy. Capitalizing on the dyadic effect, therapists talk about problematic areas of their lives, thereby enabling clients to accomplish the goals of therapy. However, therapists find many dilemmas with the use of this strategy. Some therapists assume that there is an expectation to remain neutral in the therapeutic setting (Lane & Hull. 1990). Revealing private information compromises the "objective" nature of the therapist's position and may shift the balance of intimacy.

The difficulty of soliciting disclosure through reciprocity may mean therapists gradually alter the nature of their relationship with clients. In addition, therapists must consider how the client's knowledge of the therapist's personal issues influences the goals of therapy. Because soliciting private information through reciprocity reinforces the role of deliberate confidant, sometimes clients might feel that there is an expectation to model this behavior. When the client also takes on the role of deliberate confidant and begins to analyze the therapist, there is a potential for difficulty.

Basescu (1990) points out that some self-disclosure from the therapist may be helpful. However, there are conditions that work against the therapeutic goals, such as when the disclosures reflect the analyst's personal needs, when they are responses to manipulations of the client, when they reflect a need to impress the client, or when the therapist discloses defensive behaviors.

Lane and Hull (1990) identify a set of questions that captures some of these paradoxical issues. They ask whether the client should be the only member of the dyad to self-disclose. To be an active member of this relationship, should the therapist engage in self-disclosure in return?

> Does the personal self-revelation make the therapist seem more humane, leading to greater self-revelation on the patient's part . . . thereby enhancing therapeutic progress? How much and what types of personal information should the therapist share? Self-revelation for some patients might have an opposite effect, setting back the therapy or even harming the patient. Do a therapist's candor, authenticity, and openness mean the same thing to all practitioners and all patients? How should the decision around self-disclosure be influenced by variables such as age and sex of the patient, and the stage of therapy? (Lane & Hull, 1990, pp. 31–32)

In addition, the intensity, depth, and timing of the personal disclosure may also play a role in its success. Salient to this discussion is Dindia's (1994) insightful argument that the reciprocity of disclosure may be rotational. The idea that reciprocal revelations work in a paced, one-for-one manner is unrealistic. Instead, the work of Miller and Kenny (1986) offers a more realistic solution. They propose that there are two kinds of reciprocity, individual and dyadic.

Individual is the more general of the two; people who typically disclose about themselves receive general disclosures from others in return. However, the therapist and client are more likely to engage in dyadic reciprocity; for them, disclosure transactions are embedded in their relationship. The kind of information exchange that takes place is measured against managing the reciprocation of revealing unique to their relationship. The reciprocity that takes place is contingent upon the expectations of the relationship, tends to occur over time, and is cumulative (Miller & Kenny, 1986).

The reciprocal nature of the interaction creates a sense of responsibility to the relationship for both the discloser (client) and confidant (therapist). This is not a one-for-one disclosure pattern. Instead, it is an interconnected series of disclosive statements. These may serve as a reason to reveal private information later in the sequence of interactions over the course of the therapist-client relationship. For this dyadic exchange, the client produces the largest amount of disclosure initially in the relationship. After a therapeutic goal has been set, the therapist may engage in disclosure periodically as needed to reach these goals. In this manner, the sequence for reciprocity is set in this relationship.

The burden in this kind of management, however, falls onto the therapist. When the therapist is both a deliberate confidant and a self-discloser, the nature of enacting these roles may be responsible for difficult decisions confronted by the therapist. The client may also be faced with stresses that complicate the outcome of therapy. Consequently, judicious self-disclosure is often advocated as the best approach, where the client is assessed to be an able recipient of the information (Lane & Hull, 1990). Personally private information may be revealed by the therapist when it provides useful illustrations of an issue or when there are special circumstances such as pregnancy or illness.

The therapist is trained to handle disclosure from clients. However, friends and family members who solicit private information often learn more than they want to know. This sometimes turns them into reluctant confidants, even though they started out as deliberately wanting to know. Thus, the family member or friend may receive too much information, resulting in a paradoxical situation because the person requested the disclosure. Miller and Berg (1984) argue that disclosive actions provoke feelings of responsiveness in the receiver, who often feels obligated to live up to those expectations.

Typically, people feel compelled to lend social support to a person for whom they care (Wills, 1985, 1990). There are many benefits to the discloser in this situation; however, the confidant may not be prepared to hear the depth or breadth of information revealed. For example, when a daughter tells her mother about the exploits of a friend, the mother faces a dilemma. Should she be responsible to the friend's parents and inform them of their daughter's actions? If she informs the parents, she has breached her daughter's confidence. Where do her loyalty and responsibility lie? Research by Ashworth, Furman, Chaikin, and Derlega (1976) indicates that, at times, those who listen to disclosure may be put in an uncomfortable position.

Miller, Berg, and Archer (1983) investigated the role of the deliberate confidant in the contexts of conversational openers outside of the therapeutic setting. Among other issues, they developed an Opener Scale that focuses on people's interpersonal skill at getting others to open up. Using their scale, they are able to determine high and low disclosure openers. In other words, people who are high openers solicit disclosive information more frequently. Thus, they are deliberate confidants more often than low openers.

Miller et al. (1983) point out that the characteristic of attentiveness seems to be an important aspect of high openers' ability to elicit disclosive information. People who engage in opener behavior may be perceived as having goals that involve an interest in listening to others. Strategies or plans are used to enact these goals. Interpersonal skills are significant in assessing the way others perceive one's role as solicitor. However, high and low openers appear to differ in the number of strategies and plans they use. Thus, Miller and Read (1987) suggest that those deliberate confidants would report

> that they have a number of goals, strategies, resources, and beliefs that we hypothesized would be consistent with engaging in a set of responsive behaviors, encouraging others to disclose, enabling people to feel comfortable, and encouraging the development of friendships. (pp. 46–47)

From the research by Miller and Read (1987), it seems that high openers are also relatively successful in reaching their objectives. These researchers found that high openers are more successful in obtaining disclosure than low openers. Interestingly, those scoring as low disclosers tend to reveal more intimately to high openers than they do with low openers. Deliberate confidants also seem to benefit from their role. Miller et al. (1983) found that women who are high openers appear to be better liked than low openers and report having more close friends. As deliberate confidants of disclosure, high openers tend to be perceived in a positive light by the disclosers.

The deliberate confidant may benefit personally from functioning in this role (Cohen & Willis, 1985). When disclosers perceive that the confidant is willing to listen to their troubles, they often feel positive toward the recipient (Barrera & Baca, 1990). The deliberate confidant may also experience a sense of power from helping others and the information received might result in an elevated status for the deliberate confidant. However, eliciting disclosure is tricky because there is an implicit contract that suggests the recipient is aware that he or she is expected to keep the information confidential. Breaching that tacit agreement may result in negative outcomes for both the discloser and the deliberate confidant. However, if the deliberate confidant is aware of the implicit responsibilities, the knowledge of helping another person can be very positive.

**Inferential confidant.** The inferential confidant is in the position of expecting disclosure or soliciting disclosure if the situation calls for this supportive action. Because the inferential confidant role is connected to the relational context, the way that individuals disclose and the outcomes for the confidant are often complicated. For example, Cutrona, Suhr, and MacFarlane (1990) found that when seeking support, marital couples frequently used direct request strategies that were often disclosive in nature. Thus, marital partners might ask for emotional support from a spouse by stating, "I just need you to listen to me."

Direct or explicit disclosure messages have high certainty for response choices. In other words, the recipient spouse knows what the partner wants (Petronio, 1991). Yet, while clarity may be helpful for understanding the demand, the confidant is left with fewer options for response. If the disclosing spouse wants the partner to listen, the confidant must listen according to the disclosing spouse's expectations. Thus, the burden of fulfilling the request means that the inferential confidant has few options but to honor the demand.

The inferential confidant also may grapple with the timing of the response. If a direct disclosure is made about the stress a partner experiences, delays in a response to the revealed problem may result in difficulties for the relationship (Eckenrode & Wethington, 1990). In addition, offering advice that seems inconsistent with the problem, responding with less enthusiasm than expected, or giving a reply at the "wrong" time might lead to a negative outcome for the confidant (LaGaipa, 1990). The inferential confidant may feel handicapped by an implicit assumption that he or she should periodically elicit disclosure in return to show support.

The underlying theme of asking for help through disclosive messages is somehow seen as prompting an obligation for marital couples. In general, eliciting emotional support is associated with higher levels of relational satisfaction (Cutrona et al., 1990). However, making no effort to elicit support is viewed as problematic for marital couples. Thus, when a spouse plays the role of confidant, there may be risks if no attempt is made to find out why the partner is feeling stressed.

Even when inferential confidants seek disclosive information, they may be unable to genuinely help. The difficulty for this type of confidant may be in knowing enough about the experience to be beneficial. For instance, if a family member is diagnosed with cancer, the confidant may not have any personal experience with the disease. Efforts to comfort or be helpful might result in making the family member more anxious (LaGaipa, 1990). Consequently, the confidant might feel bad about exacerbating the problem instead of reducing the stress.

The extended family is mobilized for support at times of personal crisis (LaGaipa, 1990; Wortman, 1984). Although depending on family is normative, there are situations when members are less able to be effective confidants. For example, if resources are limited, members might resent being expected to listen and be helpful to the family. Often in families, the wife is counted upon to be a confidant for her relatives and her husband's relatives. She may feel troubled by the assumption that she must fulfill this role for everyone. To be an effective inferential confidant, trust is a critical factor as is the sense of obligation a family member feels toward the discloser. If there is little trust, or displeasure about fulfilling the role, the inferential confidant may feel that being privy is a burden. Clearly, under these circumstances, the inferential confidant might not be willing to play an active role in listening to disclosures by family members.

**Reluctant confidant.** When disclosers select others to hear their private information, they place these individuals in a role that recipients do not necessarily select for themselves (Petronio, 2000c). Being an unintentional or reluctant confidant occurs in a number of different circumstances. The literature representing the stranger on the train, plane, or bus phenomenon is discussed from the perspective of the discloser (Jourard, 1971).

However, the confidant is often unsuspecting and frequently a captive audience for such experiences. In these cases, reluctant confidants are expected to attend to the problems and difficulties of people with whom they have no relationship. For the disclosers, this circumstance is frequently ideal because they will not encounter the individuals again. However, it is also likely that they will not find a satisfying solution. For the confidants, the situation may prove to be a burden because they might be expected to help solve problems in which they have little or no investment.

Reluctant confidants also find themselves in this role when extraordinary life events occur. For example, illness, broken bones, dental problems, or pregnancies tend to elicit disclosures by others. Most people experience this type of disclosure when one or more of these events happen and are obvious to others. Hospitalization for major illness often prompts others to tell the ill person about their own personal experiences whether or not they are solicited. Many times, long, detailed explanations of medical encounters are disclosed to a person currently in the same circumstance. For example, the pregnant woman in her last trimester faces many others who want to share their personal stories of birthing (Petronio & Jones, 2001).

These situations place the confidant in a somewhat different role than typically considered in the disclosure literature. However, reluctant confidants hear in-depth personal disclosures of experiences when they have not asked for the information. The difference in this type of circumstance is that the discloser does not expect the confidant to contribute to a solution. The discloser may be revealing to socialize or educate the recipient instead of seeking something from the confidant. This expectation is not true for certain professions where involuntary confidants are assumed to contribute to the well-being of the discloser.

People expect they will be able to disclose their problems to those who hold certain occupations, such as bartenders, hairdressers, nurses, and flight attendants, and use these workers as confidants. Although *occupational confidants* may find they must cope with the disclosed information, they may also enact strategies that curtail the amount of disclosure they receive. For example, bartenders may anticipate disclosure from regular customers. If they are tired or somehow unwilling to fulfill their role, they may use protective strategies like washing glasses and pretending they are busy to overcome the potential of being targeted as a confidant (Petronio, 2000c).

At times, anticipatory strategies may not be effective in discouraging disclosure. In these cases, workers might be forced to consider alternative options such as venting backstage in the comfort of other bartenders (Goffman, 1971). Additionally, the workers might feel it necessary to relieve their own burden and tell others about the disclosures they hear from customers. Although there are a number of different options workers utilize in these kinds of positions, the expectations of their jobs necessitate learning coping strategies to protect their privacy while presumably functioning in the role of reluctant confidant.

## Position of Confidential Co-Owners

As the discussion above illustrates, understanding the position of confidants requires a multifaceted approach. The ability to cope with the stressful event and the use of personal resources contribute to assessing the position of a confidant (Pearlin, Lieberman, Menaghan, & Mullen, 1981). However, these factors have more import when they are contextualized within a framework of roles that confidants play. The deliberate confidant actively seeks out information from others resulting in unique consequence for the confidant. The inferential confidant performs both the soliciting role and the listening role. This dual nature of fulfilling the inferential confidant position creates idiosyncratic problems for the individual.

The inferential confidant role is also dependent on the nature of the relationship with the discloser. *Relational audits* tend to be necessary for individuals in this role (LaGaipa, 1990). They are in the position of checking to see if they are meeting or failing expectations. Fulfilling the partner's needs as a confidant may be very positive for the relationship. However, deficiencies as a confidant may be negative for the relationship. Consequently, the burden in this role is somewhat more complicated than in other roles.

The reluctant confidant role is an example of how individuals often take helping behavior for granted. In other words, individuals frequently assume that when they are hurting or in need of a sympathetic ear, they only have to talk to another to find support. There is little evidence in the literature that the discloser considers the impact such telling might have on the receiver. This is most evident when the receiver is a stranger. If the discloser assumes that he or she will not encounter this person again, disclosive information flows. In the process, so does the implicit assumption that the confidant will respond to the issues revealed. Private information also flows when a person expects to see an individual again, but the discloser might then be somewhat more inclined to consider the recipient.

In other cases, reluctant confidants are placed in this role because others want to give advice or educate them. The individuals may tell private information to make their point. The information revealed is unsolicited; however, the outcome may not be very positive for the confidant. Through the unsolicited information, confidants may find out more information than they wish to know about the issue. As this discussion suggests, being positioned as a confidant can be both a positive and negative experience. Whether confidants gain or lose from being a disclosure recipient depends on the consequences of the experience.

### Consequences of Confidential Co-Ownership

The ramifications of serving as a confidant bridge a number of related issues. To understand the obligation experienced as a confidant, it is useful to consider an underlying theme. Most encounters revolve around the ability to provide support for the discloser (Notarius & Herrick, 1988; Pennebaker, 1995). However, recent research suggests that providing support through listening to traumatic accounts leads to stressful consequences for the confidant (Coyne et al., 1987; Kessler, Price, & Wortman, 1985; Notarius & Herrick, 1988; Perrine, 1993). Perrine (1993) argues that "listening to someone who is in distress may be perceived as a negative social interaction and therefore have deleterious health consequences" (p. 372) for the confidant.

The degree of strain may rest on four factors: (a) the confidant's appraisal of the situation; (b) the confidant's ability to cope; (c) the amount of distress; and (d) the personal resources on which the confidant depends (Petronio, 2000c). This is not to say that all confidant situations lead to negative or stressful outcomes. Still, when they do, the four delineated issues are the more typical results. In addition, the kind of consequences faced by confidants influences their ability to negotiate privacy rules for managing private information they have received from others. Thus, the extent to which the disclosure encounter is perceived as stressful by the confidant bears on how the person defines his or her co-ownership of the private information. Overall, grasping the consequences of being a confidant requires consideration of an interface between the intentions and assumptions of the discloser and an assessment of the confidant.

**Appraisal of the situation.** Often disclosers have embedded beliefs about how others will support them. These expectations may not be compatible with the way confidants define the situation (Petronio, 1991). Some people might want confidants to show a great deal of sympathy but refrain from offering directives about what they should do to correct their problem. Others might want confidants to take a proactive role by telling a third party off.

Disclosers may also believe that each revelation will be treated with discretion and trust (Derlega et al., 1993). Because the assumptions about the interactive character of disclosure vary, the confidant may not hold the same beliefs or make the same assessment of the situation as the discloser (Petronio, 1991). For example, research suggests that a close friend or intimate may provide unconditional positive regard after disclosure, even at the expense of perceived accuracy. The confidant may assume that the best way to help the discloser is by providing unqualified support.

Nonetheless, the discloser defines feedback as less accurate if provided by a close friend, rather than by an acquaintance (Derlega et al, 1993). Confidants who choose to be unconditional about acceptance of the discloser because they see this as the best way to define the situation may be discouraged by their choice of unrestricted support if the discloser dismisses their support attempts. Sometimes a person who is an intimate partner may be given less credibility because "of course they would/should respond in a positive way." Hence, both parties may feel frustrated because the confidant's appraisal of the discloser's needs suggests unconditional support; however, the discloser sees this response as the confidant's "doing what he/she is supposed to do," thereby diminishing the import of the support.

In addition, there are situations where the information disclosed may be defined by the listener as stressful. In contrast, the discloser may not view the event as problematic (Hobfoll & Stokes, 1988). For example, older individuals often disclose about their medical problems to younger adults (Henwood, Giles, Coupland, & Coupland, 1993). Although the younger adults may see the disclosure as painful because it is about significant medical problems, the elders might view the information simply as a topic of conversation. They would tell anyone, not necessarily finding the disclosure to be a problem. When the younger adults are confidants, they might perceive the medical information as something to hold in confidence and as a cue to provide support. When the misperception is discovered, the younger adults may feel uncomfortable or embarrassed by assuming their interpretation is correct.

Appraisal of the situation also refers to times when disclosers expect the confidant to do something with the information that may be contrary to the content of the message. These *disclosure warnings* discussed earlier, such as "don't tell anybody, don't tell mom, don't tell Jimmy, don't tell Aunt Sara," set the parameters for third-party disclosures (Petronio & Bantz, 1991). In these cases, confidants are clearly told who should know the discloser's information. However, the intent of these regulators may be contradictory to the actual message.

For example, Jane may say to Mary, "Don't tell anybody that I just received a huge raise." If Mary complies by keeping the information confidential, Jane may act frustrated by Mary's compliance. Sometimes information is crafted to give the impression that it is intriguing by the very act of restricting who knows. However, these actions may be motivated by a contradictory desire to let everyone know. Jane may have calculated that her information would be considered "hot gossip" if she acts protective of who could know. She may have hoped that Mary, the confidant, would tell others so she did not have to reveal the information herself. Jane may have wanted to inform her coworkers without appearing to sound presumptuous so she used Mary and tried to convey how intriguing the message was by restricting its dissemination. In this paradoxical way, the definition of the situation was inconsistent for the discloser and confidant. Appraisals, consequently, tend to be tricky, but necessary for those in the confidant role.

**Ability to cope.** Another reason confidants are susceptible to feeling discomfort from receiving private information is that they may not be emotionally able to provide the kind of support anticipated by the discloser (LaGaipa, 1990). The confidant may not be equipped to cope with the discloser's expectations. Barbee (1990) argues that helping a depressed person when a request is made restores some of discloser's ability to take responsibility. However, frequent interactions with a depressed partner may lead to verbal or physical abuse for the confidant when discussing the problems.

Repeatedly hearing attacks from a partner may dampen the desire and capacity of the confidant to respond in a supportive manner.

Not only does the frequency of these difficult situations hamper confidant effectiveness, but so does the timing of disclosures (Eckenrode & Wethington, 1990). In some cases, for support to be skillfully used, the response to a disclosive demand for help is more beneficial if offered quickly (Eckenrode & Wethington, 1990). Unfortunately, the confidant may not be able to produce an instantaneous response. Confidants may therefore feel inadequate or disappointed that they are unable to fulfill these needs (Eckenrode & Wethington, 1990). The person in need of support may also exacerbate these feelings by berating the confidant for his or her lack of support. This reprimand may not be deserved because the confidant may not have been reasonably able to meet the discloser's needs. In addition, confidants may not have been initially aware of how significant the request for help was for the discloser.

Sometimes it is difficult for confidants to know how to respond. A person might just hint at a problem and not elaborate. The confidant may not have processed the meaning of vague references to some issue. When confidants catch on, they may berate themselves for their tardiness in identifying a call for help. For example, research shows that sexually abused children often preview the actual telling by hinting at the abuse (Petronio, Reeder, Hecht, & Mon't Ros-Mendoza, 1996). Confidants may not recognize the full force of these preview statements and thus treat them with much less importance than if they recognized that these were disclosures about abuse.

People are also more likely to become delibrate confidants when they believe that they can cope with the needs of a discloser. When disclosers seem to be actively working on their own problems, confidants appear more willing to offer support than if the disclosers expect the confidants to solve the problems for them (Schwarzer & Weiner, 1991). The ability to cope with information from a discloser may depend on how competent the discloser is perceived to be and how probable it is that the confidant will be able to find a solution to the problem.

**Amount of distress.** Pennebaker (1990) suggests that burnout may occur when too much information is revealed, making the coping process difficult for the confidant. Sometimes, in an effort to ease tensions, individuals reveal in-depth information about their problems (Stiles, 1987). Stiles refers to this as the "fever model of disclosure" (p. 259). People tend to disclose more when they are psychologically distressed (Stiles, Shuster, & Harrigan, 1992).

However, distress increases attention to internal states such as thoughts, feelings, and wishes, often at the expense of attention to other people or events (Pennebaker, 1995). For example, when people are in the midst of a divorce, they may not consider another person's feelings. They need to talk about their divorce proceedings to relieve the level of distress they are experiencing. Because the confidant's feelings are not a priority, recently divorced people may unload negative experiences onto a confidant without regard for that person.

Nevertheless, the burden may be too much and as a result, confidants may feel they can exercise little control over outcomes for themselves and for the discloser. When people are concerned about their friends or family members, they often ask for details of their troubles. Disclosers may find it a relief to be unburdened and the request gives them a license to enter into a catharsis with the confidants. However, the kinds of problems faced by these individuals may increase the amount of distress that the confidant experiences. The recipients might not be able to persuade disclosers to follow a particular route to solve their difficulties. Because confidants are only advisors, they have less control over the way the problems are solved. This may result in frustration and anger on the part of the confidants.

Confidants who are repeatedly confronted by other people's problems may have nowhere to turn themselves. They may have to keep the confidences of the discloser. The knowledge of certain disclosures may result in intensifying feelings of distress for confidants. For instance, a woman is told that her brother-in-law has AIDS but she is sworn to secrecy. The woman may find it stressful to keep that information to herself. She may wish to tell her sister, the brother-in-law's wife. The confidant is obviously in an awkward and uncomfortable position. Knowing too much about situations creates problems in the same way as knowing information about situations over which the confidant has little control (Pennebaker, 1990).

**Personal resources.** Confidants may also find that their intentions are positive, but that they do not have the personal resources needed to provide the support. This experience may result in feelings of frustration and anger or disappointment on the part of the confidant and the discloser. LaGaipa (1990) argues that "support is sometimes discussed as a perfectly matched provision of resources to needs, but the matching of support to real needs of a person is often not done effectively in real life" (p. 124).

For example, when someone has had no experience with cancer or death it may be difficult for that individual to serve as a confidant for someone dealing with these experiences. The discloser may not consider whether a confidant has any experience or direct knowledge about the issue. Being in the position of confidant without firsthand knowledge may make it difficult for confidants to feel competent. The support offered may be perceived as ineffectual because confidants do not have enough knowledge about the experience to be comforting.

Although a person may want to provide comfort, confidants' abilities may range from more to less sensitivity in the way they carry out the support (Burleson, 1985). Some people consistently employ strategies that legitimize other people's feelings and others use less sensitive strategies, which diminish the feelings of disclosers. The intention of the confidant may be well-meaning, yet the personal resources available to confidants make it difficult for them to provide support. The burden for the confidant results from the lack of employable personal resources.

This discussion suggests several issues that arise from being a confidant. Yet, as we probe deeper into the meaning of the confidant role, there seem to be some distinctive characteristics that can be discerned. First, not all confidants experience the same ramifications. Second, the critical variable that distinguishes among differential confidant burdens is the kind of role a person plays. Some people may find that their personal resources are adequate for playing the confidant role because they are prepared to meet the demands. Others may have previous knowledge about a situation and understand that they are expected to develop good listening skills.

Third, confidants may also be caught completely off guard and experience the most negative ramifications because they are the least prepared for the role. The nature of the consequences may depend on the type of confidant role a person enacts. As the discussion of confidant roles illustrate, more information is needed about the disclosure receiver. Most individuals have played this role, but as researchers and theorists, we know little about why choices are made in response to disclosure. To complete our understanding of the disclosure equation from a dyadic point of view, we need insights into both the discloser and the confidant.

## CONCLUSION

This chapter has considered the apparatus necessary to understand what boundary coordination is and how it works. Coordination is necessary when we disclose to others, create a collective boundary, or join an existing privacy boundary. We use boundary linkages to connect, shape, and change the ties we have to share private information. Boundary permeability plays a role in determining the degree of access or protection collectives manage for mutually shared boundaries. Boundary ownership is the third dimension used in boundary coordination to identify boundary lines. In all, these factors reflect the way people regulate and manage private information for which they are mutually responsible.

Finally, this chapter focuses specific attention on the role of confidant or co-owner because the way people become confidants and cope with co-owning private information matters greatly to the coordination process. In the next chapter, we examine boundary coordination on multiple levels. As this chapter explains, we manage many different types of private information housed in corresponding boundaries. Chapter 4 highlights some of the issues that people face at each boundary level.

# 4

# Cases of Boundary Coordination

As discussed in chapter 3, there are both personal and collective boundaries involved in managing private information. However, when we examine collective boundaries there are specific issues that help define coordination on the collective level. This chapter first considers the patterns that emerge when people are seeking boundary coordination. The remaining portion of this chapter presents in-depth information on the way certain types of collective boundaries, such as those that are relational, familial, and organizational, coordinate privacy management.

## COLLECTIVE COORDINATION PATTERNS

There are numerous ways that coordination takes place. Currently, CPM has identified three general coordination patterns that collectives use to manage mutually held privacy boundaries. Because we are dealing with collectives, these patterns are in addition to the way people manage their personal privacy boundaries. Coordination patterns represent the way people synchronize their efforts. General kinds of patterns grow out of the different ways people engage in privacy management.

Although three different general patterns can be identified at this time, many more patterns are likely to emerge in the future. The patterns include *inclusive boundary coordination, intersected boundary coordination,* and *unified boundary coordination.* Although each pattern is framed within a dyadic mode for ease of discussion, conceivably, these patterns can accommodate the way privacy is managed on group, familial, organizational, and societal levels. For each pattern, we see alternative implementations of the rule management processes. As a whole, these patterns illustrate the modes of change for the dialectic of privacy-disclosure as managed in a collective manner.

### Inclusive Boundary Coordination

The central issue represented in *inclusive boundary coordination* is that of power. The power stems from person B giving up privacy control to person A (see Figure 4.1). There are many reasons why privacy control is given over to someone. In a study on nursing homes, older adults often discussed the trade-off of privacy for safety (Petronio & Kovach, 1997). They clearly were willing to relinquish many kinds of privacy. For example, these older adults gave up control over their finances, allowed others to bathe them, and left their bedroom doors open so that they could have a "safe" environment in which to live. By giving up control over their privacy, these individuals gained a sense of security. Thus, as the figure shows, person A manages more of person B's privacy than person B does for person A. For these older adults, this pattern works to the benefit of both individuals.

Sometimes giving up privacy control does not lead to such a positive outcome. Instead, when one person has more power over another's private information than the individual does him or herself, the level of vulnerability increases significantly for the person giving up privacy control. One critical issue determining whether inclusive coordination is positive or negative revolves around the reason for surrendering privacy control. A way to consider the nature of this pattern is to understand the basis on which the boundary is formed. To do that, we turn to the characteristics of boundary linkages for the inclusive coordination pattern.

### Inclusive Boundary Linkages

Given that this pattern is based on a power differential, there are three ways in which boundary linkages may be defined for inclusive coordination. First, there are *coercive linkages* that are formed when person B is forced to give up personally private information to person A. Issues of disclosure compliance, through either humiliation or manipulation, force the linkage leading to inclusive boundary coordination. The situations that take place with sexual abuse also represent an example of linkages based on coercion. The perpetrator invades the victims' privacy and then the perpetrator controls the boundaries around the private information about the abuse. The victims are coerced into allowing the perpetrator to determine boundary rules for disclosure about the crime and have to relinquish control. These coercive linkages are destructive to individuals and underscore the negative consequences of inclusive patterns when one party is forced into this kind of linkage.

Second, there are inclusive patterns that form out of *role linkages*. For example, person B, as a function of his or her role relationship, becomes involved in an inclusive coordination pattern that manages private information with person A. The role linkage is established when individuals hold positions that dictate who is privy to private information. The parent-child relationship is an example of a role linkage where the parent has more

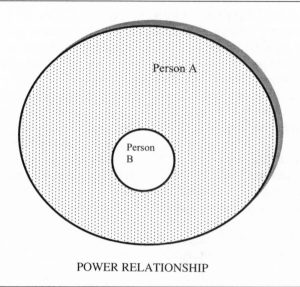

POWER RELATIONSHIP

**Figure 4.1**
Pattern 1: Inclusive Boundary Coordination

control over the child's private information than the child has over the parent's information by virtue of their role relationship.[1] The inclusive pattern in this case may be mutually beneficial for both the parent and child. However, as the child advances into adolescence, the willingness of the child to give over control to the parent becomes challenged. As we saw in chapter 2, and will see later in this chapter, there is a need to shift out of the inclusive pattern and into other ways of dealing with privacy needs when children move into more adult roles.

As mentioned earlier in this discussion, another example where the inclusive coordination pattern arises is seen with older people when they depend on caregivers in nursing homes. The older individuals often must give up control over their private information in order to obtain help from others. However, in this circumstance, the pattern produces a mutually beneficial collective boundary. This pattern is also observed in other types of health care relationships such as with nurses in hospitals, doctor-patient relationships, and with therapists. In each case, the role of caregiver defines

---

1. Of course, during adolescence, one of the main goals in the deindividuation process is to redefine the boundary coordination and shift the boundary lines for privacy management to a more equitable level between the parents and children.

a differential level of privacy information revealed and managed in a collective boundary resulting in an inclusive coordination pattern.

Third, inclusive coordination patterns are also produced through *susceptibility linkages*. These are defined as situations where individuals engage in inclusive boundary coordination because they inadvertently disclose more information than do their confidants or recipients. Thus, they are linked into this type of coordination system because they did not monitor themselves and ultimately find they have exposed more personal information than did the receivers. These individuals have potentially put themselves in a vulnerable situation where the recipient has more power to control the discloser's information than the discloser has. This may happen when a person has a high need to disclose because of a stressful circumstance such as immediately following a divorce or when a person is not good about self-monitoring personal information. Nevertheless, it leads to power incongruity where the confidant, willingly or unwillingly, is privy to a great deal of personal information that has the potential to become a power source.

Although all three linkages have the prospect of negative implications for person B, the level of vulnerability depends on how person A treats the co-owned private information. Thus, there are a number of ways that co-ownership might be defined. Each has implications for the way person B will be treated within the inclusive boundary coordination system.

## Inclusive Boundary Ownership

How boundary ownership is considered depends on the extent to which person A uses the power differential gained by knowing person B's private information. In a most general sense, there are three ways ownership parameters can be defined. One, there may be *benevolent ownership*, where person A, who is in control of person B's private information, may define this position as one of responsibility to person B's wishes for third-party revelations. Thus, being a benevolent co-owner means that person A would work to coordinate with person B about the limitations on who can know, how much they can know, and to what information they might be privy.

Two, there may also be *manipulative ownership*, where person A's responsibility as co-owner may mean that he or she tries to completely dominate how the information is managed. Person A takes charge of the information leaving little room for person B to have a say in how the information is disclosed or protected from others. The example of sexual abuse victims mentioned above speaks to this situation. Not only is an abuse victim coerced into a linkage, but that person experiences manipulative ownership by the perpetrator. The perpetrator does not allow the victim any rights as to how information about the abuse is controlled. Manipulative ownership also influences boundary permeability. Thus, the rules regulating the boundary around the abuse guard against any leakage to others. These rules are counterproductive for the victim and extremely useful for the perpetrator.

Three, we also find *obligatory ownership*, where person A's responsibility for the information requires him or her to take control, but person A does so out of necessity. Person B may not have the ability to determine for him or herself, the best way to judge appropriate rules for disclosure. For example, a parent who has Alzheimer's may require his or her adult child to take over complete ownership of private financial information. Although the adult child takes on the responsibility of managing this information, he or she may not want the level of control necessary to effectively take care of the parent's finances.

### Inclusive Boundary Permeability

For inclusive boundary coordination, the rules regulating boundary permeability dictate that person A has more influence in determining the conditions for access to B's information than person B has for deciding access to his or her own information or that belonging to A. Thus, because of the power discrepancy, person A has license to make decisions for person B in choosing the rules for disclosure or protection of the co-owned information. Although person B still has control over the remaining information that stays personally private, the co-owned information previously revealed by person B is now under the command of person A.

Since person A is in a power position, the permeability of the privacy boundary and regulating rules are within person A's control. Hence, for person B to have any influence, he or she must persuade person A to change the rules if they do not meet the needs or desires of person B. How much influence person B has on the kind of protective and access rules used by person A may depend on ownership parameters and the initial reasons for boundary linkages. Thus, if linkage is based on coercion and the ownership of person B's information is defined as manipulative, person A may not consult person B before he or she tells others about the private information.

As one might assume, all combinations of situations may take place in any inclusive boundary coordination system. Also readily apparent is the fact that linkage, ownership, and permeability interrelate with each other. In addition, there may be other types of ownership, linkage, and permeability parameters found in the inclusive system. However, those mentioned here set the stage for investigating the conditions found when person B gives up more private information than person A.

## Intersected Boundary Coordination

*Intersected boundary coordination* reflects an equitable measure of private information exchanged between people (see Figure 4.2). No one individual has more control because the level of depth, amount, and breadth of the information revealed and concealed over time tends to be perceived as comparable though not identical. This pattern is also marked by specific ways that boundaries are linked, permeable, and owned.

### Intersected Boundary Linkages

Boundary linkage is determined through several different kinds of relationships. First, linkage may occur because of a desire to achieve a mutual or common goal. *Goal linkages* target mutual objectives to enter into a significant relationship, friendship, attain an outcome such as mutual helping, or use disclosure to accomplish an outcome that requires a collective effort. For example, if two people wish to develop a significant relationship, their disclosure of private information is revealed with this goal in mind.

Linkage may also occur because person A and person B have a common identity. The *identity linkages* evolve when two or more individuals disclose similar amounts and kinds of private information because they are both going through comparable experiences. For example, individuals who are HIV positive are more likely to disclose to others who also have the disease (Greene & Serovich, 1996).

There may be other reasons that people come to an intersected pattern of boundary coordination; however, common goals and identities are substantial bases on which this kind of pattern emerges. Later in this chapter, we will see several examples of groups striving to accomplish certain tasks or marital couples aiming for a common goal linking their privacy boundaries around certain kinds of information to achieve an outcome important to them.

### Intersected Boundary Ownership

Boundary ownership for intersected coordination assumes a shared responsibility for the mutually owned information. The assumption is that each individual gives approximately the same amount, kind, and level of information in situations where co-ownership is treated equitably by each person in the boundary system. No one person has any more or less responsibility for managing the information. Each person is a reciprocal contributor to the jointly held disclosed information that is the property of

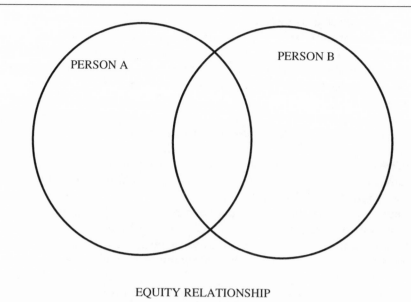

EQUITY RELATIONSHIP

**Figure 4.2**
Pattern 2: Intersected Boundary Coordination

both person A and person B. Consequently, for individuals in this pattern, each has an expectation that the others in the boundary will adhere to rules established by all parties having membership in the boundary. If a person breaches the agreed-upon rules, the other members will enforce the sanctions that are generated to keep everyone on common ground.

**Intersected Boundary Permeability**

Boundary permeability is regulated through mutually agreed-upon rules for revealing and concealing. The protection and access rules are known to each party and determined collectively so that the shared information is controlled in a consistent manner. Thus, the assumption is that the rules will be synchronized so that the people within this boundary all work toward the same type of management goals.

As with the issues of ownership, if one party assumes too much control and makes independent decisions about when private information owned by the collectivity should be shared or concealed, others in the boundary are likely to find this unacceptable and they would impose negative sanctions. All parties are expected to use the same regulation rules that have been determined by the group. Any variation means a breach of confidence and the result could start a shift in the boundary coordination pattern. This coordination system works by having full cooperation of the members in following access and protection rules for boundary permeability.

## Unified Boundary Coordination

*Unified boundary coordination* represents a pattern where the private information belongs to everyone together and no one person in particular (see Figure 4.3). The establishment of this system does not necessarily depend on every member giving equally; instead, the body of private information typically found in this type of coordination often predates all members and new members make contributions, yet the information belongs to the body of the whole. For example, families co-own a body of private information that belongs to the all members and no one person has jurisdiction over the collectively owned information individually. Later in the chapter, we will see how this type of pattern is found in families as they develop and maintain private information that belongs to all members. We will also see the way that this same system can be found in organizations.

## Unified Boundary Linkages

Boundary linkage is determined by membership in a group. Once a person is deemed eligible, a marker of membership is whether the person is told private information that is held in common by all members. For example, when couples become engaged, often one member of the family becomes an ambassador, telling the new person collectively held private information. Often we hear someone state, "Now that you are going to be a member of this family, I need to tell you about our family secrets so that you understand what we are talking about." Thus, the telling of private information signals group membership to the incoming member.

## Unified Boundary Ownership

Boundary ownership assumes that no one person has special rights or privileges over the collective. The private information belongs to everyone. No one person is presumed to have more control than anyone else. Often groups institute sanctions that limit or work to control the parameters of

ALL MEMBERS

PARTICIPATIVE RELATIONSHIP

**Figure 4.3**
Pattern 3: Unified Boundary Coordination

ownership rights. The difficulty is that, because the information belongs to everyone in general and no one in particular, mistakes can be made about regulation rules managing permeability.

**Unified Boundary Permeability**

Boundary permeability for this kind of coordination pattern needs to be adjusted cooperatively for the system to work effectively. The access and protection rules for the jointly held private information have to be agreed upon by each member. When many people are involved, the task of coordination is more difficult. Determining permeability rules demands negotiation and conformity. Unfortunately, some members may define ownership differently, impacting which rules (personal or collective) prevail.

## DYADIC PRIVACY BOUNDARIES

The characteristics and formation of dyadic boundaries may reflect a number of types, including *relational privacy boundaries* and *marital privacy boundaries*. Typically, dyadic boundaries result from disclosed personal information (mutual or individual disclosure) that is shared with one other person (Derlega & Chaikin, 1976). In this sense, two personal boundaries may become linked to form a dyadic boundary, or someone's personal boundary extends to incorporate another individual. In the first case, the private information from both parties blends to become dyadic, similar to the intersected pattern. In the second case, the private information may remain defined as belonging to only one of the individuals, but there is a collective responsibility of both parties for that personal information making it dyadic. This situation may be an alternative of the inclusive coordination pattern where person B (the one disclosing) has more control over his or her own information, whereas person A is accountable for managing that information but has much less control. Of course, there are also circumstances where marital couples, who have a dyadic privacy boundary, enact a unified pattern of coordination regarding collectively held private information.

The communal nature and reciprocal responsibility for regulation of this information changes it into dyadically held private information once the linkage is formed. Boundary permeability, or access to this information, is managed by agreed-upon rules for disclosure. Each person in the dyad has an obligation to maintain and protect the dyadic boundary around shared private information. Depending on the coordination pattern that emerges, the ownership of the information definition may vary; however, to some degree both dyadic members are held accountable.

The size of dyadic boundaries, including relational and marital boundaries, may grow larger as individuals share information with each other (Derlega & Chaikin, 1977; McCall & Simmons, 1966; Petronio & Kovach, 1997). Although the initial boundary may start with a personal disclosure from one person, once a dyadic boundary is formed, private information may become mutual, where flow from both parties add to the amount of information within that boundary (VanLear, 1991). This may be particularly evident in long-term, intimate relationships such as marriage, due to the nature of the relationship and amount of time available to disclose. As this discussion suggests, relational and marital relationships offer a specific way to understand the nature of collective boundary management for dyadic boundaries.

### Relational Privacy Boundaries

Managing boundaries around private disclosures often results in the explication of relational borders (McCall & Simmons, 1966). Revealing or concealing may be a fundamental activity that is essential to interpersonal ties with others (Derlega et al., 1993; Huston & Ashmore, 1986; Ludwig, Franco, & Malloy, 1986). Derlega et al. (1993) argue that disclosure functions as a transformation agent for relationships of all kinds, but particularly for close relationships. As people gain knowledge about each other, they become interdependent through the mutual sharing of private information. Thus, to understand how significant relationships form, it is useful to examine the way couples establish linkages that transform a personal privacy boundary to a dyadic boundary.

The boundary rules for permeability that partners develop also bind the relationship, and sanctions work to provide relational parameters for the individuals. Violating or misunderstanding these rules once they are developed for the dyadic boundary may lead to strife. Because rules for determining access to co-owned private information need to be agreed upon mutually, the way they are determined and sustained matters to the relationship.

## Relational Development

The road to relationship development often depends on the way personal boundaries are transformed into dyadic boundaries through disclosure of private information. Existing literature gives us insights into how this transformation takes place. For example, Altman and Taylor's (1973) concept of social penetration depends on disclosure as a vehicle for relational growth. They offer an in-depth explanation of relational development and its motivating forces. Altman and Taylor suggest that depth and breadth of disclosure, and uncovering the layers to increased intimacy, characterize the way relationships grow. They propose that rewards and costs motivate this movement toward relationship development, thereby broadening an explanation of how and why people become intimates (Taylor & Altman, 1975; Taylor, Altman, & Sorrentino, 1969).

Certainly, in Altman and Taylor's (1973) approach, disclosure plays an integral part in the development process. As a relationship becomes deeper and more disclosive, a relational boundary around co-owned private information grows to reflect the shared intimacies. Because there are many issues associated with disclosure in relationships, Derlega et al. (1993) maintain that issues such as relational definition, time, attributional processes, liking, reciprocity, and goals reflect how disclosure is used in relational development.

The way individuals characterize a relationship, for instance, serves as a factor in how privacy boundaries are managed. Over time, revealing is the basis for the relational boundary of shared intimacies. Partners establish boundary rules that maintain the communal sense of connectedness.

For example, most people identify "sharing private thoughts, dreams, attitudes, beliefs, and fantasies" (Waring, Tillmann, Frelick, Russell, & Weisz, 1980, p. 473) as important for intimacy.

A study on the evolution of relationships by Davis (1977) also presents some noteworthy findings for understanding boundary growth at the relational level. Davis suggests that when responsibility is reciprocated rather than set by one partner, individuals develop an agreed-upon set of guidelines or superordinate aims for the evolution to intimacy. The joint construction of expectations allows for consensus about the progress toward intimacy using disclosure. Through mutually held rules or guidelines, individuals control their progress toward intimacy. This may be explained as one way relational privacy boundaries are developed. Negotiations of privacy rules between the partners may coconstruct expectations for the level of intimacy.

Other aspects of the relational level are also salient for understanding the profile of relational privacy boundaries for revealing and concealing. For example, maintaining topical relevance is important in highly intimate relationships and so is the way individuals structure interactions when they are intimates (Berg & Archer, 1983; Hornstein, 1985). From their study on reciprocity of disclosure at the individual and dyadic levels, Miller and Kenny (1986) argue that the most disclosure

> appears to be due to the unique adjustment individuals make depending on who they are disclosing to within a particular relationship. . . . It seems likely that disclosure in close relationships is apt to reflect the unique adjustments and modifications individuals make in working out their individual relationships. (p. 718)

The relational level of reciprocity was found to be more important than the individual level in this study (Miller & Kenny, 1986). That is, the extent to which individuals disclose to their partners apart from how much they disclose in general is an important factor. Thus, as individuals become more intimate and the relational boundary grows, they may change the way they reciprocate to accommodate the expectations of the privacy rules for dyadic boundaries.

## Challenges for Relational Boundary Coordination

Revealing and concealing patterns may best be understood in terms of the way relational privacy boundaries are defined, ownership is understood, and linkages are made. However, because boundary coordination is not always smooth and synchronized, there are circumstances that may lead to challenges in coordination. If coordination does not go smoothly, ultimately the disturbances may result in boundary turbulence. Three issues provide examples of challenges to coordination practices for relational privacy boundaries.[2]

First, although boundary linkages may give rise to relational intimacy, once established, the coordination process may be compromised by *disclosure paradoxes*. Second, there are some situations where the private information is significantly risky such that establishing linkages requires careful weighing of potential costs and benefits. *High cost disclosures*, therefore, may present linkage predicaments. Third, coordinating privacy rules regulating permeability often requires *calibrating* such things as how much to tell, when to tell, frequency of telling, and breadth of the information. Although the process can go smoothly, sometimes it is tricky. There are situations that arise where adjustments are needed to change the rules controlling permeability. Consequently, if these adjustments are not made in a way that is productive, asynchronicity may result for the relational boundary.

**Disclosure paradoxes.** There are any number of examples illustrating disclosure paradoxes. This kind of paradox often changes the way coordination is enacted in relational boundaries. One curious pattern found over time in some long-term relationships is a tendency for commitment in long-term relationships to generate more caution in disclosing (Gilbert, 1977; Hendrick, 1981; Taylor, 1979). On the other hand, when a relationship is characterized by less commitment, disclosure appears to be more open (Thibaut & Kelley, 1959). In other words, personal boundaries may be drawn tighter over time when there is a higher degree of commitment.

Because a great amount of sharing has already occurred in long-term relationships, the relational privacy boundary may have grown large enough to sustain this long-term relationship. However, the information that remains in a personal boundary after a significant amount of disclosure has occurred is possibly someone's deepest, darkest secrets, which may have a greater potential for risk to the person or relationship. Thus, long-term partners likely weigh the consequences to the relationship and themselves in determining the benefit or cost resulting from revealing. On the other hand, telling strangers information that is more personal often means the risk of negative consequences are minimal by comparison to those in a long-term relationship.

---

2. These challenges, while not specific to relational privacy boundaries, are discussed in this section because they are more obvious for relational boundaries than other types of privacy situations.

This tendency may also explain the findings identified in a study by Tardy, Hosman, and Bradac (1981). Investigating students' disclosure to friends and family members, these researchers report that with a same-sex friend, disclosure is more negative, intimate, honest, and frequent than with a parent. Conceivably, commitment to family members might be perceived as stronger, perhaps making disclosure more risky than with friends. The potential for revealing certain kinds of information to a friend may be less detrimental to the relationship than disclosing that information to a parent. As with intimate partners, the information disclosed by children to their parents may be of a more risky nature because so much has already been revealed. What remains to be told potentially may have a higher impact on the parent-child relationship than the same information has on a friendship relationship.

**High cost of disclosure.** Although many examples may be used to illustrate coordination with high-risk information that might be disclosed within a relational privacy boundary, disclosure of sexual orientation is seen as particularly difficult. Because of society's inability to openly accept individuals who choose a particular sexual orientation, the desire to reveal this personal information to others presents a set of risk issues. For example, in a study by Wells and Kline (1986) that examined disclosure of gay or lesbian sexual orientation, the respondents reported that their greatest perceived risks of rejection are in disclosure to friends, family members, and coworkers. Although Berzon (1979) advocates disclosure to friends and family as a way to develop a positive gay or lesbian identity, the respondents in this study reported the risk of revealing to be too great. Wells and Kline note that even though most "detested lying about their sexual orientation, they often believed they had to resort to lying and deception to protect themselves" (p. 196). These authors argue that while many of the respondents wanted to reveal their sexual orientation in order to develop relationships, they were not willing to risk rejection. Thus, disclosure would make them feel better, but disclosure also carries vulnerabilities that the respondents seem unwilling to chance.

In a study of nurses, Deevey (1993) investigates lesbian self-disclosure. This author reports several strategies used to introduce the topic of sexual orientation into a conversation. Deevey (1993) recommends verbal strategies that may be used to control boundary access and initiate discussion about sexual orientation. For example, in the course of an interaction, statements such as "I know you know this already, but I wanted to bring this out into the open" (p. 22), "You are an open-minded person, so I know you will not have a problem with this" (p. 22), "I need your support for a risk I want to take" (p. 22), or "I want to share something with you" (p. 22) she suggested as ways to bring up the topic or preview the disclosure about sexual orientation.

A statement about being a lesbian typically follows these types of preview statements. They are used to set the stage or mark a shift in the boundary lines that might take place after revealing one's sexual orientation. Deevey (1993) implies that these kinds of statements may help the individual feel more in control of access to this information and alert the receiver to the riskiness of the information. Nevertheless, the potential for rejection may lead gay men and lesbians to be very selective, thereby drawing their boundaries tightly when it comes to trust and management of private information. Because of the risk, gay men and lesbians may have many more rules they follow for disclosing this information.

Thus, the initial boundary linkage is difficult for gays and lesbians partly because they are assessing the way recipients might handle the subsequent boundary coordination defining ownership responsibilities and permeability rules. Often the function of a preview statement is to gauge the way confidants will function within the boundary once linkage has occurred (Petronio, et al. 1996). Due to the high-risk nature of the information, gay men and lesbians clearly see the effort of investigating subsequent responses as a necessary step in forming a relational privacy boundary.

**Calibrating relational privacy boundaries.** For relational privacy boundaries, individuals are engaged in significant relationships that often require certain considerations of the confidant (Petronio, 1991). As the discussion on disclosure paradoxes indicates, the stakes are often higher than in stranger interactions for relational boundaries. Consequently, boundary management within a relational sphere often requires calibrating such choices as how much to tell a partner, when to tell, and how to reveal private information.

Revealing too much at one time, or when the other person is not ready to hear a disclosure, is sometimes costly for partners, both individually and as a couple. When they are not ready to hear the information or if they perceive there is an implicit demand that they are not able or willing to address, the boundary coordination process is compromised (Petronio, 1991). People may expect friends or partners to disclose, but when personal boundaries are opened too freely and partners are told more than they can handle, the calibration process has not been adjusted to accommodate the needs of the recipient. As a result, there is too much permeability of the personal boundary, making it difficult for the relational boundary to have clearly defined borders.

To cope with this coordination problem, people in friendships or romantic relationships may have to recalibrate the amount, frequency, and depth of personal information they disclose in consideration of their relational boundary around dyadically private information. The excellent research by VanLear (1991) on openness cycles gives significant insights into how the coordination system might be modified to restore synchronicity. When people match the amplitude of their openness cycles to fit their partner's and are concerned with the timing of when they are open, they use these indicators (timing and openness) to adjust the flow of personal information to relational boundaries (VanLear, 1991). Consequently, they are better able to revise personal boundary rules to develop relational privacy boundaries more adequately.

Cycling patterns may indicate the actual negotiation of rules for relational privacy boundaries and access-rule modification with the personal boundary. Change in this pattern may signal a transition to termination of the relationship or a desire to advance the relationship. People who are striving to coordinate their privacy boundaries want to maximize the way they communicate with each other. Those who are looking to exit a relationship may have off-cycles that are at odds with achieving boundary coordination.

We know that as people move out of a relationship, the amount, breadth, and depth of information they share is significantly reduced (Tolstedt & Stokes, 1984). There seems to be little reason to continue telling someone with whom you want to terminate a relationship your innermost secrets. However, the whole system of boundary coordination has to change in order for the couple to break apart. This situation results in boundary turbulence (see chapter 5 for discussion about the way boundary coordination is disrupted and how people try to work back to synchronicity). Though we have separated relational boundaries from marital boundaries, many of the same issues are salient. As we move to private marital and family boundary levels, it is clear that these kinds of issues become more complex.

## Marital and Significant Partner Privacy Boundaries

Marital and significant partner boundaries are somewhat different from general relational privacy boundaries. The linkage that moves private information from personal boundaries to marital boundaries is more complicated with possible long-term relational effects. Couples link through transforming personal information into dyadically held private information. Couples expect that disclosure will take place and that coordination of the privacy rules concerning ownership and permeability will be synchronized (Derlega et al., 1993; Petronio, 1991). Further, when turbulence occurs, it needs to be addressed. If it is ignored, turbulence can become very disruptive to the marital relationship. For example, inappropriately telling private information that is considered to belong to the marital privacy boundary violates synchronized rules and often results in feelings of embarrassment for the partner who was betrayed (Petronio, 2000d).

## Coordinating Intimacy

Often, there is an implicit rule that couples should exchange private information to advance their relationship. Most frequently in marital relationships, the privacy rules regulating permeability, granting or denying boundary access, speak to intimacy and relational maintenance. For example, Waring (1980) states that intimacy is comprised of affection, expressiveness, compatibility, cohesion, sexuality, conflict resolution, autonomy, and identity. What, where, when, and how disclosure of private information is regulated tends to be a critical determinant of intimacy and, therefore, is significant to its development in marriage. Because failure to establish a close, trusting relationship in marriage through granting access to private information has been linked to psychosomatic symptoms (Waring, 1980), non-psychotic disorders (Hames & Waring, 1980), and marital dissatisfaction (Waring, McElrath, Lefcoe, & Weisz, 1981), the rules for regulating the way personal privacy boundaries become dyadic is critical.

According to a study on clinical and nonclinical married couples by Chelune, Waring, Vosk, Sultan, and Ogden (1984), marital couples find disclosure to be important in expressing intimacy. However, the valence of private information plays a significant role in the way partners respond to these revelations. Consequently, the rules for managing the kinds of disclosures that are made can have a lasting effect on the marital relationship. For example, when one partner opens his or her personal privacy boundary revealing information that is positively valenced, the disclosure is more likely to be associated with increased marital intimacy (Chelune et al., 1984).

## Issues of Satisfaction

Similarly, Cutler and Dyer (1965), in their investigation of young married couples, suggest that sharing negative feelings, such as violations of expectations, may be problematic for the marital relationship. Levinger and Senn (1967) also found that the valence of the information revealed makes a difference in perceived levels of marital satisfaction. Thus, increased marital satisfaction appears to be more related to pleasant disclosures than unpleasant ones. Although the empirical explanations are not altogether clear, perhaps couples find it increasingly more difficult to cope with high-risk disclosures from their spouses as their relationship continues. Privacy boundaries are drawn tighter as couples deal with high-risk information. This uneasiness is apparently reflected in feelings of marital dissatisfaction (Morton, 1978).

For many of these reasons, Gilbert (1976) advises that there may be a curvilinear relationship between martial satisfaction and disclosure

(Cozby, 1973). Thus, there comes a point when increased disclosure may in fact decrease satisfaction in the marital relationship. Simmel (1964) makes a similar argument, stating that too much disclosure over time may contribute to marital difficulties.

In a study on family role satisfaction, Petronio (1982) suggest that if husbands disclose more frequently than their wives need or want, this may contribute to difficulties in role satisfaction. Further, Davidson, Balswick, and Halverson (1983) report that people in marriages who feel they receive more or less disclosure than they give to their partners are more likely to report lower levels of marital adjustment.

Levinger and Senn (1967) comment that the dilemma of disclosure in marital relationships may be best solved by "selective disclosure" (p. 246). In other words, spouses need to regulate the way they make private information available to their partners. They may be better able to manage their relationships if they consider rules that take into account when and how they should tell, and if they contemplate their spouse's role before they open up their personal boundaries (Miller & Berg, 1984).

Although there is some empirical support for Gilbert's (1976) proposition, others question the validity of the curvilinear approach. For example, Jorgensen and Gaudy (1980) tested the marital disclosure-satisfaction relationship by examining 120 couples, comparing three models: linear, curvilinear, and social desirability. They report that their data provided substantial support for only the linear model. Even when they controlled for confounding effects of social desirability, they continued to find the linear model prevailing. They state, "the consistent linear relation between marital disclosure and satisfaction would suggest that the chances for fulfillment in marriage increase in proportion to the *frequency or quantity* of self-disclosure present in the relationship" (Jorgensen & Gaudy, 1980, p. 266).

Schumm, Barnes, Bollman, Jurich, and Bugaighis (1986) also address Gilbert's (1976) curvilinear proposal, considering a reinterpretation focusing on an interaction between quantity and quality of disclosed private information. Although the results are not consistent with expectations, these authors believe that part of understanding the relationship between disclosure and marital satisfaction is predicated on acknowledging the need for selective disclosure or boundary rules regulating revealing and concealing.

Like Levinger and Senn (1967), Schumm et al. (1986) maintain that "selective self-disclosure will be associated with higher levels of marital satisfaction even though the results did not produce the type of interaction effect expected with Gilbert's (1976) model" (Schumm et al., 1986, p. 245). Selectivity suggests that boundary rules may be a critical factor in marital success. When couples develop rules for disclosing that consider the other person's needs, the process of revealing and maintaining co-owned private information may be more productive.

## Strategies for Disclosing and Responding

Marital couples apply privacy rules to regulate linkages, boundary owner-ship, and permeability, as do those within other dyadic boundaries. How-ever, a significant part of how the rules are used depends on the communicative strategies couples employ to disclose (Holtgraves, 1990; Petronio, 1991). Because a personal disclosure creates a link that forms a dyadic boundary, once a marital partner reveals the partner's response is critical to the way the couple coordinates within the dyadic boundary. Con-sequently, it is "the sequencing of messages in conversations and the sequencing of conversations in relationships" (Pearce, 1976, p. 17) that gives insights into the boundary management process. The original CPM proposal sets up a scheme that capitalizes on an interactive, sequential mes-sage pattern between disclosing spouses (Petronio, 1991). The partner's response is critical to understanding how dyadic boundaries form and unlocks secrets of the disclosure process as a whole.

CPM argues that at least two different message strategies might be used to disclose (Holtgraves, 1990; Petronio, 1991). They include direct and indirect messages that communicate certain kinds of intrinsic or extrin-sic demands (Petronio, 1991). The demands do three things. First, they indicate the personal privacy rules the discloser used to reveal. Second, the message demands convey rules that the discloser expects others to use to control permeability for third party disclosure of the information. Third, there is an embedded expectation in the message that suggests the way the recipient "should" respond.

For direct messages, the kind of private information and the purpose of disclosing tend to be more clearly understood by the recipient. Likewise, the demands for particular responses and the assumed privacy rules to reg-ulate the information in the dyadic boundary tend to be more obvious. There is high certainty for the receiving partner regarding the rule expecta-tions a disclosing spouse has for a response. However, for indirect mes-sages, the rule and response expectations are less conspicuous. These statements are more ambiguous, yet, interestingly, they afford the receiving partner more control over response options. Unlike the direct approach, the indirect message may be misconstrued with fewer penalties because the expectations are less concrete. "Disclosing spouses who couch their demands in hints, prompts, and pre-requests afford their partners the choice of more varied responses" (Petronio, 1991, p. 318).

Considering how to respond to these disclosive messages involves three processes that illustrate conditions necessary to regulate personal pri-vacy boundaries for the recipient. To fully understand the dyadic linkage, it is necessary to recognize that the receiver or confidant partner also man-ages both a personal boundary and the emerging dyadic one. To do that,

CPM proposes that at least three processes are used by the confidant: (a) evaluations of expectations, (b) attributional searches, and (c) determination of a message response strategy. Evaluations of privacy rule expectations suggest that the confidant partners have a better chance of regulating their own privacy boundaries and producing successful responses if they assess their level of ownership (i.e., determine ownership for personal, as opposed to the dyadically held private information) for the disclosure and the degree of autonomy perceived in responding.

The curious point about ownership is that spouses have the right to ask for shared responsibility and reciprocal disclosure (McLaughlin, Cody, & Robey, 1980). Given that they are probably already functioning within a mutually owned boundary of private information, there is a duty to respond. This notion has been seen in the research on obligation and is part of the "egocentric bias" (Ross & Sicoly, 1979) found in marriage suggesting that partners over-attribute responsibility for events to themselves (Roloff, Janiszewski, McGrath, Burns, & Manrai, 1988).

Attributional searches are also important in determining how to respond (Petronio, 1991). Relational memory, content of the message, context of disclosure, the environment, and nonverbal cues are important in deciphering the best approach to responding and in determining privacy rules for controlling the permeability of the boundary (Petronio, 1991). The message strategy used by the disclosing spouse plays an important role in how the couple negotiates privacy rules, as does the emotional level of the revelation.

Consequently, there are several message strategies that confidant partners use to respond (Petronio, 1991). They may be responses that suggest a high degree of certainty in responding to the disclosure message or a low level of certainty in reacting to the revelation. However, the more important issue is the level of boundary coordination resulting from the intersection of the disclosure message and the response message used by the confidant partner. Thus, the degree of fit between expectations in the disclosure message and the response message is critical as to how boundaries are coordinated.

### Message-Centered Coordination Fit

When considering the communicative messages used to reveal private information, the meta-messages embedded in disclosures, and responses by recipients, boundary coordination may result in at least four types of fit: (a) satisfactory, (b) overcompensatory, (c) deficient, and (d) equivocal. The type of fit represents the degree of need complementarity achieved in the interaction (see Figure 4.4). "The degrees of fit are contingent upon the integration of message strategies from the disclosing spouse and the receiving marital partner" (Petronio, 1991, p. 325).

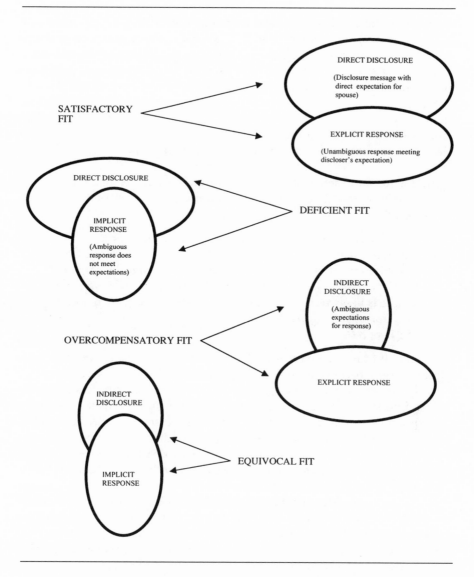

**Figure 4.4**
Boundary Coordination: Message-Centered Fit

**Satisfactory fit.** In a satisfactory coordination sequence, the disclosing spouse uses a direct and explicit disclosure message and the partner uses a direct response in return. Because the expectations for rules and reaction are clearly articulated in the disclosure message, and the partner chooses to meet the demand in a straightforward manner, the fit is satisfactory for the marital partners in this interaction. For example, Ron says to his wife Joan, "I wouldn't want anyone else to hear this, but I think that in this last week I have made progress on coming to terms with the problems I am having at work, doesn't it seem like it?" Joan replies, "Yes, you have talked through the major issues and found a place for a lot of the things that were bothering you and I can understand why you wouldn't want others to hear this." Ron's expectations about the nature of a response and his privacy rules for the boundary parameters are clearly embedded in his message.

**Deficient fit.** In a deficient fit, the disclosure message is again direct and lacks ambiguity about the expected response and corresponding privacy rules, but the response is one of low certainty.

> Thus, whether the receiving partner has met the expectations is not necessarily clear to the disclosing spouse. As a result, there is a different fit between the demand message and the response by the partner. Because of the ambiguity of the response, the spouse is likely to feel that his or her expectations have not been met, and there is, therefore, a perceived deficient fit. (Petronio, 1991, p. 326)

This kind of fit may be seen as problematic from the perspective of the disclosing spouse because his or her demands or expectations were not met.

However, for the receiving partner, the outcome may be less problematic and possibly beneficial. The receiving partner may not have been ready to respond or able to cope with the disclosed information. Because timing plays a role in how privacy boundaries are coordinated, the discloser may have overlooked the need to consider when to reveal the information to advance the development of a dyadic boundary with co-ownership.

**Overcompensatory fit.** In the case of overcompensatory fit, an indirect disclosure message is used, but the partner responds with a high-certainty response. The disclosing spouse chooses a strategy that is implicit and ambiguously conveys embedded expectations for a type of response. The disclosing spouse more tightly controls his or her personal privacy boundary by leaving much of the meaning uncertain. The receiving partner responds to this ambiguity by using a highly certain, unambiguous response. Thus, even though the disclosing spouse did not let too much private information flow out of his or her personal privacy boundary, the receiving partner replied by making assumptions about hidden meanings in the disclosing spouse's message. In this way, the receiving spouse overcompensated for information that was not available but presumed. For example,

Alex says: "how was your day, Carol? I called but I guess that you were busy. I found out that my mother is ill." Carol says in reply: "I suppose that you are angry now because I wasn't around when you called. How was I supposed to know that your mother is sick?" (Petronio, 1991, p. 327)

Carol responds in an overcompensatory fashion given that her husband only mentioned the fact that his mother was ill. Interestingly, as the recipient, Carol is contributing more disclosive information to the dyadic privacy boundary than is her partner. Her response may be more than her husband expects and more than he wants. He may not be ready to cope with his mother's illness, and by her making this kind of statement, she forces the issue.

**Equivocal fit.** For the equivocal type of boundary coordination, the disclosing spouse uses implicit messages that have a more ambiguous meaning. The receiving partner responds by also using an indirect or implicit message. The clarity of meaning for both discloser and respondent is low. Hence, the expectations for response, rules, and boundary parameters are not apparent in either case. Each is able to maintain his or her personal privacy boundary, but the developing dyadic boundary may suffer. The couple likely dance around an issue that needs attention in their marriage where equivocal fit is concerned, never achieving a level of revelation that is satisfying to either.

Equivocal fit, consequently, can lead to skirting around the edges of issues or artfully ignoring them. A person once described a scenario in which she and her husband had resorted to equivocal fit too often. She said that her marriage was filled with "area rugs" on which she could no longer walk. With equivocal fit, over-compensatory fit, and deficient fit, emotions can run high because the boundary coordination occurring is disharmonious.

## Emotional Disclosure

Especially for marital and significant partners, an affective dimension of the privacy-disclosure dialectic enters into the equation in considering how couples treat each other. Shimanoff (1987) argues that considering face needs when disclosing is very important for marital partners both when the disclosure pertains to the partner and when talking about others outside the relationship. Partners who are confidants tend to feel more honored and, therefore, may express a higher degree of co-ownership when the discloser presents the information in a way that is sensitive to their feelings (Shimanoff, 1987).

However, the kind of emotions expressed about someone not present in the interaction and outside of the relationship seems to change the level of ownership commitment a partner (recipient) feels. Curiously, partners feel even more honored and more willing to claim co-ownership over the disclosed information if they receive disclosures that represent hostile emotions about an absent other rather than face valuing statements (positive regard) about an absent other. In addition, face valuing and hostile emotions about absent others tend to increase intimacy more than other types of messages. Shimanoff (1987) reasons that:

> since VOs and HOs [face-valuing and hostile emotions of absent others] were combined with a request for help to avoid the negative effects of absent others, the greater cohesiveness associated with these types of emotional disclosures probably is due to a "we versus they" mentality, as well as to the hearer's feeling more honored, as noted above. (p. 96)

As these findings show, the kind of emotional dimension inherent in the disclosure message is significant to the spouses' interactions, particularly in the extent to which they are willing to claim co-ownership rights. For marital privacy boundaries, the decision to disclose something and share feelings with a spouse, particularly information that reveals negative emotions about someone else, may show the spouse how much he or she is trusted and needed to help overcome the negative emotions. If a spouse feels honored to receive the information, it is likely that he or she will become a loyal co-owner of the information and treat it responsibly.

## Marital Types

Besides the message dimension, there is also a structural aspect that influences revealing and concealing. Marital type may change the disclosure patterns, the boundary linkages, and ownership of boundaries between marital partners (Fitzpatrick, 1987). Fitzpatrick's portrayal of marital couples helps isolate a way to consider boundary coordination. She proposes three basic couple types, *traditionals*, *independents*, and *separates*. For each, a different pattern of boundary coordination might emerge.

*Traditionals*, for instance, display a great deal of interdependence in their relationship and have a high degree of companionship. It is likely, therefore, that they have an integrated boundary management system of accessibility to private information. This couple type might typically have a larger marital boundary than separate personal (individual) boundaries. The marital privacy boundary grows large in this couple type because they disclose a great deal about themselves to each other. *Independents* have a high level of companionship and share in their marriage. However, although they develop a marital boundary, they also equally maintain their own personal privacy boundaries. They value being both connected and autonomous from their spouses.

*Separates* are much less interdependent in their marriage, emphasizing personal privacy boundaries rather than developing marital boundaries around shared disclosures. Consequently, these individuals have a smaller marital boundary around collective private information and a larger personal boundary around private information held separately. Fitzpatrick (1987) argues that these couples represent the pure types but that there are also mixed categories as well. Although we have separated the marital privacy boundary and examined it as enclosing dyadic information, the marital boundary around co-owned private information is often found embedded with a larger family boundary.

## FAMILY PRIVACY BOUNDARIES

Families have a complex set of boundary linkages. They own and co-own different kinds of private information for which they establish rules regulating linkages, permeability, and determine levels of ownership. The information is jointly held and controlled at different levels. There are also sanctions that help manage these boundaries. In chapter 5 on boundary turbulence, we talk about how families cope with rule violations; in this chapter, we discuss the nature of family boundaries.

### Boundary Spheres

In the most basic way, families have two intersecting boundary spheres that they manage. One is an exterior boundary for regulating private information to those outside the family. Another is a set of dyadic and group boundaries that function internally within the family around linkages between and among family members. The outer or exterior boundary is the one that regulates all family private information to nonfamily members. Access and protection rules guiding permeability that families use focus on managing the flow outward from the immediate family to others.

The interior boundaries represent linkages that may form around private information between marital couples, siblings, parents and children, or internal family collectivities. Often these two boundary spheres function interdependently and the rules for each are similar. On the other hand, the rules that families develop may be different for the outer boundary and the inner boundary.

This argument is similar to, yet differs somewhat from Karpel's (1980) proposal that families control secrets on several different levels. He suggest that they include *individual secrets*, where one family member keeps secrets from others in the family; *internal family secrets*, where at least two people keep secrets from another member; and *shared family secrets*, where all members know the secret. He notes that "the boundaries created by them [secrets] depend not only upon who knows the secret but *knowing who knows*" (Karpel, 1980, p. 297).

CPM proposes only two distinctive privacy boundaries, external boundaries that protect private information belonging to the whole family and internal privacy boundaries within the family. In addition, CPM argues that families develop and socialize members into rules used to manage the revealing and concealing of private information. These privacy rules can be explicit or implicit. When they are implicit, violations, or boundary turbulence, often bring the rules into the open. As illustration, Waterman (1979) argues this case by focusing on violations that take place in dysfunctional families. She points out that,

> in many dysfunctional families, the person expressing the family hurt and receiving psychotherapy is often the one who states the family's covert secrets out loud or discloses them to outsiders. Because he or she is not following the unspoken rules concerning family disclosure, the family defines that member as the problem in the family. (p. 237)

Rules for exterior family privacy boundaries may be clearer than for internal family boundaries.

### Exterior Family Boundary

The boundary around commonly shared private information, constructing an outer family border, has obvious significance for the family. We see many examples of both positive and negative outcomes of families regulating their exterior privacy boundary. On the positive side, these borders determining ownership provide the family a backstage place where its members can try out ideas, attitudes, beliefs, and positions on issues (Berardo, 1974). All types of privacy are tested in this protective environment (Burgoon, 1982). Thus, the family privacy boundary gives its members a buffer, a degree of latitude in adhering to societal norms, and self-protection from the outside world (Berardo, 1974). As such, the exterior family privacy boundary is important to its members and to the family as a whole. Consequently, family members collectively work to maintain the integrity of this boundary.

On the negative side, family privacy boundaries can also restrict the flow of information that would otherwise be beneficial if revealed. For example, when families keep their knowledge of incest tightly within the family boundary and do not allow others outside the family to know, the secret has a potentially devastating impact on the family. Likewise, tightly keeping information about members who are drug addicts, abuse alcohol, are known felons, or have severe psychological problems may not be in the best interest of the family as a whole. Obviously, protecting and granting access to a family's exterior privacy boundary can have both a positive and negative impact. Nevertheless, this outer boundary is regulated according to established rules that guide ownership, linkage, and permeability. The same is true for internal privacy boundaries for the family.

### Interior Family Boundaries

Because of the number of different interior boundaries that exist for families, understanding them is complex (Caughlin et al., 2000). The complexity stems from the numerous combinations of potential linkages that form within a family system. Hence, at a minimum, there may be a marital privacy boundary, relational privacy boundaries, sibling boundaries, and parent-child boundaries within a family. Of course, this does not take into account the possibility of families that are single-parent households, blended families, and the like. For each family structure, the complexity of the privacy boundary system necessarily incorporates the linkages among the family members.

Given that we have already discussed marital privacy boundaries and the socialization of children into family boundaries (see chapter 2), this section focuses on parent-child borders as an example of another interior family privacy boundary.

**Parent-child interior family boundaries.** The research on disclosure has identified several patterns for parent-child interactions that give insights into interior boundaries and internal privacy rules families use. One of the most consistent patterns found in research on parent-child interactions concerns the rule about which parent typically receives information. As a boundary access rule, it is interesting to find the consistency with which members tend to practice this rule.

Particularly for adolescents, mothers tend to be the preferred target of disclosure, whereas fathers seem to receive less information overall (Daluiso, 1972; Denholm-Carey & Chabassol, 1987; Jourard, 1971; Komarovsky, 1974; Rivenbark, 1971; Tardy, Hosman, & Bradac, 1981). This may occur because adolescents perceive their mothers as more nurturing and supportive, using a motivational criteria for disclosure (Doster & Strickland, 1969; Franzoi & Davis, 1985; Komarovsky, 1974; Miller, Berg, & Archer, 1983; Schneider & Eustis, 1972).

Although fathers receive much less information, the educational level of fathers is positively related to disclosures heard from children (Franzoi & Davis, 1985). In addition, females who identify with their father tend to disclose more frequently to them than to their mothers (Doster, 1976). Self-esteem also appears to be an important factor in adolescent disclosure to parents overall (Abelman, 1975). The degree of parental affection is likewise linked to the degree of self-disclosure (Snoek & Rothblum, 1979).

Concerning boundary coordination between an adult child and father, a difference exists in the way that they manage their linkage from personal to dyadic privacy boundaries. For example, fathers tend to be more honest, positive, and intentional in their disclosures to adult children, whereas the young adults exercise more control over their boundaries, reducing the amount and depth of revelations (Martin & Anderson, 1995). Motivation as a factor in determining rules is likely, given that fathers, desiring emotional closeness, are more honest and affectionate and reveal more private information about themselves when interacting with their adult children (Martin & Anderson, 1995).

Comparing best same-sex friends with parents, Tardy et al. (1981) found that personal disclosures to parents are more positive, but less honest, frequent, and intimate. Tardy et al. also found that the undergraduates in their study reported disclosing more about social relationships and schoolwork to their close friends than to their parents. In addition, they reveal more intimate information on these topics to their close friends than they do to either parent. From these data, we see the emergence of privacy rules these children use to determine dyadic boundary transformations.

Age also is a factor in determining privacy rules for linkages. In studying disclosure across children in fourth, sixth, eighth, tenth, and twelfth grades, Rivenbark (1971) found that disclosure to peers tends to increase with age. Papini et al. (1990) report similar findings, suggesting that, in particular, adolescent emotional disclosure to best friends increases from the ages of 12 to 15 years. Thus, while 12-year-olds prefer to disclose to their parents, 15-year-olds choose their friends instead. Taking into account this set of findings, as children reach young adulthood, they apparently rely more frequently on friends than parents as confidants when they reveal personally private information. Hence, the privacy rules children develop to regulate permeability and linkages to form collective boundaries change with time.

The way the family internally treats collective boundaries of privacy has an impact on the success of family relationships. Unlike the development of dyadic boundaries between two adults, within the family structure children start out with very small personal boundaries and larger dyadic privacy boundaries. As children develop, they form their personal boundaries, adjusting the size to fit their needs of privacy control through the life cycle (see chapter 2 for more detail). This means that the personal privacy boundary develops for the child while the parent-child privacy boundary is still maintained even though it may shift and change. Through the maturation of the personally private boundary, autonomy may be developed. However, the boundary ties to the parents continue to exist. As this discussion illustrates, the interior and exterior family privacy boundaries intersect in a variety of ways.

### Intersection of Interior and Exterior Family Boundaries

Although it is fruitful to examine various interior family boundaries, we also need to consider the intersection of interior and exterior boundaries. One way to consider the intersection of internal and external family privacy boundaries is to examine the characteristics that define coordination within and across both levels. Generally, for both internal and external privacy boundaries in a family, the nature of rules might be more permanent because families develop privacy values out of concretized rules over time (Berardo, 1974). Thus, decisions about permeability, ownership, and linkages might likely be determined in families by a value for privacy that has evolved over the course of time. For example, when members disclose, the particular orientation that their families have toward privacy (values) will prevail, despite which member is disclosing. Hence, there is likely to be a degree of stability in how family members manage boundary coordination in general. Nevertheless, the idea of a privacy value for families emerging out of long-term use of privacy rules does not mean that boundary turbulence is nonexistent.

Although these rules may be more clearly understood by families, any number of circumstances exists where members breach these privacy rules and compromise the value structure of the family. However, when these values are resisted, such as the father telling the mother their child received bad grades, these incidents often signal a need for change in the coordination system. Thus, while the privacy values for a family contribute to a level of consistency in rule usage, there is still the possibility of turbulence.

Whereas families may depend on privacy values, it is also clear that the kinds of privacy rules derived from those values may vary for interior and exterior family boundaries. Just as likely, the rules may be consistent across both levels. Accordingly, privacy rule orientations for privacy management of exterior and interior boundaries follow several patterns. Thus, there are families that manage both interior and exterior boundaries in comparable ways and those that depend on dissimilar privacy rules across interior and exterior boundaries.

## Family Privacy Rule Orientations

To frame a discussion of rule orientations for families, it is useful to keep in mind that both levels (exterior and interior boundaries) are important. Second, the kinds of privacy rules frequently transformed into orientations are those controlling permeability. Considering that individuals control access and protection of their privacy boundaries, there are three ways in which boundary permeability might become stabilized for families. Some families may rely solely on protection rules to control boundaries, tightly erecting thick walls, and thereby significantly reducing the permeability of the borders. Hence, this orientation might be defined as privacy management that makes boundaries *difficult to permeate.*

Other families may loosely control the boundary walls, allowing the boundaries to become *highly permeable.* As a third option, there is the possibility that families construct rules that allow for a more *moderate* degree of *permeability* in the boundaries around private information. With a focus on these three types of boundary permeability, they can be applied to describe the intersection of interior and exterior privacy boundaries in families. As these three levels of permeability are employed to regulate interior and exterior family boundaries, there are times when they represent privacy orientations that control permeability in a consistent manner across interior and exterior boundaries, thus producing congruent privacy rules at both levels. At other times, the way permeability is control led differs for interior and exterior privacy boundaries resulting in incongruent usage of rules at each level (see Figure 4.5).

### Congruent Privacy Rule Orientations

On one end of the spectrum, families may have a privacy rule orientation of high permeability for the exterior boundary and the same type of boundary control is used for the interior boundaries (EHP/IHP; exterior high permeability/interior high permeability). This means that the family uses a similar kind of rule orientation for managing permeability within the family among its members and for outsiders. The boundary walls are loosely held and there is a high rate of disclosure to both family members and to outsiders.

Families may also have an orientation that restricts disclosure internally and externally (ELP/ILP; exterior low permeability/interior low permeability). Therefore, these families hold their exterior and interior boundaries with the same degree of tightness, using privacy rules that manage a restricted amount of private information disclosed to outsiders and to members within the family.

In addition, families may grant a moderate level of permeability for both the interior and exterior boundaries (EMP/IMP; exterior moderate

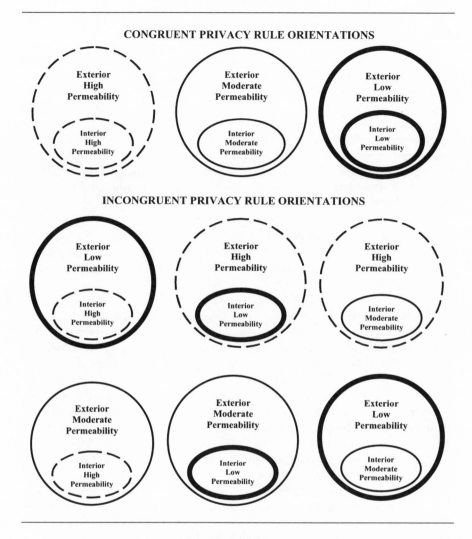

**Figure 4.5**
Family Privacy Orientations

permeability/interior moderate permeability). The rules for moderate permeability regulate the privacy boundaries in a way that never keeps the information flow too restricted or too open.

**High permeability rule orientation.** Families may have privacy rules that allow permeable boundary access to private information belonging to the family for both external and internal boundaries. Thus, the exterior boundary is loosely controlled, and the families do not impede or constrain but instead encourage disclosure to those outside the immediate family. Within the family subsystems, the orientation also reflects open access. Hence, members, when talking within the family to parents, siblings, or marital partners, tend to be open about their dyadically or personally private matters. For example, discussions held between a mother and daughter are shared with other members, private matters revealed between a sister and brother are discussed openly, and the rules for managing privacy among family members tend to be nonexclusive.

Most likely these family members are highly enmeshed (Olson, Russell, & Sprenkel, 1984), given their openness with each other and with others outside the family. However, while they may be highly bonded, this closeness may come at the expense of autonomy for the individual members because they are expected to tell private information to all family members. The rules are nonexclusive, meaning a high probability of full disclosure. Consequently, autonomy is sacrificed for these highly bonded family members.

**Low permeability rule orientation.** These families restrict access for both the exterior and interior privacy boundaries. In this case, families expect that no one will talk about private matters to outsiders. However, they also have the same rule for members' interaction within the family. This orientation is the most restrictive, representing a closed system where the members are expected to solve their own problems without depending on others for help. The low-permeable rule orientation is the most secretive. The privacy boundaries are very tightly controlled, and little information is revealed. The rules that function for low-permeable boundaries protect privacy and control the flow of information by confining it within the boundaries.

Thus, there is limited or little awareness of the problems and concerns among family members and none to those outside the family. These families have more taboo topics than most and members make more of a conscious decision not to tell, restricting the scope of people who know their secrets (Baxter & Wilmot, 1985; Vangelisti, 1994; Vangelisti & Caughlin, 1997). This secretive orientation, restricting access, may have a negative impact on family relationships (Vangelisti & Caughlin, 1997).

For example, withholding topics from some family members, possibly without a clear explanation for ownership rights, may influence family satisfaction (Vangelisti, 1994). In addition to affecting feelings about family relationships, the kind of secret differs depending on which boundary level is being maintained (Vangelisti & Caughlin, 1997). Thus, taboo topics are more often identified with whole-family secrets or those kept within the exterior border, regulating information for outsiders. However, rule violations of private information tend to be more frequently seen as individual secrets, or those within a personal boundary (Vangelisti, 1994).

Although this family type may generate independent, autonomous members, they may also be disengaged from each other. For this type of family orientation, the members may have low bonding with each other and not depend upon each other, nor demand loyalties in the same way some of the other types may expect. These families may also have difficulty responding to change. However, they have established rules that are more protective than penetrable, keeping family information private within the boundary borders. Consequently, the members may be rigid, reducing their ability to cope with change because they keep their boundaries so tightly controlled it is difficult to accommodate new or different ways of dealing with issues.

**Moderate permeability rule orientation.** Families may define both their exterior and interior boundaries according to moderate access and protection. Hence, when interacting with people outside of the family, members may tell only a certain portion of the collectively owned private information to others. The privacy boundaries are controlled by rules that represent a set of conditions agreed upon by the family members. For example, we would never talk about my mother's breast cancer to people outside the family.

Internally, there may also be times when permission is granted to allow permeability and disclosure of certain information to particular family members. Thus, a daughter may confide in her father and reveal something private. She may stipulate a linkage rule that the information not be disseminated to anyone in the family except her mother. The rule specifies moderate permeability and controls access to certain kinds of private information. However, when families have a moderate permeability orientation, there is more room for filtering the information. As a result, this can alter the levels of awareness members have about private issues.

*Levels of awareness.* As suggested by Karpel (1980), there may be different levels of awareness for family members, especially with the use of rules regulating family privacy boundaries. Glaser and Strauss (1967) proposed at least four levels of awareness within a network of people. There are *open* and *closed* awareness, where people either know or do not know certain information. They also suggest that people may have *suspicious* awareness, where a person suspects certain information has been shared among or between others. Last, people may have *pretense* awareness, where both interactants are fully aware that the other knows the information but pretend not to be aware.

If family boundaries depend on a moderate permeable rule orientation, members may experience different levels of awareness that change depending on how much information they receive or give. Some members may be denied linkage, resulting in *closed awareness*. For example, when a sibling says, "Don't tell mom this. I don't care if dad knows; he won't tell her," the boundaries are restricted to maintain closed awareness for the mother while the siblings keep an open awareness among themselves. The same seems true for children with their peers. Among children, there is a tendency to restrict disclosure to friends, thus limiting the boundary linkage possible, closing off access, restricting possible co-ownership, and ultimately obstructing awareness for those outside the friendship (Rothenberg, 1995).

Another example of closed awareness may be witnessed in a letter to Dear Abby:

> Dear Abby: My beloved aunt died more than a month ago. I found out a few days ago when I called the rest home to check on her before the visit I was planning. I was devastated by the news. (Van Buren, 1997, p. C6)

Apparently, the sister who lived closer to the rest home where her aunt resided made all of the arrangements for the funeral and burial without notifying the writer of this letter. The writer attributed the lack of awareness to a conflict a number of years before between her husband and her sister. To maintain closed awareness, the sister tightly controlled the boundaries around the death of the aunt even though it could be argued that ownership should have been shared.

On the other hand, there are circumstances where particular members or all members are granted *open awareness*, as with the father in the above example. The boundaries become permeable and there is a linkage afforded those family members targeted. Co-ownership is consequently expected once all members have been made aware of the information.

More compelling is the idea of *suspicious awareness*. Often parents exercise suspicious awareness about their adolescents' actions and feelings. For instance, parents may suspect that their children are doing something they might not like. Yet, because the children have not disclosed, the parents can only surmise whether it is true. Suspicious awareness confounds the boundary coordination process because family members might breach privacy borders and compromise ownership rights to learn what they imagine is happening with their children.

The idea of suspicious awareness where private information is concerned has many applications in family interactions. Besides the issues in parent-child relationships, married couples might become suspicious of being kept in the dark about some issue. The most obvious is an extramarital affair. Many times, spouses might ignore signs of affairs. However, when some patterns in words and deeds have been altered, partners may become suspicious of their spouse's behavior. They might try to open personal boundaries to claim the information they believe they rightfully co-own.

Families also may find that members use privacy rules resulting in *pretense awareness*. For example, a husband knows that his wife is having an affair and the wife knows her husband is aware. Nevertheless, because neither is ready to talk about this situation openly, they both *pretend* they do not know. Pretense awareness may work as a hiatus for people who are not ready to link personal privacy boundaries with existing dyadic boundaries for certain private information.

As this discussion demonstrates, when the exterior and interior boundary orientations are similar, there is continuity for the way families control accessibility. The members coordinate their rules and are unified in the way they synchronize controlling private information.

### Incongruent Privacy Rule Orientations

Although there are families who coconstruct congruent rules that give them an optimal way to coordinate their privacy boundaries, there are also situations where families have inconsistent orientations to managing their interior and exterior privacy boundaries. Using the three main orientations, there are six combinations representing how families manage interior and exterior privacy boundaries (see Figure 4.5).

**Exterior high/interior low permeability rule orientation.** In this orientation, the exterior boundary is managed using rules that allow for open access and the internal boundary management reflects protective, low permeability. This family grants right of entry to outsiders regarding private family information that belongs to the collectivity. However, while these members are open with people outside the family, they are less open with each other. They tend to restrict access and institute protective rules where revealing among them as a whole is concerned.

This family type is more trusting of those outside the family than they are with each other. The members have more autonomy within the family but depend on people outside the family to help them solve problems. They are willing to reveal to friends and confidants outside the family. However, protective rules function when talking to family members. No apparent privacy rules for boundary control limit disclosure with those outside the family. Perhaps these are the people more prone to disclose to bartenders or to strangers on the train, plane, or bus because there has not been a high level of trust developed with their own family members collectively.

Families adhering to this orientation are not well bonded, seeming to be closer to people from outside the family. Thus, internal family cohesion may be low except for those dyads in which family members have chosen to reveal to each other. Hence, these family members may tend to be disengaged from each other. In addition, they may also find it difficult to adapt to change that is generated internally or externally. The permeable external orientation is problematic because the options that guide privacy management are limited to openness and, for the protective internal orientation, the options are limited to restricted access.

**Exterior moderate/interior low permeability rule orientation.** Families may also adopt a rule orientation that regulates privacy boundaries with moderate permeability for the exterior boundary and low permeability for the internal boundaries. These families set conditions for revealing private family information; for example, only certain people may know the information, if the conditions are right to tell the private information, and only if the person is trusted. Internally, they restrict access to each other. They are not completely trusting of outside members the way families are if they have permeable exterior boundaries. Nonetheless, they are more apt to tell nonfamily members their problems or private matters than they are to tell their family. Hence, the rules they use limit the frequency of disclosure or amount of information known by other family members. This orientation to privacy assumes that each family member will solve his or her own problems and keep information within personal privacy boundaries. Consequently, these families are more cautious about revealing in general, and especially to each other. On the continuum, they are more open than the low permeable orientation, but less open than the next orientation of moderate permeability.

Moreover, these families are more disengaged in terms of cohesion. Because the rules protect privacy rather than regulate the give-and-take of private information, family members are more distant. However, in comparison, these family members open their boundaries to outsiders more often. They are also more rigid regarding change. Negotiating privacy boundaries is difficult for this type of family. When change is necessary, these families may find it easier to redefine the outer boundary and change external rules than to change within the family.

**Exterior high/interior moderate permeability rule orientation.** Families may also have permeable rules for the exterior boundary and moderate permeable rules for interior boundary coordination. For these families, the members are very open with outsiders but only reveal private information to other family members under certain conditions. The boundaries are managed according to rules regulating when to discuss private matters with members of the family, yet, these same family members view people outside the family overall as more trusted recipients of personally and family private information.

For these families, the level of bonding is very high with people outside the family. They tend to be more dependent upon nonfamily members to solve problems, although they do select certain family members in whom to confide. The extent to which they establish a sense of cohesiveness with each other is dependent upon the regulatory rules the family uses for controlling privacy. These families also find it difficult to cope with change from the outside regarding privacy issues; they tend to respond in a chaotic fashion. Nevertheless, they are adept at responding to change within the family because the privacy rules are more accommodating to changing needs.

**Exterior low/interior moderate permeability rule orientation.** Families may combine orientations where the exterior boundary is protective and the interior boundary orientation gives partial access. The members use protective rules that keep private information within the confines of the family. They tend to be distrusting of people outside the family network and somewhat more willing to disclose to certain family members, linking them within a dyadic or group boundary if the circumstances meet their criteria.

With these families, the exterior boundary is controlled tightly and bonds with people from outside the family are not often established. Within the family, the members are more connected; however, they continue to maintain separateness through partial access to private information. This family type is also more accommodating of change internally, yet resists change that is imposed from the outside.

**Exterior moderate/interior high permeability rule orientation.** Families may combine moderate permeability for their exterior boundary and high permeability for their interior family boundaries. Thus, there may be certain circumstances under which information may be revealed to outsiders, for example, when the target person is able to keep confidences and is a trusted friend. However, within the family, the members are very open with each other about their private matters and have only one rule of nonexclusion. There are no restrictions disallowing disclosure; instead, the members are encouraged to be open with each other and expected to co-own the disclosed information.

These families may be highly enmeshed and bonded because of the expectation for open internal boundaries, leading to a high degree of interdependence among the members. By comparison, these members are less connected to people from outside the family. They have coconstructed rules that specify the extent to which they may disclose to others and use outsiders as confidants.

For these families, adaptability within the family may be more chaotic, given that the rules for regulating private information are limited to openness. By contrast, the rule orientation guiding the exterior boundary is more flexible and may respond to changing needs with a larger range of options. Hence, these families may adapt better to fluctuations in their privacy needs when they concern interacting with people outside the families.

**Exterior low/interior high permeability rule orientation.** The last privacy type combines a protective, low permeable orientation for the exterior boundary with a high permeable orientation for the inner boundaries. This family has a distrust of outsiders and protects the privacy boundary around personal family matters. Yet, internally, the family is very open with each other. Family members are willing to give access to their boundaries and talk about personal, dyadic, and group matters with each other without restraint. They may be viewed as interdependent, using each other to test out ideas and work through problems. This is useful, because linking with outsiders is not an acceptable option in this family.

These members are disengaged from those outside the family and more highly enmeshed with the family members. Although the members, admirably, take ownership issues seriously, a disadvantage of this perspective is that the family does not encourage opening up privacy boundaries to outsiders. Consequently, the orientation to privacy tends to restrict the ability to connect with people from outside the family. Nevertheless, boundaries are loosely held internally among family members, encouraging a high degree of cohesion. Being committed to strong ownership values about private family information means that these families assume each member will keep confidences. The exception to this rule becomes problematic and divergent.

All nine family privacy orientations focus our attention on the integration of two levels of information: (a) collective private family information, and (b) private information that may be specific to dyads, triads, or the individual family member. Because these orientations are constructed socially or phenomenologically, there may be times in the life of the family that the rules change and the family's orientations are challenged. This typology provides a framework for thinking about the way families orient to regulating private information.

However, family systems are not static. Wolfe and Laufer (1974) suggest in their life-cycle dimension of privacy that there are various stages and times of maturation where family members' "needs, abilities, experiences, desires and feelings change, and as a part of this change, the concept and patterns of privacy should also change" (p. 31). Change may occur on the individual level and the collective level throughout the life cycle. Although the system functions because all members acknowledge that they must work cooperatively, they are also individuals who may challenge the expectations of the family as a whole.

One of the sources of challenges and change is the integration of individual criteria for privacy expectations with a family's basic orientation. This is best understood by examining the way children learn the privacy norms that the family follows and how they attempt to develop their own. Parents tend to develop the orientation that the individual family adopts (Wolfe & Laufer, 1974). Their decision is based mostly on negotiating a combined perspective that integrates their own family-of-origin approaches.

As children grow, they are taught "where they have autonomy and where they must comply" (Wolfe & Laufer, 1974, p. 34). The balance of each is largely dependent upon the parent's perceptions of "whether the child is an independent being capable of understanding and being responsible for his [or her] own behavior" (Wolfe & Laufer, 1974, p. 34). As children reach a point where they are considered independent, they may begin to form an individual set of criteria or rules for privacy regulation over information that is considered personally private.

These rules may differ from family privacy orientations. An older child may be willing to adhere to family rules that maintain the exterior privacy boundary with outsiders, yet be unwilling to use the same rules for his or her own personal information. The other family members may see this divergence from a general orientation to private information as a challenge. The willingness to acknowledge the individual's right to regulate his or her own privacy boundary according to idiosyncratic rules may depend upon the type of privacy orientation the family has developed.

Another challenge for family members occurs when a marital relationship is being established. Each individual comes into the marriage with a definition of how he or she independently maintains a personal boundary around private information. When the partners are married, they must coordinate their personal privacy rules. Sometimes, it is difficult to move from an individual to a dyadic level. The rules that maintain the boundaries need to be negotiated; however, not everyone is able to coordinate boundary fit successfully.

The negotiation period between the partners, especially if they have inconsistent views on how personal information should be treated, may result in conflict and influence marital adjustment. For example, Davidson, Balswick, and Halverson (1983) found that spouses receiving more or less disclosure than they gave experienced problems in marital adjustment. It is likely that the reason couples have contrary expectations is because they come from different privacy orientations. The dyadic effect that Jourard (1971) identified suggests that people expect rates of disclosure that are similar to their own. Using differing rules means the expectations of both partners are violated. Therefore, they feel less satisfied than when they share similar orientations toward privacy (Jorgensen & Gaudy, 1980).

There are many other challenges to navigating family privacy boundaries. The chapter on boundary turbulence extends this discussion, focusing on several factors that help isolate the privacy issues that families face. However, matters that confront families attempting to cope with privacy relate to a more general discussion of maintaining group boundaries.

## GROUP PRIVACY BOUNDARIES

We belong to many different kinds of groups. At work, we might participate in task groups; in the community, we are affiliated with parent-teachers organizations, baseball teams, reading groups, and homeowners' associations. Groups are fundamental to our lives, yet in some groups we are more likely to consider whether to reveal or conceal private information. Social support groups are the most obvious because they are geared to fulfill needs that require some disclosure to succeed.

However, even in "reading groups," we might find that some discussions of the books lead the members to talk about private matters. In this way, the members construct boundary linkages and determine the level of co-ownership. There are some clues to ways people formulate these linkages. For instance, we know that people are more cautious about disclosing private information to out-group strangers than to in-group members, especially during initial interactions (Brems, Fromme, & Johnson, 1992; Egan, 1970; Higbee, 1973). In addition, when comparing dyads and triads, people tend to be more inclined to disclose private information in a dyad than they are in a triad when the target is an acquaintance (Taylor, 1979).

Yet, there are some gender differences suggesting variance in disclosure rules. Since CPM argues that men and women develop their rules based on a different set of criteria, it stands to reason that disclosure patterns are dissimilar. Thus, men disclose more in dyads than in small groups, whereas women disclose more in small group settings (Pearson, 1980). The amount of information also varies: Women reveal significantly more than men do in small groups.

Although gender criteria are important, other aspects of boundary coordination are also observed in group disclosure. For example, group members might be more inclined to conceal personally private information when they are coerced or harassed by others to disclose (Petronio & Braithwaite, 1987). The method of soliciting private matters obviously makes a difference in whether members contribute to the collectively held private information. Learning about each other helps establish a bond among the members. Ultimately, the preference of concealing may interfere with the goals of the group. However, if the information is not given freely, the environment is hampered from facilitating an open exchange of ideas in the group.

Although coercion and harassment are likely to block group members from revealing personally private information, so are other kinds of strategies. One tactic that is apt to restrict entry to personal boundaries is a show of indiscretion. When one group member learns private information about another member and then shares it with the group, the target member is likely to draw his or her borders more tightly.

These cases illustrate the way people link personal and dyadic boundaries with group boundaries where there is no relational history among members. The linkages reflect internal group interactions. They depend on sharing personal or dyadic private information that becomes the collective property of the group. An initial disclosure linking others may stimulate reciprocal revelations that add to the transformation of the private information from its original personal status to becoming property of the group members.

To reflect co-ownership, the group appropriates all the disclosures made by the individuals as belonging within the group privacy boundary. Just as a single person contributes to a group, transforming it into something new, so do individual disclosures grow into private information that belongs to everyone in the group. This process of linkage represents a way that we define boundary parameters around group-owned private information. Once it is clear that the group possesses the information, the members begin to develop privacy rules for maintaining the borders.

The way this linkage happens is supported, in part, by the fact that disclosure is different for groups than it is for dyads. Taylor, De Soto, and Lieb (1979) point out that perhaps this is due to the revealer needing to feel confident that his or her disclosure is safe with the group members. There are more possibilities for violations within group privacy boundaries than in the dyadic boundaries. Some members may not accept responsibility for co-owned private information. They may use different privacy rules than those established by the larger group to protect revelations.

## Group Confidences

One way that members demonstrate their loyalty to a group is by keeping the disclosures of its members confidential. For example, Daniels (1970) talks about a case of group sensitivity training that takes place within a military psychiatric residency. The group included all first-year students, with the involvement of some second and third-year students. Although there was little agreement about the purpose of the sensitivity group,

> some saw this group as private and personal, i.e., as "our group" and "the staff have nothing to do with it." These residents felt that the secrecy of the group was important to its integrity. They refused to speak about the group in their interview and warned

that no residents would speak of these matters. Their prediction
was not borne out. Eleven of the seventeen residents discussed
the group quite freely. Some of these had never accepted what
they saw as "the myth" of secrecy. (Daniels, 1970, p. 235)

The conversations conducted within the group, including many disclosures
by individual group members, were considered private. As a whole, the
information revealed in the group was seen by some of the members as
their collective responsibility. Thus, boundaries around the private information shared by the group members defined their ownership lines, sepa-
rating the residents from outsiders such as their supervisors.

Several residents recognized the boundary lines as articulating access
rules such as restricting the staff from knowing what the group members
said to each other. However, most group members did not follow the general rules for protecting the information. They developed their own privacy
rules for the way they managed revealing the private information belonging to the group. In this way, boundary permeability shifts depending on
whether members adhere to the privacy rules they establish or use their
own rules for managing access to the information (Putnam & Stohl, 1990).

Changing from group rules for privacy management to personal
boundary rules may lead to intra-group conflict. Breaching an agreement
to support certain access or protection rules belonging to the group jeop-
ardizes the trust of some members. Members may alter their privacy rule
focus (e.g., from the group to the personal level) for many reasons. For
example, they may change the rule because they are more committed to
their personal needs than the needs of the group. Group members might be
new to the group and not yet fully integrated or socialized. They may also
disagree with the consensus achieved about the privacy rules for handling
group private information. Thus, their allegiance is more toward their personal needs and individual privacy rules than group goals.

The members may also shift to personal rules because they are uncertain about the group rules. One of the difficulties in coming to consensus
about boundary rules managing privacy may be neglecting to explicitly
state them (Petronio, 1991). Relying on indirect messages or implicit
assumptions to establish the way group disclosures are handled may lead
to ambiguities about the expectations for access and protection rules. As
with other decision-making situations, "it is vital for a group to understand
fully the matter with which it is confronted if the members are to proceed
through subsequent phases of the decision-making or problem-solving
process and ultimately make an appropriate choice" (Gouran, Hirokawa,
Julian, & Leatham, 1993, p. 584). When the privacy rules are vague, group
participants may depend on their own decision criteria to disclose, rather
than sort out ambiguous rules or comply with ones they do not like.

## Reinforcing Group Boundaries

Although many groups may experiences the difficulties of inconsistent adherence to privacy rules, some groups work hard to reinforce unwavering compliance with the rules. For example, magicians are bound to the faithful adoption of privacy rules for disclosure. "Concealment creates property, something that is possessed, and the existence of this special property distinguishes possessor from nonpossessor and alters the attitudes of both toward the thing possessed" (Luhrmann, 1989, p. 136). Magic is necessarily concealed. Protecting the boundaries around magic allows us to believe in its powers (Luhrmann, 1989). Knowing too much diminishes the intrigue of magical experiences. For magicians, "secrecy is central to the practice of these different groups. Most members, for obvious reasons, keep their participation hidden; conventional civilians rarely take the assertion of witchhood with nonchalance" (Luhrmann, 1989, p. 136). For some groups involved with magic, it is important to keep activities, symbols, or the type of magic concealed. Magicians must keep the way they perform magic secret.

For magicians, the privacy boundaries are typically drawn tightly, with rules that emphasize protecting the knowledge needed to be part of a magician's group. Thus, to participate in a coven that practices witchcraft, a pagan group, or a general occultists' group, the rules for privacy protection need to be followed by all members because there are risks for revelation. Disclosing may decrease the intrigue or worth of the claims. By revealing, those practicing magic might also risk skepticism or rejection and possible persecution. For example,

> keeping the magical identity secret prevents it from being challenged by outsiders while retaining the sense of power and daring that makes it exciting. It seemed to me that participants quite liked the fact that their neighbors remained ignorant of their activities but would be shocked by them if only they knew. One woman who led an otherwise drab housewife's life spoke eloquently of feeling special and more alive through magic. It gave her something different from her husband. Moreover, when he drove me to the station he asked me what we did at the meetings. "She tells me very little." (Luhrmann, 1989, p. 141)

All members, either out of fear or of risking problems as a group, necessarily adopt concealment. The individual is less than the whole as we see in unified coordination. One only needs to think of the image created by historical accounts of the Salem witch trials to recognize the hazards. However, members are also mindful of giving up their powers by telling too much. The consequences are great enough to see that privacy rules have been routinized over time to give worth to magic and to balance the risks of others knowing too much.

The most complicated aspect of considering group privacy boundaries is in accommodating the multiple levels at work. Sometimes people who function as "privacy spanners" bring information from one group to the next (Huber & Daft, 1987). At other times, the information flow is kept within the confines of the group, as we see with the magicians. Variations occur depending on whether the groups have a long-term history (i.e., bona fide groups) or are zero-history groups (Putnam & Stohl, 1990). Although understanding the way groups negotiate boundary coordination is complex, for organizational privacy boundaries there is an added layer of coordination issues.

## ORGANIZATIONAL PRIVACY BOUNDARIES

Like the group and family boundaries, the organizational boundary houses multiple layers of private information where individuals coordinate permeability, linkages, and ownership. When affiliated with an organization, individuals manage personal, dyadic, and group boundaries in addition to those that surround private information belonging to the organization (Bok, 1982; Roth, 1991; Steele, 1975). The dyadic and group boundaries for private information reflect salient structures within the work environment and may include the superior-subordinate relationship, dyadic coworker relationships, or work groups collaborating on a task

Although there are fewer studies focusing on disclosure per se, scholars in organizational communication have targeted the concept of openness as a critical issue in the work environment (Baird, 1977; Jablin, 1982). Steele (1975) argues that the concept of openness typically conceived of in organizational research is similar to the notion of disclosure. Like the scholars advocating a dialectical framework of disclosure, Steele asserts that there is both a negative and positive side to openness, with costs and gains found in the patterns used by workers in the organization. Thus, disclosure in an organization can both enhance and impede workers' performance.

### Superior-Subordinate Boundaries

The focus on an open organizational environment presumes that the best policy is to encourage workers to provide a permeable boundary in the superior-subordinate relationship (Jablin, 1982). Facilitating an open environment between a superior and subordinate requires a receptive and willing listener for both participants. However, certain kinds of message strategies are likely to increase or decrease the possibility of experiencing an open environment (Jablin, 1982). Hence, the message strategies are critical in determining the permeability of all types of privacy boundaries.

For example, personal privacy boundaries may be more tightly guarded when disconfirming responses are given between superior-subordinate interactions (Jablin, 1982). In an open organizational environment, subordinates tend to be more receptive to confirming messages. Jablin states that,

> subordinates who perceived an open climate of communication between themselves and their superior felt that it was inappropriate, regardless of the object of the message . . . for a superior to react to a subordinate's message with a repudiating or disconfirming response. In contrast, subordinates who perceived a closed communication relationship with their superior judged the appropriateness of a superior's response by not only the type of response expressed, but by *whom the message was about* (superior or subordinate). (p. 305)

This concern for both the conversational and relational level in responsiveness is similar to an argument made by Berg (1987). He suggests that in the disclosure equation, individuals are responsive and open their privacy boundaries in two ways. Recipients may exhibit conversational responsiveness by showing, through message content and interest, an understanding of the disclosed information.

People also convey responsiveness relationally by acknowledging the obligations of the relationship in responding to disclosure. Both are important in understanding the relative importance of how recipients respond to disclosure. Jablin (1982) states, "in a truly open communication relationship between superior and subordinate, both individuals possess a freedom to respond to the other's messages" (p. 296).

However, workers also have rules that they use in order to reveal in an organizational environment. For instance, when subordinates are seeking help with work-related problems, they disclose to people with more authority (Burke, 1982). When they need help solving personal problems, they turn to peers and coworkers rather than superiors. Employees differentiate between levels of information and privacy boundaries, particularly when they are making choices about where and to whom they will reveal.

## Vagueness as Privacy Protection

Although many scholars have advocated an open organizational environment, there is an argument for limiting the information flow between privacy boundaries internally within the organization and externally to outsiders (Eisenberg & Witten, 1987). Ambiguous messages, similar to indirect strategies discussed in the section on marital couples, give both the freedom to respond and the complication of responding. Indirect disclosure messages also afford the person revealing the opportunity to veil the content in a way that protects his or her privacy boundary.

With vague and ambiguous messages, internally, supervisors may shroud a disclosure about poor performances, forthcoming layoffs, or other unpleasant information. Likewise, subordinates may reveal problematic information to their coworkers or supervisors in an ambiguous way. Vagueness protects both the discloser and recipient from dealing directly with problems. Sometimes this elusiveness is a way for workers to selectively reveal private information that is personal, owned by work groups, or belonging to the organization.

For example, "After a secretive campaign to throw its leading competitor off track, Johnson Controls Inc. has introduced what it maintains is the next generation of computerized systems to control heating, security and other functions in buildings" (Shapiro, 1990, p. 2). The Johnson company's employees talked about how they tried to keep their competitor from finding out about their new product and the ways in which they worked to mislead Honeywell. Johnson Controls actively tried to keep proprietary information about its product from leaking out by using several strategies to protect this organizational privacy boundary. For instance, they invented code names, misled Honeywell by launching a big campaign for a minor change in an existing building control system, and made up new product names (Shapiro, 1990). They were successful in drawing the borders of the privacy boundary tight enough to keep out the competition. Vagueness and attempts to maintain organizational privacy by the corporation is only one way that openness is being considered. However, because openness is embedded in a dialectical tension with privacy, privacy rights from the perspective of the employee become an important issue.

## Employee-Employer Privacy Rights

Currently, there are a number of salient points being made about employee privacy. Some argue this is the new "employee relations battlefield" (Hubbartt, 1998, p. 1). Do employers have the right to require preemployment tests, such as physical exams, drug and alcohol screening, background checks, and reference checks, and require the prospective employee to take tests to prove his or her abilities? So far, the answer is a resounding yes (Alderman & Kennedy, 1995).

Arlene Kurtz learned that workplace privacy concerns begin at the start of the employment process when she applied for a job as a clerk typist with the city of North Miami, Florida. The city had developed a policy that all job applicants must sign an affidavit stating that they had not used tobacco products for one year before seeking city employment. The city had implemented a no-smoking policy in 1990, claiming that smokers create higher health costs, as much as $4,611 per year more than nonsmokers. When Kurtz refused to sign the affidavit, she was not hired. She then filed suit against the city alleging that the no-smoking rule was an invasion of privacy. (Hubbartt, 1998, p. 3)

Ms. Kurtz lost her suit because the courts argued that the health issues outweighed her claims of privacy invasion. The battle lines are drawn between personal privacy boundaries and organizational expectations for employee openness. Employees are often required to give up some measure of private information in return for being considered for jobs, promotions, and positions in the organization. However, the exchange of information is more like a parent-child relationship and less like an equal relationship between two adults. Thus, we see how inclusive boundary coordination functions within an organizational context. Employees are expected to give more private information than they get from employers. In some cases, the employees learn little about the internal workings of the company; however, they are expected to give a great deal of their personal information away.

### Conflict of Interest

Because disclosing can make a person vulnerable, crossing boundary lines by telling personally private information in the organization can potentially lead to problems for the individual as an employee. For instance:

During her career, Roulon-Miller met and began dating a fellow IBM employee, account manager Matt Blum. Blum left IBM to join a competing office product company called OYX. Blum and Roulon-Miller had dated on and off for several years, and IBM management was aware of their relationship. Shortly after receiving a $4,000 raise, Roulon-Miller was called in to supervise Phil Callahan's office. Callahan confronted her about whether she was dating Blum, stating that the dating relationship created a conflict of interest. Callahan told Roulon-Miller to stop dating Blum. When Roulon-Miller protested against the company's intrusion into her private life, Callahan dismissed her. (Hubbartt, 1998, p. 11)

The organization claimed that Roulon-Miller's dating habits created a conflict of interest for her and hampered her abilities to perform her duties effectively. Employers have insisted that couples not work for the competition, refrain from working in the same departments, and resist the temptation to comment on each other's work performance. All of these decisions have a basis in a logic that is geared to protect organizational privacy and internal organizational functioning. However, the boundary lines are often blurred, not taking into account the full complement of issues that boundary coordination requires.

Although employees cope with managing their personal privacy within organizational boundaries, companies also must handle privacy issues of their own. As the earlier example of Johnson Controls illustrates, organizations aim to regulate the kind of information that is revealed about their products. At times, it is difficult for companies to keep track of the many ways they can become compromised. The sheer volume of people within the privacy boundary and the number of potential issues compounds the concerns for boundary coordination. People are taught boundary rules regulating organizational privacy, or managers are expected to develop a set of rules controlling dissemination of organizational information. In both cases, the effectiveness of learning and communicating the rules may be incomplete.

For example, managers may go to great lengths to develop and train employees in how to judge appropriate revealing and concealing for organizational information. However, the company may not be able to control employee misconduct. For example, unauthorized disclosures can throw product development back years and give the edge to the competition. Additionally, the employee may use private information belonging to the company against it by *whistle-blowing*.

## Whistle-Blowing

Bok (1982) defines whistle-blowing as "revelations meant to call attention to negligence, abuses, or dangers that threaten the public interest" (p. 211). Sounding the alarm about internal organizational abuses means that the employee brings private company information to people outside. The difficulty lies in the fact that disclosing is not only problematic for the organization, but it will also be risky for the whistle-blower (Bok, 1982).

"The message of whistle blowing is seen as a *breach of loyalty* because it comes from within" (Bok, 1982, p. 214). The insider brings the organization's dirty laundry outside into the public domain. This act, while often motivated by the need to reveal negligence or abuse, sends a message about the whistle-blower as much as it does about the action prompting the transgression. Others may find the organizational abuse thorny, but they also feel uncomfortable about the employee who is willing to break a code or breach the privacy boundary rules that implicitly suggest workers should be loyal to their company and responsible co-owners of the information.

Consequently, the employees seek to expose the seemingly inappropriate behavior of the company but, in the process, has their own privacy violated. One of the reasons that whistle-blowers become vulnerable is because they are pointing a finger at unfulfilled organizational expectations. However, in the process they also compromise their role as a person accountable to the organization to keep confidences. They are assigning responsibility and showing how that responsibility was not honored by the company when, in fact, they are doing the same thing. This rocks the very core of the organizational structure and is therefore damning. For example, the University of Michigan had to pay a researcher $1.6 million dollars in damages because she blew the whistle on her supervisor who stole her data (Hilts, 1997).

Dr. Phinney revealed that her supervisor used her data on issues of aging and claimed it was hers.

> She had just solved the core of the problem, and her supervisor, Dr. Perlmutter, a recognized researcher in aging, suggested that she write up that and other research in applications for research grants. Dr. Perlmutter promised Dr. Phinney that she would be listed as the first author on papers resulting from the work as well as [receive] a job at the Institute of Gerontology, Dr. Phinney said. But after Dr. Perlmutter had Dr. Phinney's research and grant applications in hand, Dr. Phinney asserted, Dr. Perlmutter said the work was her own. (Hilts, 1997, p. A13).

Dr. Phinney was not only awarded money for fraud; she also received additional damages because of retaliation by the university officials.

As Bok (1982) notes, "the whistleblower's accusation . . . concerns a present or an imminent threat. Past errors or misdeeds occasion such an alarm only if they still affect current practices" (p. 215). In this case, Dr. Phinney's accusations were at the core of academic research and the relationship between supervisors and subordinates. The presumption in an academic organization, that intellectual property is preserved, made Dr. Phinney's problem salient and threatening.

Whistle-blowing illustrates the integration yet separation of multiple-boundary privacy management within organizations. Employees regulate these privacy boundaries on many levels. They are interrelated in ways that are at times barely visible until there is boundary turbulence. In chapter 5, this book explores other types of disruptions people face as they traverse the many layers of private information.

## CONCLUSION

This chapter focused on boundary coordination that takes place in collectively held privacy boundaries. As we incorporate more layers into our control and take responsibility for more information, the coordination process becomes additionally complicated. However, we can see some patterns emerge that generalize about managing personal and multiple boundaries.

The regulation of permeability depends on the same kind of rule development, whether it is for personal privacy boundaries or the more complicated collective boundaries. Generating rules is contingent on the fundamental criteria people use in addition to evaluating the risk-benefit ratio. Generally, when there are several layers of boundaries, as in families and organizations, we can see the emergence of privacy management for internal and external borders. When boundary coordination works in synchronicity, the members successfully regulate privacy. However, as the next chapter shows, sometimes a tension exists between these borders complicating how they are managed. Ownership can become problematic because people vie for either relinquishing responsibility or incorrectly claiming someone else's information as their own. The mishandling of boundary linkages, ownership, and permeability often results in boundary turbulence.

# 5

# Rule Management Process 3

## *Boundary Turbulence*

Due to the complexity of boundary coordination, sometimes the process fails. When coordination becomes asynchronous, turbulence erupts, disturbing the harmony of boundary management of private information. When people are unable to collectively develop, execute, or enact rules guiding permeability, ownership, and linkages, the coordinating efforts of privacy management are confounded and boundary turbulence occurs. There are times when this misstep is obvious to all involved and measures are quickly taken to correct the problem (Coupland, Giles, & Wiemann, 1991). However, there are also times when an asynchronicity in rule usage is not clear until some conflict takes place and it becomes obvious that a miscommunication has occurred (see Figure 5.1).

There is a wide range of turbulence that people experience. We may encounter minor flare-ups, confusion, misunderstandings, mistakes, embarrassments, and full-fledged uproars. From the most disturbing to the least, we are able to gain insights into the boundary management process. Further, turbulence is not limited to the development of new boundary lines. Instead, we see coordination problems in established boundaries, when the boundaries are being reformulated, and when people are trying to manage multiple boundaries. In all cases, something has disrupted the boundary management process, making it difficult for the individuals involved to communicate effectively about private information.

## TYPES OF BOUNDARY TURBULENCE

There are several reasons boundary coordination might not work. This chapter examines six different precipitating factors leading to boundary turbulence, including: (a) intentional rule violations, (b) boundary rule mistakes, (c) fuzzy boundaries, (d) dissimilar boundary orientations, (e) boundary definition predicaments, and (f) privacy dilemmas. Because of

177

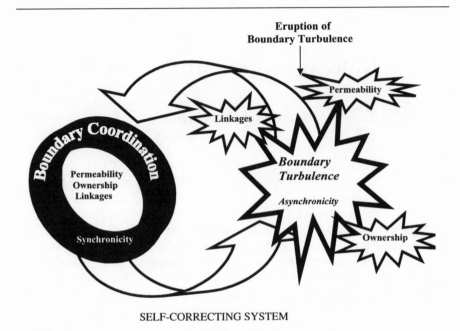

**Figure 5.1**
Coordination-Turbulence Interplay

the interdependent nature of these categories, they are not necessarily mutually exclusive. For example, people may intentionally violate rules, which compromises boundary management, making boundary lines fuzzy. Thus, these categories are used to organize the ways that coordination of boundary management falls apart and is restored.

### Intentional Rule Violations

When people deliberately tell collectively held private information without following agreed-upon rules, they violate the implicit contract for regulating the boundary. Rule violations ensue for different reasons, among them betrayal, spying, and confidentiality dilemmas.

### Betrayal

Betrayal breaches the trust of co-owners to follow boundary rules. A way to think about trust is in terms of *"trust credit points."* When a boundary is formed and people negotiate rules, they assume that the others can be trusted to follow these rules. In other words, they give each other a fair amount of trust credit points up front, believing that they will abide by the privacy rules. Trust points can increase or decrease from that moment on. Nonetheless, people start out in the black. As they use the rules according to their agreement with the co-owners, they may gain even more points. If individual co-owners breach the trust, however, they lose these points, sometimes significantly, as occurs with betrayal.

**Case of Monica Lewinsky.** Betrayal is one explanation for the case of Monica Lewinsky and Linda Tripp. A newspaper account states that Monica Lewinsky was betrayed by Linda Tripp because she (Linda Tripp) allegedly tape-recorded a conversation (in secret) with a "friend" (Monica Lewinsky) about Ms. Lewinsky's affair with the President of the United States (Parker, 1998). Over the course of time, Monica Lewinsky and Linda Tripp had many "confidential" conversations about Ms. Lewinsky's love life.

Because we do not know all of the details, we might assume, as did Monica Lewinsky, that Linda Tripp understood she was mutually responsible for the disclosed information. In other words, Linda Tripp was accountable for Ms. Lewinsky's disclosures because they were revealed with the assumption of confidentiality under the pretext of a "friendship" relationship. Linda Tripp repeatedly listened to and commented on Ms. Lewinsky's alleged relationship, forming a dyadic boundary around this private information.

Given that rules for third-party disclosure are negotiated, we can imagine that Ms. Lewinsky and Ms. Tripp talked about whether other people should be told this information. If rules for boundary access were established and Linda Tripp ignored them, she is guilty of intentionally compromising this privacy boundary. Third-party disclosures without permission trespass on rule expectations for information flow. When violations take place, other members may perceive the breach as a disloyalty and feel betrayed.

Accounts suggest that Ms. Lewinsky thought Ms. Tripp would use protection rules to keep the information confidential. This seems reasonable because we know that "when a close friend tries to strike up an unwanted conversation and violates another's privacy, interaction control strategies are more likely to be used than when the violator is either a stranger or an acquaintance" (Hosman & Siltanen, 1995, p. 71). Monica did not perceive any ulterior motive on Linda's part because she trusted her intentions. Consequently, Ms. Lewinsky was open with Ms. Tripp and responded positively to attempts at soliciting more details. It appears that Linda Tripp lost many trust credit points with her betrayal, not only with Ms. Lewinsky but with others observing her betrayal.

This example also illustrates another dimension of intentional violations, besides breaching trust. As Ms. Tripp's behavior suggests, sometimes people claim more ownership of the information than is appropriate or desired by other co-owners. Although a certain level of responsibility is expected for the information (that is what makes it dyadic), people acting like Linda ignore the shared nature of the information, taking over control. At the extreme, people mentally shift the information into their own personal privacy boundary, making them feel they have complete and unitary rights to regulate without consulting others in the boundary. While Ms. Lewinsky seemed to define coordination as equitable, Ms. Tripp appeared to define coordination as inclusive, taking over control of Ms. Lewinksy's information.

*Inappropriate claims* may explain why some people breach confidences and seem perplexed that others complain. In their minds, the shared private information becomes solely theirs to do with as they wish. Turbulence erupts because this assumption is rarely acceptable to other co-owners. Ignoring the mutuality of the information and acting in ways that contradict presumptions of dual ownership are problematic for boundary coordination. Negative sanctions are put into place to right the wrong of inappropriate claims such as these.

**Don't ask, don't tell rule.** The U.S. Navy's actions against Timothy R. McVeigh (not related to the Oklahoma City bombing) are another example that highlights the problems associated with betrayal. The "don't ask, don't tell" rule for military personnel concerning gay or lesbian sexual orientation was allegedly violated for Mr. McVeigh:

> McVeigh . . . ran afoul of Navy prosecutors last autumn after sending an email message to the wife of a fellow submarine crewman. The message contained the screen name "Boysrch," which was linked to McVeigh's profile page. That page was signed "Tim" . . . listed the author's marital status as "gay" and expressed a sensual interest in young men. (Graham, 1998, p. A11)

In this case, two levels of privacy rules were compromised. On one level, Mr. McVeigh's personal privacy boundary was invaded thereby ignoring any protection rules Mr. McVeigh might have had for his privacy boundary. On another level, the organization violated its own "don't ask, don't tell" rule when a Navy investigator called AOL (an online computer service) anonymously to attain the identity of Timothy McVeigh. Hence, an initial betrayal was compounded by ignoring yet another set of privacy rules installed to protect confidentiality. One federal court judge stated that Navy personnel intentionally "embarked on a search and 'outing' mission in ordering the dismissal of a sailor accused of homosexuality based on information obtained from an online service" (Diamond, 1998, p. A3).

Because gay men and lesbians are often stigmatized, the management of privacy boundaries surrounding their sexual orientation is a burden (Dindia, 1998). Particularly in the armed services, where there is potential for emotional and physical harm, gay men and lesbians are hampered by maintaining a veil of secrecy. Individuals keep tight controls over boundaries around sexual orientation in order to prevent unpleasant outcomes. The military's establishment of the "don't ask, don't tell" policy is an attempt to provide a legitimate organizational boundary around the information for the protection of service men and women.

However, in the case of Timothy McVeigh, the circumstance that led to these actions compromised the protection of information about his sexual orientation. His inadvertent disclosure occurred when sending an electronic message to a civilian Navy volunteer about a toy drive for crewmembers' children (McVeigh v. Civil Action, 1998). Because his screen name "Boysrch" appeared, she initially accessed the profile and found a person named "Tim" who identified "gay" under marital status. The Navy was notified and the actions discussed above took place. Through an unintentional disclosure, Mr. McVeigh made the crewman's wife a member of his dyadic privacy boundary surrounding his sexual preference.

Perhaps because of how she obtained the information and the uncertainty about the person's identity, she demonstrated little loyalty or obligation when it came to keeping the information within a privacy boundary. Because there was no opportunity to establish mutually agreed-upon privacy management rules, the wife acted based on her own judgment of appropriate action concerning the information. The woman apparently felt it necessary to enact a "third-party" disclosure to Navy personnel. This situation illustrates choices that are made when there are weak ties between the discloser and recipient. Further complicating the situation, Navy personnel, pursuing private information about sexual orientation, breached Mr. McVeigh's personal privacy boundary. However, they justified their behavior by maintaining that Mr. McVeigh violated the "don't tell" rule, thereby redefining the rights Mr. McVeigh had over his own private information. Thus, they argued, that by sending the information to AOL, he was making a public statement (McVeigh v. Civil Action, 1998).

For Timothy McVeigh, the betrayal comes from AOL, which identified him, and from the officer's wife, who judged that the information in his account should be revealed to Navy personnel. Whether AOL legally violated federal law or not, using a code name implicitly suggests a presumption of privacy. The wife presumably felt compelled to reveal information about this man, even though she appears not to have asked permission from Mr. McVeigh. Mr. McVeigh's case is just one example of how employers invade employees' privacy. There are other situations where betrayal by supervisors constitutes breaches of employee privacy.

**Supervisor betrayal.** Supervisors may solicit confessions about personal problems from employees, telling them that they will keep it confidential, and then tell that information to their superiors in the company. This type of betrayal sends a message of disrespect. Soliciting private information suggests that a person is concerned about another. However, giving the private information to someone who has even more power over the employee without asking permission leaves both the worker and supervisor vulnerable.

The worker is vulnerable because he or she may have these personal matters used against him or her. The supervisor soliciting the private information may become vulnerable because, although the employee feels obligated to open personal boundaries, he or she may not feel good about the situation. Telling a superior compounds the discontent the worker may feel.

Most likely, privacy invasion works against the supervisor in three ways. First, because the supervisor knows about the employee's personal problems, the subordinate may feel free to use that information as an excuse for behavior that the supervisor may find objectionable. Second, the subordinate may feel that it is acceptable to pry into the supervisor's personal life because of a reciprocity norm. Third, the betrayal to the superior may prompt feelings of resentment that interfere with the worker's productivity.

Several issues govern employees' choices to restore a level of coordination synchronicity after violations occur. For example, if subordinates anticipate that their privacy will be invaded, they use more blocking strategies and confrontation than do their supervisors and co-workers (Le Poire, Burgoon, & Parrott, 1992). By comparison, subordinates appear to be much more proactive and reactive to invasion than workers in other positions. Consequently, privacy violations trigger a number of negative reactions and, after repeated incidences, proactive behaviors that are nonproductive.

## Spying

Spying, like betrayal, is problematic because boundary ownership is compromised. The case where two employee trainers at Nissan kept in touch through e-mail and experienced "boss spying" is a typical example. A newspaper account states, they coordinated training efforts, discussed projects and occasionally traded barbs about upper management. Then one day, their boss called them in and issued them reprimands. Management had been reading their messages all along. The employees complained to superiors in the company that their privacy had been violated and sued for invasion of privacy. Nissan argues that, as owner of the computer system, it has the right to object to the way employees use their computers. ("Electronic Spying by Boss," 1995, p. A14)

Ownership rights are being questioned in this case. Who owns the information and, therefore, the right to regulate its flow to others? The employees believe that they own the rights to control the level of permeability to third parties. However, the boss and company argue that ownership rights apply only to the machines and thereby invalidate the employees' ownership claims. Consequently, the employees see the action as invasive and the company maintains that its ownership rights over property supersede any claims by the employees about their boundary ownership rights over the e-mail messages. Therefore, there is boundary turbulence because the company (i.e., the boss) and employees are unable to coordinate their claims of ownership effectively.

### Dilemmas of Confidentiality

Intentional violation may also arise when someone has agreed to the privacy rules, and then finds a need to breach them for the benefit of the discloser or another person (Petronio, 2000a). For example, Robert Berke is a physician who faced such a predicament. He learned that one of his patients had apparently infected nine women with the HIV virus and that half of them were infected after he found out his HIV status (Thompson, 1997). The doctor was bound by issues of doctor-patient confidentiality, but, for Dr. Berke, the dilemma concerned whether to tell about the HIV status for a greater good. Therefore, disclosing meant that the man's HIV status became known; however, doing so protected others from being infected.

This case illustrates some of the complexity of decision making for physicians. The physician in this example apparently made limited disclosures to law enforcement agencies after he learned of the patient's arrest. To solve his dilemma, the doctor informed the authorities, shifting responsibility for the information to another group. He violated the man's privacy, but on a restricted or "need to know" basis.

The physician's actions, in turn, led to a judge's ruling that the confidentiality of the man's HIV status needed to be violated because he was a threat to the community. This resulted in a greater intrusion for the person who was HIV positive. Namely, his picture was displayed in the vicinity where he lived, on posters warning others not to have sex with him. The decision to breach confidentiality when there are two equally unpleasant alternatives is a difficult choice to make. Physicians are particularly vulnerable on this front because their position as doctors requires a commitment to keeping confidences.

## Boundary Rule Mistakes

In addition to intentional invasion, boundary turbulence may be an outcome of *rule mistakes*. Instead of intentionally compromising boundary coordination, people erroneously apply privacy management rules that are at odds with other members' perspectives. Rule mistakes may happen for many reasons. People might be irresponsible and make mistakes about the rules because they have a momentary lapse, they are not paying attention to rule development, or they do not understand the privacy rules. Nevertheless, the action is not deliberate. Thus, three such mistakes illustrate this case. People make errors in judgment, in timing, and bungle topic rules all leading to boundary turbulence.

### Errors in Judgment

This first type of rule mistake occurs when people inadvertently tell collectively held private information to a third party without recognizing that they have breached confidences. This happens when people act *irresponsibly*, making erroneous assumptions about target confidants, and when they *misunderstand rule expectations* (Steele, 1975). In order to act responsibly as a collective member, co-owners must take into account privacy rules for choices about a target recipient. When an individual member of the collective boundary neglects to respect the wishes of the group regarding who has access to collectively owned information, he or she carelessly discloses.

Sometimes members believe that their judgment about a target is more accurate than the group's. Other times, the disclosing member makes a bad decision about a target, assuming that person will protect the boundaries and negative reactions will not result from the disclosure. The disclosing member misjudges the level of boundary security he or she might enjoy. In other words, because individuals typically assume that once private information has been disclosed others will act appropriately and not tell others, or will follow privacy rules that have been established by the group, a sense of security results. However, when the rules are not followed, that sense of security is shattered.

Once a revelation has been made, it is difficult to maintain control over the next iterations of disclosures. Therefore, the issue of trust is extremely important in the decision to reveal against the wishes of the group. Whether a confidant can be trusted is always an issue; however, when a person is breaching the confidentiality of a collective privacy boundary, assessing trust is an even bigger concern. The stakes are higher because more people may become vulnerable. Thus, when a member selects an inappropriate recipient, he or she overlooks potential ramifications for the group and for him or herself.

For example, a wife and husband are having marital difficulties; they have agreed to keep their troubles confidential within the dyadic privacy boundary. However, the husband feels an increasing need to talk about his marital problems. He has few friends with whom he can talk about his marital difficulties. To alleviate his burden he turns to his next-door neighbor, telling her the most private aspects of his relationship with his wife. Unfortunately for the husband, the neighbor is closer to his wife than she is to him, and her loyalties to the wife are stronger. Consequently, the neighbor tells the wife everything the husband said.

The husband irresponsibly chose the neighbor because he did not assess her relationship with his wife. As it happened, the neighbor had a much more dependable relationship with the wife than with the husband. In turn, the neighbor irresponsibly disclosed because she ignored the husband's request to keep the information confidential. Thus, weak ties between the husband and neighbor lead to instigating boundary turbulence. The husband assumed that the neighbor would "of course" keep confidences, and the ramifications seemed obvious to him if she did not. In this case, boundary turbulence erupted and everyone was hurt.

As this example illustrates, people can give boundary access irresponsibly when they misconstrue the collective rules for revealing or concealing. Sometimes even when the target person seems appropriate, the misjudgments are not clear until disclosure has taken place. For example, an older man came in for appointment with a cardiologist and his adult daughter accompanied him. The physician asked if the patient wanted the daughter to be present for his evaluation. The father agreed. During the course of the interview, the doctor disclosed that the father had terminal cancer, a fact the father had not told his daughter.

The doctor assumed that, since the father wanted his daughter included in the visit, he must have told her about his condition. Unfortunately, that was not true. The physician's presumption about rules for permeability of the boundary around the father's condition included his daughter because the physician relied on the circumstances as a guide for discerning access and protection rules regarding the health status of the father. However, he made a mistake in judgment.

Errors in judgment may also occur when rules are mistakenly applied to one or more members. When dissimilar rules govern different members of a collective, boundary turbulence takes place. For example, a family learns that one of the nieces is pregnant. Everyone agrees not to tell the grandmother because she has recently undergone surgery and cannot handle the information in her fragile state. The members are linked into a boundary around mutually owned private information at the family level. However, an error in judgment happens, in this case, when one of the brothers misunderstands the fact that everyone in the family has agreed not to tell the grandmother and he mistakenly discloses the information to her. He is using a rule that is not acceptable to the other co-owners, but did not realize that everyone else collectively decided to exclude the grandmother from this information.

## Miscalculations in Timing

People often make mistakes about when to conceal or reveal private information. Boundary turbulence results because the rules for appropriate timing are not followed. The irresponsible person does not intentionally aim for turbulence; however, by not taking into account certain expectations about the way people keep information or tell it to others outside the boundary, the discloser causes problems.

For example, after dating for some time, a woman was hoping that her partner would ask her to marry him on an upcoming vacation. After planning the trip, arriving at a beautiful hotel, and having several days of fun, the woman thought her partner would propose. During a lovely dinner, he told her he wanted to tell her something important. She was excited with anticipation. Her partner hemmed around a little trying to get the right words. Finally, he told her that he was gay and did not want to be in the relationship any more. The timing of this revelation was a problem because the partner made a confession after leading the woman to believe that she was going to receive a marriage proposal. Given the setting and the fact he did not provide any clues about his feelings, she felt betrayed.

Sometimes partners raise issues when they know that neither is going to be able to respond in a useful manner. For example, errors in timing may be enacted on the way to the airport when a spouse is departing for a long journey or when the discussion must take place in front of others. Choosing to make personally private information dyadic at a time that limits the ability to discuss all relevant meanings imposes a burden on all parties involved. Coordination is difficult because there is not enough time to explore what the information signifies or the way it might impact the nature of the existing dyadic boundaries. In addition, there is little time to develop satisfying privacy rules for boundary management.

One of the more devastating events happening within the medical profession is the poor timing of revealing traumatic news about health status. Nurses and doctors alike have called patients at their place of business in the middle of the workday and have told them that they have cancer, that they have hepatitis C, that they are HIV-positive, or that they have tested positive for drugs, in addition to revealing other significant maladies. The bad timing of these calls has a devastating effect on the patient. Making the calls when a person is not in a private setting precludes the possibility of keeping the information private because of the emotional reaction to the information. There are numerous other situations where the timing makes it difficult to easily coordinate the nature, permeability, and function of boundaries.

### Bungling Topic Rules

As with errors in timing, people also make mistakes about concealing or revealing certain kinds of private information. There are many examples of this mistake. For instance, on a woman's twenty-first birthday, a relative came to a party her parents gave for her. The relative began to drink and soon she was talking about the time when she first saw the young woman as an infant. She said that it was right after her parents had signed the adoption papers. The woman was stunned because her parents had never told her she was adopted. This was irresponsible of the relative and caused turbulence for the parents, the woman, and the relative herself.

Mistakes regarding topic rules are made by many people, including health workers. They may tell someone private medical information when they should not. For instance, a technician doing a mammogram, trying to be helpful, reveals that she saw "only a small lump." She continues, "but it is probably nothing to worry about." This type of disclosure is made to relieve the tension of uncertain medical status. The difficulty is that the technician, while competent in her job, is not licensed to evaluate the person's health status. Making an unreliable assessment of a person's health condition simply to alleviate the tension a patient is feeling during the interaction is not responsible in the long term.

Health care workers might also mistakenly conceal conditions from family members, even when concealment is not in anyone's best interest. Doctors may believe that it is best not to tell a son about his father's condition, thinking that the son cannot handle the information, when that may not be the case. It is dangerous to assume that individuals are not ready to hear the truth without taking steps to assess the situation more carefully. Telling half-truths that confuse patients and relatives also contributes to boundary turbulence.

Another kind of topic rule mistake comes from erroneously assessing the situation. Sometimes people presume certain privacy rules prevail. Only after they reveal or conceal do they discover their blunder. This tends to happen when rules are implicit or when individuals do not pay attention to the expected privacy rules for boundary management. We see many demonstrations of this behavior in everyday life. Individuals are routinely insensitive to other people's circumstances, especially when they have a need to disclose. One person recently made such a statement, commenting, "I don't really understand why people can't see how difficult it is for me to be around women who don't work." Unfortunately, this individual made this comment to a woman who chose to stay home with her children.

Making *insensitive disclosure* mistakes can lead to conflicts and misunderstandings. For instance, presumptuously claiming more rights than have been negotiated in a dyad or other kinds of collective boundaries may be problematic:

> A 31-year-old man undergoes surgery for the removal of his cancerous spleen. Seven years later, he learns that without his knowledge, his doctors had replicated his cells in a laboratory, obtained a patent and used the cells to develop a new anticancer drug. (Hales, 1991, p. 52).

In this situation, the doctors concealed an important fact from the patient, never disclosing their activities. It is likely the physicians did not consider the possibility that the man would find this behavior problematic, so they did not disclose.

Inappropriate or negative disclosures also are made by mistake. A former Miller Brewing executive, who won a suit against the company for firing him, is a good example. He discussed an episode of *Seinfeld* with a female coworker and she found the executive's rendition and the contents of the episode offensive:

> Jerold Mackenzie was fired from his $95,000-a-year job in 1993 after he told Patricia Best about the episode and she complained. "You should be able to talk to your co-workers. You should be able to talk to subordinates as you would talk to anybody else," he [Mackenzie] said. (Brooks, 1997, p. A8)

The executive's interpretation of the episode and the way that he expressed his feelings about it made the subordinate uncomfortable. The executive did not intend to make her feel that way; nevertheless, she responded with a negative reaction.

Sometimes people believe that honesty is the best policy. However, depending on the valence of the information, consideration may not be given to the recipient's ability to handle such brutal honesty. In the abstract, honesty is considered desirable, although it is risky because knowing exactly how someone might think can be unpleasant (Rosenfeld, 2000). When people mistake the desire for honesty to be the only acceptable policy for disclosure, thereby ignoring circumstances when discretion is a better option, there is likely to be boundary turbulence.

For example, a physician, in talking to a 90–year-old woman, stated that she should recognize that because of her age, her hip pain was likely to get worse. Having an operation on the hip would do little, and she needed to realize that she would have to live with this considerable pain. He stated that he "just wanted to be as honest as he could," so that the woman would not have any false hope of recovery. The woman left the office and became clinically depressed for two weeks after the interaction.

Although the information the physician gave his patient was factually true, giving absolutely no hope of any relief was mentally and physically devastating for the woman. If he had offered some hope, even if little changed in her condition, she could have handled the situation better than she did in dealing with his brutal honesty. The counterargument might state that this honesty helped prepare her for long-term pain. However, in this case, it did the opposite, making her depressed and physically unwell.

Being blunt means that people do not exercise face-saving and discretion:

> At its best, discretion is the intuitive ability to discern what is and is not intrusive and injurious, and to use this discernment in responding to the conflicts everyone experiences as insider and outsider. It is an acquired capacity to navigate in and between the worlds of personal and shared experience, coping with the moral questions about what is fair or unfair, truthful or deceptive, helpful or harmful. Inconceivable without an awareness of the boundaries surrounding people, discretion requires a sense for when to hold back in order not to bruise, and for when to reach out. The word "tact" conveys the physical sense of touching that these boundaries evoke. (Bok, 1982, p. 41)

Brutal honesty versus discretion often comes down to the level of boundary responsibility a person is able and willing to take to save face. Goffman (1967) argues that in communicative interactions, people assume that "face" will be preserved. "Out of *considerateness*, communicators exert effort to save the feelings and maintain the face of other people" (Cupach & Metts, 1994, p. 3). In many cases, we do not want the other person to be insensitive to our feelings and tell us information that we do not want to hear in the name of "honesty." First, if we find out someone's opinion of us and it is not pleasant, we may become angry. Second, if we find out something about someone else, we have to take responsibility for the information. We may not want to know the things a person is being "honest" about, yet, when we find out, we must take the information into account even if we were better off not knowing. Later in this chapter, we will see a discussion about privacy dilemmas. Often, where there is a lack of discretion, honesty forces individuals to be accountable for information they did not want to know.

### Fuzzy Boundaries

Fuzzy boundaries occur when people are ambiguous about who owns or co-owns the private information, changing the rights to determine rules. One person within a marital boundary, for example, may define private information at the personal level, while the spouse may see it as belonging to both of them at the dyadic level. Because boundary lines are fuzzy, the wife, for instance, may refuse to disclose information about a previous husband to her current spouse. The current spouse thinks the information belongs to both of them in their dyadic boundary and accuses his wife of lying to him. The wife thinks that this ownership definition is not true. She sees the information as belonging to her alone (part of her personal privacy boundary) and, that consequently, she has the legitimate right to conceal the information if she chooses.

   Fuzzy boundaries may lead to people believing that lies are being told. Instead, people may have different ways of defining ownership. If we think the information belongs to us, we perceive we have the right to regulate it according to our own rules of revealing and concealing. Turbulence arises when others see the same information as collectively owned and managed according to mutually established rules. When one person assumes the information is personal and another thinks it is dyadic, group, or family information, the individual using a collective definition may believe the other person is withholding the truth. On the contrary, they are not trying to deceive; rather, they do not think others have the right to tell them how to disclose.

### Is Privacy Deception?

Although deception is a factor in other kinds of boundary turbulence, it seems most salient to the question of boundary ownership. The issue that transforms deception into privacy or privacy into deception is the *reason* for the message. Deceptive communication has been defined as *"message distortion resulting from deliberate falsification or omission of information by a communicator with the intent of stimulating in another, or others, a belief that the communicator himself or herself does not believe"* (Miller, 1983, pp. 92–93, italics in original).

However, deliberate falsification or omission may be the route to privacy. What better way to retain ownership of information than to deliberately keep it protected? The question for deception is not the deliberateness of an attempt to protect, but the reason for denying access to the private information. If the reason is to preserve privacy, then it may not be judged as deceptive by the person protecting his or her information. If the reason is to protect others, the person expecting to receive the information may perceive the action as deception if he or she disagrees with the boundary definition. If the reason is to hurt the other by denying access, then both parties may consider it deception.

Rosenfeld (2000) points out: "research and personal experience show that even communicators with the best intentions are not always completely truthful in situations where honesty could be uncomfortable" (p. 9). Thus, the reason may be protection of private feelings, information, or behavior for self and other. However, when a recipient claims that a person *should have* disclosed when he or she did not want to, the cry of deception might be a persuasive device to force the resistant communicator to reveal.

Research that identifies reasons people lie appears to support the thesis of either self-protection or protection of others. For example, in one study, people reported that they lied to: (a) save face, (b) gain power, (c) guide social interaction and make conversations run smoothly, (d) avoid tensions and conflict, and (e) facilitate or deter interactions (Turner, Edgely, & Olmstead, 1975). Lying has also been associated with protecting face, which is another way to think about privacy (Metts, Cupach, & Imahori, 1992).

Being vague about disclosure of private information to save face allows the revealer the ability to control the amount, depth, or breadth of information told. Using indirect strategies to reveal affords people options in the way they want to talk about personal matters or matters that belong to a larger group. However, does the very act of selectively revealing constitute deception? Selective disclosure may only be considered deception from the perspective of the receiver and, again, we have to ask whether it is deception at all or a matter of differing boundary definitions.

## Determining Ownership Rights

In our current world, the information explosion makes fuzzy boundaries a common occurrence. Branscomb (1994) points out that, a great deal of information we consider to be highly personal, and of interest only to ourselves and the town gossip—our names, telephone numbers, marital status, educational accomplishments, job and credit histories, even medical, dental, and psychiatric records—is now sold on the open market to any one who believes he or she might be able to use chic information to turn a profit. (p. 4)

It is somewhat frightening to learn that the "average consumer is on approximately a hundred mailing lists and in at least fifty databases" (Branscomb, 1994, p. 11). In a free market, private information has become a commodity. The new plastic cards issued by supermarkets may save money, yet the companies find out exactly what each of us is buying for breakfast, lunch, dinner, and snacks. Many of us receive advertisements targeted at these eating habits. Even more serious, there is a definite possibility that people we do not know have access to our medical histories. In attempting to obtain and utilize private information, we are facing many paradoxes. Strangers often can gain access to our own private information more easily than we can. The *incongruity of access* makes the sense of privacy violation more accute. While we have to work at obtaining information about our bank account, medical history, and credit report, others enter these boundaries with ease.

Remembering the AIDS victim in chapter 3 who sued a drugstore because a pharmacy clerk revealed to his family that he had AIDS, his case clearly suggests the incongruity of boundary ownership lines. Because the clerk's teenage son told the man's children at school, even though he had hoped to keep the information from his children until he was on his deathbed, the HIV-positive father was forced to open his boundary and share ownership with his children before he was ready.

Because some people believe they have rights to control certain private information, though others disagree, the coordination process regulating revealing and concealing is compromised. Cases in which medical students have sold confidential records to malpractice lawyers, or where a convicted rapist working for a hospital purportedly tapped into the hospital's computer records looking for young women and girls, speak to *contradictory assumptions* in the control over ownership rights (Gordon, 1995). Some represent instances where people genuinely believe they have mutual rights, and others reflect known breaches of boundary definitions. Nevertheless, the presumption that having access means automatic control over information, or that having a relationship with someone means shared rights, is problematic.

## Gossip

One of the more thorny types of fuzzy boundaries is seen in the way people gossip. The distinction between gossip and legitimately being an owner of private information is the *"pretend factor."* People make believe that they own the right to reveal and conceal private information for which they have no rights whatsoever and try to convince others of their entitlement.

A gossip message is about someone else's private information that may only be partly true (although the person may wish it to be entirely true), or that may not be true at all. However, the message need only appear true. Because of the way that it is communicated, recipients presume there is a relationship between the person gossiping and the target of the gossip (Bergmann, 1993). In order for the gossiper to be effective, he or she also needs to have a relationship with the recipient (audience). The content of the gossip is necessarily of a private nature, or at least the gossiper tries to make others believe it is restricted to the target's personal boundary. However, to be of interest, it must be news that entices and has meaning for the gossiper and audience. Gossip is always about someone. Yet, that person is rarely in the loop of conversation (Bergmann, 1993).

The target of the gossip also needs to be known to those telling and listening. As a test of this thesis about ownership, people rarely, if ever, consider revelations about partners or close family members to constitute gossip (Bergmann, 1993). One could argue that because people see the disclosing person within an existing privacy boundary as co-owner of the information, he or she has rights to make that information public. People may reason, then, that the person is not gossiping because he or she has factual and reliable information about intimate matters.

As members of intimate relationships, we are recognized as guardians of private information belonging to our family and friends. Others assume we will not betray our responsibility to hold back damaging information or refrain from speculating about intimates' private lives the way we might about acquaintances. These assumptions differ from gossip about well-known people such as movie stars or politicians whom we do not know personally.

Ample sources of information for gossip are available to provide us with details about a famous person's private life. In U.S. culture, we have formalized this type of gossip by creating "gossip columnists" and "gossip magazines." Although print and television gossip may sometimes be annoying to celebrities, it is an inevitable price of fame. Their boundaries are stretched to accommodate many others because fame depends on being viewed publicly. Moreover, gossiping about celebrities has little potential for harm, certainly far less than gossip about acquaintances or friends.

While the manufacturer of gossip claims to own rights to regulate privacy boundaries, the *recipient* is invited to share this imaginary status. One issue that appears important in selecting a recipient is not choosing a stranger (Bergmann, 1993). Typically, "the recipient is a person who is familiar enough with the target of gossip to appreciate the information and well enough known to the manufacturer to allow him or her to be open without fear of criticism or betrayal" (Bergmann, 1993, p. 68).

Once the information is passed on, the recipient and the manufacturer become coconspirators, bound together in their joint knowledge. Interestingly, once the gossip is shared, the recipient can become a manufacturer, repeating the gossip to others. The gossip manufacturer and recipient might even become competitors, each vying for the right to tell others first.

Although individuals only claim they own rights to the information, the way they coordinate is similar to the coordination of legitimate co-owners. The point that makes gossip part of boundary turbulence is the fact that the manufacturer is only feigning partnership with others who actually have boundary control rights. In fact, the information is not necessarily true, but its power is in the manufacturer's and recipient's acting as though it is true. In this way, the boundaries become fuzzy.

### Dissimilar Boundary Orientation

Boundary turbulence takes place when boundary members depend on dissimilar boundary orientations stemming from concretized rules. In keeping with the way privacy is valued, there are situations in which individuals are not flexible about rule changes and are dependent on privacy rules that are firmly held. For example, marital partners may grow up in families that have different ways of regulating their boundaries around private disclosures. One family might concretize their privacy rules according to a strong orientation toward impermeability while another family may lean toward a permeable orientation.

From data collected on marital privacy, one respondent stated that:

> We were very open within the family you know moving, decisions and whether or not to, you know major purchases and grandma's really sick and those kinds of things, we all knew all about them. But, they never went outside the family. (Petronio, 2000d, Interview 2, p. 4)

Her husband's family was more private about discussing matters, typically talking to his mother.

Growing up in different orientations makes it difficult to negotiate privacy rules managing a new dyadic boundary. One newlywed couple illustrated this point when the husband complained that his wife always told her parents and siblings everything that she and her new husband were experiencing in their marriage, including problems with their sex life (Petronio, 2000e). She made these disclosures in front of her husband, who felt embarrassed and even humiliated. He explained that, although his wife came from an open family, he did not really know her family well enough to tell this information to them. He was brought up to believe that it is appropriate to conceal feelings and not acceptable to tell everyone about them.

Because each spouse came from a different family privacy orientation, both experienced turbulence. The dissimilarity of how each viewed privacy management led to conflict and problems. This type of situation underscores the need for negotiating new privacy boundaries and rules for revealing and concealing when newly married.

Dissimilarity also arises when people interact across cultures. As chapter 2 argues, culture is one criterion people use to develop their privacy rules. When cultural values override other criteria, people may have difficulty accommodating expectations about privacy. Thus, boundary turbulence erupts when people interact with others who have cultures that vary widely in their privacy values from their own.

For example, if a person interacts with someone from a different culture who has a dissimilar orientation, it may be problematic to comprehend the rule choices each is making to reveal private information. Some cultures apply highly permeable rule orientations, while others depend on more impermeable rules to regulate private information. For instance, Swedish culture relies on an "antisecrecy model" (Orfali, Saracenco, Weber-Kellerman, & May, 1991, p. 418), producing the highly permeable rule orientation used by individuals in Sweden.

"In Sweden, perhaps more than anywhere else, the private is exposed to public scrutiny. The communitarian, social-democratic ethos involves an obsession with achieving total transparency in all social relations and all aspects of social life" (Orfali et al., 1991, p. 418). Consequently, not all money matters are held in confidence. Because material success is considered very important, people want to show their wealth and talk about their riches to others (Orfali et al., 1991). People from more private cultures may be offended by being told about such riches or having Swedes expect this kind of disclosure in return.

## Boundary Definition Predicaments

Turbulence is likely when there are dissimilar definitions for the borders of the boundaries. This happens in two ways: first, when people treat public space as private and disclose private information inappropriately, and second, when people are thrust into the public domain by others in a way that forces them to change their definition of boundaries around private information.

### Private Disclosures in Public Spaces

There are many examples of people treating public space as private, compromising their own privacy by disclosing. The "private conversation" we might have in the men's or women's rest room while others come and go, the "private conversation" we have in the airplane with our spouse while others sit close by, and the "private conversation" we have in the hallway at work with a colleague while others sit in their offices are all situations that compromise our own privacy. We often put ourselves in a predicament by not recognizing when information should be kept within private boundaries, forgetting that public space is not private.

For example, two doctors were discussing the pros and cons of removing parts of a patient's lung in an elevator filled with people (Ubel, Zell, Miller, Fischer, Peters-Stefani, & Arnold, 1995). Unfortunately, the doctors were carrying on a "private, confidential" conversation in a public area. The patient's wife was among those in the elevator. The doctors defined the boundaries around their conversation as dyadically private, yet the interaction was taking place in a public elevator. In a study that was conducted on this issue, the researchers found that one out of every six rides in an elevator for a large metropolitan hospital contained instances of physicians breaching the privacy of their patients (Ubel et al., 1995).

Keeping private information confined to spaces that secure the information is sometimes a challenge for people. Perhaps we find this difficult because we define the information as privileged and, therefore, think that the situation in which we disclose does not matter. One of the most telling examples took place on an airplane. I was on a plane trip when the woman sitting next to me began a conversation but quickly stopped talking without a clear explanation. I tried to engage her, but she was writing in her notepad and did not respond to my attempts.

After the plane landed and people began to deplane, the woman turned to me and apologized for not responding. I accepted her apology and she explained that as we were talking, she overheard the two men in the seat in front of us discussing their plans for bidding on a contract. It turned out that she was their competition for the contract. She did not want to miss any of their strategies, so she listened to their conversation.

The two men treated their public space as private and disclosed information that may have lost them their bid. Sitting near a friend or colleague in an airplane gives the impression that no one can hear the conversation. However, that is not necessarily true. Goffman (1971) argues that, in these situations, people often engage in civil inattention. In other words, they *pretend* not to notice someone in first class talking on his cell phone about a real estate deal, naming people, their incomes, and the strategies he is using to increase the price of the house.

Sometimes it is difficult to overlook the information others disclose. Like the woman on the plane, the contents of the conversation might be salient, and civil inattention may be accorded in the situation, but not once the person leaves the premises. *Eavesdropping* is considered a breach of privacy when someone intentionally seeks out information by listening to others' conversations (Alderman & Kennedy, 1995). Yet eavesdropping is more difficult to assess when people breach their own privacy by mistaking public space for private quarters. When people use public space as private, they essentially open their boundaries. No one could be faulted for using the private information, because it has been made freely available by the owners themselves.

This behavior causes turbulence because it gets us into trouble. We may not know who has been listening to our "private" conversation because we often do enact civil inattention. Those people for whom the information proves relevant have certain rights to appropriate the information because of where it was disclosed. Even situations that "feel" private, like our offices at work, require certain precautions to be taken. However, people often forget to consider them.

For example, talking about an upcoming meeting, workers congregated in one person's office to plan a strategic approach to a negotiation. As the conversation turned, they started talking about the incompetence of a coworker. Because they were talking loudly, their description of this person was heard in the hallway by a number of people, including the person about whom they were speaking.

These individuals experienced boundary turbulence because they did not keep the private information within appropriate bounds. Though they did not mean the information to be accessible to everyone, the way they treated the environment in which they were speaking allowed uninvited others to hear what they said. They had little recourse because they created the turbulence by disregarding the publicness of the space used to disclose.

### Celebrities

"Fame. The instant recognition and constant adoration sometimes lead celebrities to seek the shadows—that is, until the spotlights begin to fade and the anxiously hoped for return to a quieter, private life turns difficult" (Scarp, 1998, p. D5). By implication, becoming a celebrity means a change in the way privacy boundaries are defined. However, the boundary definition is often paradoxical and, therefore, turbulent. As Gamson (1992) argues, the "ambition to stand out from the crowd is not at all new in Western culture" (p. 2).

In the United States, there is a noteworthy combination of the desire for being considered unique and the opportunity to become famous.

Braudy (1986) states that people believe others should "praise me because I am unique, but praise me as well because my uniqueness is only a more intense and public version of your own" (p. 372). People seek fame, that is, being their most public, but do not consider the toll it will take on their private lives. Since they are expected to give up much of their privacy, they may only recognize the cost after fame is achieved.

There are many examples in the lives of film stars. Much attention is paid to film stars' "personal" lives (Gamson, 1992). Many venues have been invented to satisfy the interests of fans so that they are able to learn about the stars' private lives. For instance, *The National Enquirer*, *People Magazine*, *Soap Opera Digest*, and other similar "news" outlets provide "private information" that translates the person into a public figure. The magazines are used to make a person "known" to the public; however, to do so, private lives must be on display.

Consequently, the duality of wanting to be public and private at the same time is paradoxical. To be a star means giving up a private life. Yet, most stars complain a great deal about the costs of giving up so much privacy. One way that stars have tried to maintain their privacy boundary while striving to be public is to "create" information that is seemingly "private" to satisfy the needs of their fans (Gamson, 1992).

Creating a fictitious privacy boundary gives a sense of "intimacy at a distance" (Leets, deBecker, & Giles, 1995). Fans can feel near to the celebrity, yet the star uses a fictitious privacy boundary to guard his or her real private life. Because the fans want to know about the private side of the celebrity, they actively engage in pursuing information that lets them think they know the person intimately. Creating a fictitious privacy boundary is risky because the fans presume they have open access to the information when in fact they do not. The fans assume the privacy rules for permeability privilege them. The fans come to believe that they are privy to personally private information. If they find out that the information is fictitious, they may become angry or disillusioned because they feel deceived.

Film and television stars are not the only people in the United States to experience this type of boundary turbulence. Political figures are another group who must cope with the paradoxical nature of fame. McCarthy (1972) explains how she felt when her husband ran for President of the United States. She states, "the campaign followed us everywhere—I found that we could not escape from it any place" (McCarthy, 1972, p. 313).

Their dyadic privacy boundary and personal boundaries were compromised because of the notoriety that Senator McCarthy received as a presidential candidate. By implication, his wife was also required to give up some of her personal privacy in order for Senator McCarthy to run for political office.

Fame may be short-lived and even unexpected, as those winning the lottery find out. Nevertheless, in each case, people expect the right to have private information made public for their scrutiny and consumption. By being close to fame, people feel entitled to share the halo of recognition by co-owning the "private" information of someone famous (Leets et al., 1995). Through this shared experience, real or fabricated, the mutual possession of private information elevates the fan. However, it also compromises the public figure's ability to retain control over personal or dyadically private boundaries.

## Privacy Dilemmas

> My mother asked me to clean the garage while she went to the store," said a 19-year-old college freshman. "I was working away when I moved a table and letters fell to the ground. They looked special; they had a ribbon tied around them. I noticed that they were addressed to my mother—just last year. The handwriting did not look like my Dad's. I wondered what they were, who they were from. I was afraid to open them, yet I was intrigued. My curiosity got the best of me. I opened just one to see. My world took a dive. There before me was a love letter to my mom. They were from some man I never heard of. What could she be thinking? I asked myself. And, now I knew a secret of my mom's. I told myself to calm down. I put the letters back where I found them— hidden out of view. Now what? Who do I tell? I can't live with knowing this by myself. But, if I told my Dad he would go crazy. I didn't want to be the messenger. If I told my sister, she would be a wreck. My little brother was out of the question; he could not keep a secret. Should I tell my mom? I wondered. How do I solve this dilemma? (Petronio, Jones, & Morr, in press, p. 2)

As this story illustrates, people struggle with many different kinds of privacy dilemmas, all of which cause boundary turbulence because there are no neat and clean ways to solve them. Dilemmas like this one often confuse boundary lines, suck people into a privacy boundary without having a choice, or compromise their ability to exercise control over managing the private information in a way that reduces potential conflict.

Privacy dilemmas are found in all areas of life. However, those that occur in families are significant because the ties that members have complicate the way they manage their boundaries. Dilemmas exemplify the difficulties that members have in regulating the multiple privacy boundaries within the family.

Dilemmas reflect the problem of knowing private information that, if kept confidential, has the potential to cause family problems and, if told, may result in conflict. Thus, dilemmas represent "a situation involving choices between two equally unsatisfactory alternatives" (Neufeldt, 1995, p. 168). Boundaries become turbulent when individuals are put into binds where the solutions are problematic.

Individuals must therefore determine ways to solve these dilemmas with the least amount of negative outcome for all parties involved. They consider options to assess the level of unpleasantness and degree of conflict for themselves and other family members. Doing so helps people determine ways to manage the dilemmas. If resolutions are achieved, they may not be satisfying to all members involved but is assessed to be the best choice under the circumstances.

Research shows that there are at least three different kinds of family privacy dilemmas (Petronio, Jones, & Morr, in press). First, there are *confidant dilemmas*, in which a family member is told about some problem. Second, there are *accidental privacy dilemmas*, in which members inadvertently discover problematical information. Third, there are *illicit privacy dilemmas*, in which family members snoop and find out things that have consequences for themselves and other family members.

## Confidant Privacy Dilemma

Confidant privacy dilemmas occur when one family member seeks out another member to disclose a problem. For example, a respondent in a recent study on dilemmas reports,

> One specific situation I experienced with my family was with my Uncle's recent drug problem. In confidentiality, he told me about his problem and about how he was still using drugs. This put me in an awkward situation. I either had to tell someone who could help him or I could keep it a secret like he asked me to. By keeping his problem private, I could not get him any help. By breaking my word and not protecting his privacy, I could offer him some help. . . . This situation is very stressful and difficult for me. (Petronio et al., in press, p. 16)

In this situation, the uncle selected this person to function as a confidant. However, by doing so, he put her in a quandary because there were no clear solutions to help the uncle sort out the information disclosed. The discloser built a dyadic boundary that included the recipient; however, he stipulated privacy rules that hampered the confidant's ability to react in ways that allowed her to cope with the revelation.

The confidant could select two or more possible solution paths. First, she could take a *risky path*, which might entail confronting the discloser, insisting that he take matters into his own hands and get help for his drug addition (Petronio et al., in press). Second, she could take a more *cautious path*, which would avoid addressing the problem. Silence is one option. By not talking about the disclosure, the respondent could leave the information encapsulated in the dyadic boundary as her uncle asked.

If she considers the risky path to manage this privacy dilemma, she needs to also take into account whether the action will help or cause more problems. In other words, she would have to ask whether this confrontation would lead to her uncle's getting help for his addiction. If she chooses a cautious path and remains silent, she might encounter feelings of guilt. In determining ways to manage these dilemmas, confidants often judge the chances for a viable outcome, given the choices they identify and the goals they wish to achieve. Hence, the way they manage these predicaments are tied to the estimated consequences that people perceive in a given situation.

### Accidental Privacy Dilemma

There are also predicaments where a member accidentally finds out private information about someone in the family. For this situation, a family member is not necessarily told the information directly by the person who owns it. Alternatively, there are times when someone is told private information by a third party, a family member witnesses behaviors that should remain private, or someone overhears a disclosure. For example,

> I have an Aunt who is an alcoholic. One of the first times I knew she was getting out of control [was] when my sister and I happened to be at her house. My Aunt was so drunk that she was being really mean to her kids. Finally, she hit my cousin who is around three years old. We took the kids and left. We knew we had to tell my mom about it but we were scared. (Petronio et al., in press, p. 17)

Although the women in this example were not told directly about the alcohol abuse, they observed their aunt and her behavior toward her children, which placed them in a privacy dilemma. As witnesses to this situation, they were swept into a privacy boundary without their permission and without a direct invitation by the aunt. The aunt was reluctant to have the women there and they both were adverse to be in that situation. Nevertheless, the women felt compelled to take action. The difficulty was in knowing how to manage this dilemma.

Telling their mother about the incident, in turn, also pulled her into a privacy dilemma. However, even before they could reach that point, they had to overcome the fear they had of telling their mother. They were worried she would not believe them. Initially, they managed this dilemma by waiting until they felt comfortable talking to their mother.

However, they also balanced multiple goals by (a) removing the children from harm, (b) considering how to get their aunt help, and (c) telling their mom about the problem. They did not want to go to the authorities because they might take the children away from their aunt. Telling their mother was a problem regardless of when they told. She had been denying her sister's problem for some time.

The women determined that the situation had reached a crisis level. Consequently, they had to develop some strategies to convince their mother of the problem. Getting their aunt help was contingent on convincing their mother that the drinking had escalated into a serious problem.

## Illicit Privacy Dilemma

This type of predicament reflects situations where members intentionally pry, snoop, or spy on other family members, discovering private information that results in a dilemma. Managing this type of privacy dilemma often requires a confession, which is followed by uncomfortable feelings for the snooping member.

Contrary to the other kinds of privacy dilemmas, the actions in this situation are intentional. Unlike the confidant dilemma, where the recipient does not necessarily instigate the predicament, or in the accidental dilemma, where the family member is not seeking the information, in an illicit privacy dilemma, by definition, the member is responsible for creating the situation.

Although the person may not have anticipated the outcome of a dilemma, he or she initiated the actions that led to the predicament. For example, a young girl about 7 years old went into her mother's bedroom while she was asleep. Her mother told her never to go into her desk; however, on this particular afternoon, the desk seemed very appealing. As her mother slept, the little girl went through the desk and discovered documents with her name on them. As she looked, she could not make sense of them, so she took them.

Later that day she had occasion to ask her aunt why she had a different name on her birth certificate. The aunt asked her why she went through her mother's desk knowing that she should not have breached that trust. The aunt knew that the little girl's parents had chosen not to tell her this secret until she was older. Nevertheless, she discovered it on her own.

The aunt told the little girl that she needed to tell her mother about the snooping but did not disclose that she had been adopted.

This incident illustrates the complicated nature of illicit privacy dilemmas. The aunt experienced being hauled into a privacy boundary where she knew neither she nor the child belonged. The incident was a catalyst for considering how to handle revealing the parents' well-hidden dyadically private information. To cope with this dilemma, there needed to be a multi-level approach; it required choices the aunt needed to make for herself, decisions about the child, and ultimately, decisions by the parents. Privacy dilemmas are complicated problems that lead to boundary turbulence. Because the answers require elaborate decision-making strategies, moving the boundary regulation back to a level of coordination is challenging (see a more detailed discussion in Petronio, Jones, & Morr, in press).

## CONCLUSION

As this chapter shows, boundary turbulence arises out of the inability to coordinate privacy rules and boundary management. Although coordination is a goal in interaction about private information, frequently it is an aspiration that is difficult to meet. Instead, people experience intentional rule violations and must cope with the outcome. They become familiar with rule mistakes because not all turbulence is intentional. Sometimes people misunderstand the expectations for interaction about private information. Because boundary management can be ambiguous, making it difficult for people to enact rules appropriately, the coordination process often goes astray.

We also encounter fuzzy boundaries. We are not always certain where someone's ownership of private information ends and ours begins. One reason gossip is so lethal yet so intriguing is because of communicative ambiguities. Recipients are willing to give someone leeway because they are not ready to claim unwavering certainty about who owns which information. Probably the only place individuals are certain is within their own personal privacy boundaries. Once we start managing more than that, we, no doubt, expect to experience contradictions. People do not like the feeling of turbulence; nevertheless, individuals find themselves having contradictory boundary orientations in need of resolution. We also are familiar with situations where we are caught in privacy dilemmas. They make us uncomfortable sometimes on a short-term basis and other times on a long-term basis.

In all, boundary turbulence challenges us. Yet, like any functional system, the situations where a management process breaks down help renew the system. People may become more aware of privacy rules once they experience turmoil or instability. These breakdowns are, therefore, instructional even if they are embarrassing, awkward, tricky, unpleasant, unnerving, and distressing. In striving to coordinate with others, "it is easy to overlook what 'miscommunication' may positively *contribute* to ongoing interaction and social relationships" (Coupland et al., 1991, p. 3). The next chapter highlights the way coordination and turbulence help explain issues of praxis in everyday life.

# 6

# Practices and Praxis of Communication Privacy Management

Theories are useful if they explain phenomena in the everyday world. Over the last few years, a number of scholars have employed Communication Privacy Management Theory in a variety of private disclosure cases. The beneficial nature of this theory is witnessed in the explanatory strength it provides these explorations. In essence, CPM is a practical theory. This theory gives us a way to understand the everyday practices of privacy. In the following discussion, we see samples of theory applications. First, CPM theory is used to explain physicians' medical mistakes. Second, CPM explains private disclosures by children of sexual abuse. Third, CPM theory explicates dilemmas of HIV/AIDS.

## APPLICATIONS OF CPM

The examples in this chapter illustrate ways that people manage revealing and concealing private information and present applications of the theory. The practical nature of CPM helps us see the patterns that are adopted to maintain both a public and private life in these applications. Through them, we learn the inner workings of boundary management as people come to grips with decisions about how public they wish to be with others. These glimpses into everyday practices help mark where we refuse to share, partially share, or completely allow others to experience our confidential joys and troubles.

### Medical Mistakes

Allman (1995, 1998) points out that doctors are not supposed to make mistakes. "Doctors practice medical perfection—at least that is what patients expect of them . . . and what they expect of themselves" (Allman, 1995, p. 1). For a physician to admit to mistakes possibly means an open invitation to

205

litigation and may put the confidant at risk, not to mention those involved at the hospital or the staff. However, mistakes are made (Leape, 1994a, b). For example, Leape summarizes a study of iatrogenic injury (i.e., injuries caused by physicians) among patients hospitalized in New York State:

> For New York State, this equaled 98,609 patients in 1984. Nearly 14% of these injuries were fatal. If these rates are typical of the United States, then 180,000 people die each year partly as a result of iatrogenic injury, the equivalent of three jumbo jet crashes every 2 days. (Leape, 1994a, p.1851)

The difficulty for physicians is having few outlets to delve into their feelings about these mistakes. If the revelations result in negative outcomes, it is difficult to know whom to select.

Although there are measures in place to deal with "risk management," particularly for hospitals and health maintenance organizations, coping with the reality of these mistakes is left to the physician alone (Allman, 1995). "In response to having mistakenly aborted a live fetus, [a physician] relates that he spent hours in a professional review of the mistake, analyzing what went wrong and how to institute corrective measures" (Allman, 1995, p. 9). However, this physician stated, "somehow, I felt, it was my responsibility to deal with my guilt alone" (Hilfiker, 1984, p. 119). Hence, it is no wonder that physicians reported their feelings of culpability to Allman. For example, the following physician captures the issues clearly as he states:

> I felt very badly for a long period of time and went through kind of a grieving process, which I think happens whenever a physician makes a mistake. . . . I think there's a grieving process because every time you make a mistake you lose a little part of yourself. You lose a relationship with the patient, but you also lose a certain sense of yourself as being confident. It takes away a little bit of your self-esteem, so I think you do go through a certain amount of shock and denial and sadness and needing to gradually forgive yourself over time. (Allman, 1995, p. 77)

As this physician points out, there is often a grieving process, and the doctor feels bad about the experience. One of the reasons physicians find it difficult to cope is because the medical community defines "mistakes" as private information. In a sense, there is a cultural expectation that has developed rules for managing disclosure about these errors. On the most simplistic level, physicians understand that, when in doubt, it is better not to talk about these mistakes because they are off limits to others.

The boundaries are tightly held around information about mistakes made by physicians. Rules restricting disclosure are especially evident as physicians complete their residency and graduate to the status of practicing physician. If a physician feels the need to talk, the private information must be recast into something that helps the physician appear less vulnerable (Millman, 1977).

Allman (1995) points out that mistakes are often linguistically revised to take the sting out of the prospect that physicians make poor judgments. Instead of calling them mistakes, they are technically referred to as iatrogenic injuries. Further, physicians may describe them as slip-ups, overlooking some information, a blunder, or making an "honest" error. The neutralizing language glosses the issues, not only for the physician, but also for the rest of the medical community. One physician points out that "as a serious and conscientious MD, you do not necessarily make any mistakes. You may make better or worse decisions together with your patients" (Allman, 1995, p. 61). The way those better or worse judgments are framed softens the potential embarrassment if mistakes are made and as this statement illustrates may spread the responsibility of co-ownership for the mistake to the patient.

In a sense, the physicians in this study identified a face-saving strategy that helped them fit into the expectations of the medical community (i.e., physicians do not make mistakes), while alleviating any discomfort they may have felt. The difficulty may be in not having a viable way to cope with the problems created by the mistakes. Acknowledgment may be the first step to developing a perspective on the medical error.

Using neutralizing terms hampers the physician's ability to take control of the private information about the mistake and disclose it in a way that permits him or her to come to grips with the event. Currently, rules tend to use equivocal terms to signify an error; however, the ambiguity of these terms puts distance between a clear statement of what transpired and who is responsible for the action (Bavelas, Black, Chovil, & Mullett, 1990; Petronio, 1991). As such, saying that there were "procedural complications" or that someone made an "omission" in making a diagnosis, treating a patient, or prescribing a drug does not tell the whole story (Allman, 1995).

The indirect nature of these statements to camouflage "mistakes" is illustrative of how the medical community sets rules for the way that physicians should manage their privacy boundaries. "Role models in medical education reinforce the concept of infallibility" (Leape, 1994a, p. 1852). Such messages discourage the acknowledgment of medical mistakes.

The difficulty for physicians is twofold. First, when they make mistakes, the prospect for the patient is potentially dire. Second, the physicians may be racked with guilt and need to disclose their feelings (Pennebaker, 1995). Since physicians live in a medical culture that restricts even the acknowledgment of their accountability, they are denied the vehicle of disclosure to cope with the uncertainty of their judgments.

To patients, this cultural rule about disclosing medical mistakes may seem like a conspiracy. Most physicians will not comment on their colleagues' choices because they adhere to the boundary rule of not disclosing any contrary opinions in public (Allman, 1995). In actuality, this is a prime example of how powerful the boundary rule managing privacy can be for individuals. Physicians are trained in medical school to recognize the significance of adopting this rule. They may even learn by breaching the privacy rule (Allman, 1995). All of these experiences contribute to reinforcing the power of the boundary rule set by the medical community to regulate privacy.

Adherence to this privacy rule takes its toll, however. As stated, CPM theory argues that people often function on multiple boundary levels for privacy. Allman (1995) points out that physicians must abide by the boundary rule managing collective privacy that the medical community institutes. Yet, sometimes it is clear that the rule for this collective boundary compromises a physician's personal or relational boundary rules. For example, physicians may wish to disclose the mistake to a patient, a patient's family, a colleague, or their spouses. However, with the pressure to adopt the medical community's privacy rule, physicians may feel that the decision is out of their personal control.

The problem with this privacy dilemma is that physicians must personally live with their mistakes. When silence is held, the medical community can move on. This argument does not deny that physicians would be the targets of possible litigation or public shame if they disclose mistakes. However, by disclosing, the physician has the advantage of purging guilt and regret. The physician is better able to decide if privacy rules for personal boundaries should be used and is thus better able to handle opposing needs effectively.

Most often, physicians appear to want the privacy rules for personal boundaries to take precedence so that they can justify revealing their medical mistakes instead of withholding them. Many of Allman's (1995) participants reported feeling embarrassed, ashamed, anxious, fearful, discouraged, guilty, or worried about the medical mistake they made. Often the physicians mentioned regrets as they tried to calculate what they could have done differently. They all wrestled with putting the events into a perspective they could accept.

The narratives reported by Allman (1995) appear similar in content and form to the narratives of others who have been denied the opportunity to talk about experiences that have made them uncomfortable or have placed them in untenable situations (Ray, 1996). Not being able to talk about their regrets or to acknowledge that they could have done better, means physicians have to hide these feelings from others.

Physicians are expected to isolate themselves and live with the knowledge that they caused harm to others. Thus, they are forced to face the fact that their "mistakes" are contradictory to the goal of medical care. However, concealing their actions is antithetical to their personal need for disclosure and may result in festering turned inward or resentment turned outward.

Like *forced concealment* in other situations, such as that of adult women and men who were sexually abused as children, the expectation for secrecy is strong and the consequences are potentially immense for physicians who make mistakes. The physician does not necessarily choose to keep the medical mistake a secret. The information is considered a secret because "no one is to allowed know" the event, information, or situation. This particular brand of concealment is forced by others or by expectations built into a cultural system. The common theme of forced concealment is similar for incestuously abused individuals and for physicians who make mistakes.

In other words, physicians live with a privacy rule established by the collective that reinforces the assumption that disclosing mistakes compromises not only their own medical standing, but also that of the entire medical community. The sanctions instituted by this community are clear, yet, the punishment leveled by those outside the boundary around these mistakes such as the patients, are also clear. They are forced into silence by group pressure, fear, and negative sanctions. Abused children often face the same problem. Forced concealment of this kind is "usually effected with such success that the incestuously abused child often reaches adulthood with the incest secret intact" (Frawley, 1990, p. 248).

As we read earlier, the inability to disclose after a traumatic event has the potential to harm an individual both mentally and physically. Petrie, Booth, and Davison (1995) point out that "individuals in situations that prevent disclosure of stressful situations are at increased risk of negative health consequences" (p. 224). One "of the reasons that opening up and sharing one's hidden thought is beneficial may be that disclosure starves off the negative psychological, and oftentimes pathogenic, effects produced by keeping secrets" (Ellenberger, 1966, p. 216).

Forced concealment makes the collective privacy boundary and rules take precedence over personal needs for disclosure controlling if, when, how, or to whom these experiences are revealed. One physician states that he "must be resigned to live with a lot of guilt" (Allman, 1995, p. 75). Consequently, this condition could lead to medical problems for the physician.

The discussion of medical mistakes underscores the need for people who are members of collective boundaries, though in a collective, to have a sense of boundary control and ownership over their own personally private boundaries. Being a collective member should not necessarily mean that the collective privacy boundary deprives the person a right to concurrently own a personal privacy boundary. When collective privacy boundaries take over personal information without leaving the individuals a choice, thus making it difficult for people to have control over personal information, there may be situations of turbulence.

Turbulence of this kind has the potential to negatively impact the person and the relationship with those in the collective. This argument is not to deny that others, such as patients and their families, have been hurt by medical mistakes. Yet, some acknowledgment needs to be made of the difficulties physicians have making medical decisions in the first place. Though medical mistakes are made, living with the knowledge of those mistakes when the physician's main commitment is to help others is difficult enough. When physicians are unable to come to terms with these mistakes because the ability to regulate when they can disclose the mistake, how, and with whom they can reveal their mistakes compounds the problem. Physicians need the opportunity to make their own judgments about disclosure according to personal rules for privacy management that allow them to seek ways to cope with these mistakes. Denying them this opportunity makes them feel powerless in the face of a traumatic event.

### Child Sexual Abuse

The Communication Privacy Management Theory of private disclosures has also been applied to studying children who have been sexually abused. Through this application, we learn the "voice of logic" that children use to tell about their horrific experiences with abuse (Petronio, Reeder et al., 1996, Petronio, Flores, & Hecht, 1997). Sexual abuse is a pervasive problem that invades all kinds of families (Stinson & Hendrick, 1992). Reported cases in the United States range from 200,000 to four million each year (Garbarino, 1986). However, many experts agree that sexual abuse of children is higher than these numbers indicate because many are unable or unwilling to disclose the abuse. The research that has been conducted using CPM focuses on the rules that children use to tell about these sexual violations.

Given the fact that people who are prevented from disclosing about traumatic events such as sexual abuse have an increased risk of negative health consequences, learning about ways that children try to tell is important to know (Petrie et al., 1995). Thus, this body of research provides an initial road map of indicators that adults might recognize to help these children before they are forced into a lifetime of concealment.

In taking two general concepts from CPM theory, the studies uncover privacy rules that children use for boundary access and protection about the abuse. For example, boundary access reflects the privacy rules these children used to decide whom, how, when, and under what conditions they would tell about the sexual abuse. Boundary protection represents the privacy rules for withholding the information and keeping it private. Through the application of these rules, we find out the children's logic for letting others know about the crime.

Although the abused children want to talk about the experience, the perpetrators frighten the children into forced concealment against these needs and desires (Petronio et al., 1996). However, in their own way, the children find methods of revealing. Because they are so scared, the application of the privacy rules they use tends to be unconventional or different from the rules used by adults who have not been abused. From the data in the Petronio et al. (1996) study, three privacy access rules were identified: (a) tacit permission, (b) selecting the circumstances, and (c) incremental disclosure.

## Tacit Permission

Tacit permission incorporates two strategies used by the children (i.e., responses to inquiries and reciprocity), in which the abused child discloses if she or he defines messages by others as a request to talk about the abuse. In both cases, the children are looking for permission to talk about the crime with someone. However, they need this nod of encouragement or approval before they feel comfortable disclosing.

**Response to inquiries.** Generally, this rule tends to be implicit. Inquiries communicate nonspecific concerns for the abuse survivor. "Although not explicitly demanding disclosure, the child often perceives the intent of the message to suggest that the recipient is interested in his or her welfare" (Petronio et al., 1996, p. 187). Simple questions, such as "Is everything all right?" or "Are you doing okay?" perhaps followed by "I am worried about you," were interpreted as an opening to disclose.

These questions were particularly seen as permission if the questions came from someone who was liked and considered trustworthy. In a sense, inquiries made about the child's welfare were seen as communicating a sympathetic ear to hear the children's problems. The meta-message in these probes conveyed to the children an understanding that the person was offering support. An example used in the research illustrates this point. Laura (a fictitious name), one of the children, reported the following:

> She [Theresa] asked me why I was gone all that time from school, so I told her and she didn't believe me at first. She said, "no, not you" and I said, "yea, me," you know, I just told her cause she asked. (Petronio et al., 1996, p. 188)

As the authors point out, although Theresa was asking why Laura was gone from school, Laura interpreted Theresa's inquiry to mean she was concerned and was indirectly suggesting that Laura talk about her situation. This interpretation is explained by another statement Laura made pointing out that "she [Theresa] asked, you know, and I thought that I should, she's my best friend and I wasn't going to hide anything from her" (Petronio et al., 1996, p. 188). Most of the examples of this privacy rule application concern verbal messages. However, sometimes even a smile from a trusted other was enough encouragement to broach the topic of abuse.

**Reciprocity.** A second type of tacit permission used by these children was reciprocity. The application of this privacy access rule is seen in the following example from the Petronio et al. (1996) study. Jennifer talks about her interactions with her sister concerning abuse by their stepfather. Jennifer states that,

> We were just talking about different little things. She was just basically telling me what she was doing. She wasn't living at home at the time. We were talking about her, the job she had, and stuff, and then she brought it up because she started talking about how it happened to her. Then she asked me. . . . I just said, well yes, it happened to me too. (Petronio et al., 1996, p. 189).

As Dindia (1994) points out, reciprocity may take many temporal forms. In other words, for Jennifer, the reciprocity was immediate and used to respond to her request (Petronio et al., 1996). For Hazel, another one of the children, a friend disclosed an abuse experience without knowing Hazel's situation. Hazel interpreted the disclosure as an invitation to tell about her abuse following her friend's revelation (Petronio et al., 1996). Sometimes confessing the abuse occurs right after a person gives permission through the norm of reciprocity, and sometimes the confession comes several days, or even weeks, later. Primarily, the meta-message in the initial disclosure by another is a license to tell about one's own abuse.

### Selecting the Setting

The circumstance in which children tell is also an application of the privacy rules these children used to open their boundaries. It was important that they felt comfortable in the place where they told about the abuse; for example, a child might wait until the home was free of the perpetrator, or might feel that the car or backyard gave them the needed security. Talking in a room with the door closed and, sometimes, locked, having these conversations when the parent who was the perpetrator was away on vacation, or going over to someone else's home were choices these children intentionally took into account when they made their disclosure.

The setting was also meaningful to the children. For example, the most striking point revolved around the dependence on mundane activities like watching television, washing dishes, shopping, cleaning the car, baking a cake, or making dinner. These children often spoke of waiting until they were doing these everyday tasks to talk about the abuse. The ordinariness of the circumstances may have given the children a sense of normality when they wanted to disclose something extraordinary in their lives. In addition, the mundane nature of these tasks often provided a situation where attention to other issues may be given without much compromise to accomplishing the tasks. The confidants did not have to divide their attention between two equally challenging issues. Instead, they could do these mindless tasks while concentrating on the disclosure about abuse without feeling guilty.

Petronio et al. (1996) also argue that selecting the circumstances for disclosure may be a way to attempt control over the risk of the revelation. Inviting the confidant to watch TV or asking if he or she wants help doing the dishes let the children feel they had arranged the situation in which they disclosed. They could limit the audience, direct the conversation, and select the setting. In this way, they had mastery over their privacy boundary so that disclosure about sexual abuse might be conducted according to their rules.

### Incremental Disclosure

The use of incremental disclosure also illustrates the way these sexually abused children depended on the application of privacy access rules. In many ways, this sophisticated communicative action shows how strategic these children were about their disclosure. Incremental disclosure refers to a series of statements about the abuse that started with disclosing a small amount of information and increasing the quantity and intensity of the revelation with each subsequent message (Petronio et al., 1996). These children sequentially told about the abuse, building on each subsequent message until a full disclosure about the sexual abuse was made.

The increments continued as long as the confidant responded positively to the previous statement. If, at any time, the children felt that the confidant was not responsive, they stopped the disclosure sequence. For example, a child could tell her mother that she did not like the stepfather's clothes. If the mother responded by asking why she felt uncomfortable, the child would understand that the mother was interested and cared. If the mother said something to the effect of "oh, you don't go out in public with him anyhow, why should you even care," the child might take that response as indicating disinterest. In the second case, the child might not disclose anything further.

The children talked about making these "preview statements" to test the responses of confidants. Many were generally clear about the purpose of these statements. For example, Magdaline reported that she "hinted around quite a bit" (Petronio et al., 1996, p. 191) before she actually told about the sexual abuse. The initial remarks by these children appeared to be used as a barometer to gauge the recipient's relative responsiveness to a full disclosure of their abuse. The responsiveness of the confidant is a signal to the children. The reaction should convey a degree of appropriateness and caring in order for the children to take the next step (Davis & Holtgraves, 1984). The consequences of responsiveness are important to learning more about the abuse situations (Berg, 1987).

In considering underlying issues regarding the three privacy access rules, a main theme recurs in the data. The children implicitly and explicitly talked about confidant characteristics that were central to boundary permeability. When confidants had certain attributes that these children deem important, they routed messages to them. Within these parameters, the children were willing to make their privacy boundaries more accessible. Thus, these were also rules that grant or deny passage of information about abuse to be revealed (Petronio et al., 1996).

In a second study using the same data, Petronio et al. (1997) suggest that along with tacit permission, selecting the circumstances, and incremental disclosure, there are five parameters for selecting a confidant. Deciding on a confidant is based on (a) credibility, (b) supportiveness, (c) advocacy, (d) protectiveness, and (e) strength. These characteristics determine privacy rule application for these children. In other words, they tell about the crime of sexual abuse when confidants meet one or more of these qualifications.

## Credibility

Credibility refers to choosing a confidant based on trust, prior knowledge of a similar abuse experience, or a combination of these factors. For these children, trust comes in the form of assessing whether the recipient will use the information in a careless or responsible way. "Because they fear unwanted exposure, abandonment, angry attacks, or destructive acts, these children target trust as a mainstay characteristic of a confidant" (Petronio et al., 1997, p. 104). Hence, if the abused child is able to determine that the confidant will treat the disclosure with respect, trust is given and the revelation about abuse will be made. For example, Cami explains, "I knew that he wouldn't say anything to anybody 'cause I wouldn't want anybody to know. . . . He was caring and I knew that I could trust him" (Petronio et al., 1997, p. 104).

Although a number of children depended on trusting confidants because they were considered responsible, some children used prior knowledge as a credibility measure. "Knowing about the abuse by actually having comparable encounters gives the confidant a special position of personal knowledge" (Petronio et al., 1997, p. 105). There were a number of examples where this criterion was mentioned as important. For instance, one child stated that she turned to her mother, "because my mom grew up abused and stuff so that's how I'd know she'd know" (Petronio et al., 1997, p. 105). Another child stated that she told her friend because "she's got a lot of problems at her house that are like mine. Her dad and my dad are exactly [alike], I mean to the 'T' on 'em, you know and she was abused" (Petronio et al., 1997, p. 105). The commonality these children felt with others who had been abused served as a basis for selecting them as confidants.

## Supportiveness

Supportiveness was also an essential factor as a confidant characteristic for these children. Given that support and comforting are critical in disclosing about problems, it seems reasonable that these children would seek out those who could help them overcome this horrific experience (Wills, 1990). People who were considered caring, understanding, able to show affection, willing to give guidance, and able to comfort tended to be favored as confidants by the abused children. While trust and support are characteristics that allow the child to reveal the painful experience with abuse, the next confidant quality reflects a desire for someone to stand between them and perpetrator.

## Selecting an Advocate

Selecting an advocate refers to actively pursuing someone who will relay the child's disclosure about abuse to an authority that will stop the crime. This strategy involves selecting someone who is able to accomplish a goal that the children believe they are unable to do themselves. The advocate is chosen who can adequately represent the child's position and effectively end the abuse. As the authors note,

> Selecting an advocate is another way these children attempt to
> control their unpleasant circumstances. They are not always

successful, although their judgment is not necessarily flawed. Some select their mothers only to find out that their mothers are unwilling or unable to heed their cry for help. (Petronio et al., 1997, p. 107)

Statements such as "She's the person who could do something about it" (Petronio et al., 1997, p. 107), "I knew that maybe she [confidant] could talk to him and maybe get him to quit" (p. 107), and "So she can get it stopped" (p. 108) all attest to the importance of the expectation that the confidant could intervene as a factor in choosing a recipient for disclosure.

### Protectiveness

Along with seeking a confidant who would function as an advocate, the children were looking for someone who would protect their feelings. "Protecting feelings means that the confidant shields the children from feeling uncomfortable, guilty, or upset by treating their concerns seriously" (Petronio et al., 1997, p. 109). The need for protection evolves out of the child's fear of the perpetrator. The perpetrator is often a trusted member of the community or family. A disclosure of sexual abuse has the potential to meet with reactions of disbelief (Frawley, 1990). Consequently, these children were looking for someone who would be able to protect them from those who would doubt or discredit the children's statements.

### Strength

The confidant also needed to have a level of strength to be selected by the abused child. In other words, the child needed to feel certain that the person targeted as a recipient would be able to withstand hearing the disclosure. "Because disclosing about such distressing events as abuse can be painful for the confidant, not everyone is able to handle knowing this kind of information" (Petronio et al., 1997, p. 108). These children talked about ways they eliminated certain people as confidants. For example, some mentioned that they would not tell their grandmother because the perpetrator was their grandfather.

They discerned that their grandmother would find it difficult to hear the details of abuse and believe the disclosure (Petronio et al., 1997). Confidants do not always have the strength to cope with the information revealed (Pennebaker, 1990, 1993). Disclosures about sexual abuse are traumatic enough to require the capacity to confront this painful information. The children in this study were aware enough to be concerned about whether the recipients had the aptitude to hear about the abuse.

The most striking aspect of the data is the children's ability to take control while facing such terror. They actively attempted to manage their privacy boundaries so that they, as people, were not completely lost in the vortex of this crime. These, however, are children who came forward. There are countless others who remain silent with their nightmares. Through these courageous children, we learn a number of important lessons. As adults, we have a responsibility to understand a logic and language being used by abused children to free those who remain voiceless. The privacy access and protection rules these children applied to their situations become critical to interpret. While these studies only scratch the surface, they signal the need to determine the basis on which children route their private messages to others (Petronio et al., 1997, Petronio et al., 1996). Given that the cycle of abuse recurs, it is useful to discover the logic and language that children use to reveal these crimes.

## HIV/AIDS

People manage their boundaries around all types of private information, including health problems such as AIDS (Greene, Parrott, & Serovich, 1993; Greene & Serovich, 1996; Serovich & Greene, 1993; Serovich, Greene, & Parrott, 1992; Yep, 1992, 1993a, 1993b, 1995, 1997, 1998, 2000). The HIV/AIDS epidemic continues to have an astonishing effect on our everyday world (Yep, 1998). In all facets of life, from interpersonal and emotional levels to economic and social issues, this disease has left its mark on those infected and those associated with the illness (Kalichman, 1995). One of the more problematic concerns relates to the unwillingness of infected people to disclose their status, even to partners (Greene, Parrott, & Serovich, 1993).

Fear of being stigmatized is one reason people have difficulty disclosing (St. Lawrence, Husfeldt, Kelly, Hood, & Smith, 1990). Studies show that these fears have some basis. For example, St. Lawrence et al. (1990) found that people living with AIDS are highly stigmatized relative to people who face other kinds of terminal illnesses. Dindia (1998) points out that people living with HIV/AIDS often face a dual stigma. In addition to the disrepute perceived because of the illness, many face irrational homophobic attitudes (Derlega, Sherburne, & Lewis, 1998).

The duality of the stigma for individuals with a gay or lesbian sexual orientation may lead to extreme reactions by others who accuse them of being dangerous, having less intrinsic worth, and deserving to die (St. Lawrence et al., 1990). Although there are many negative outcomes of being stigmatized in this way, social isolation is particularly problematic

(Morin, Charles, & Malyon, 1984). Out of fear of infection or out of disgust, others may withdraw from contact with individuals known to have AIDS, thereby limiting the infected individual's ability to seek social support (Donlou, Wolcott, Gottlieb, & Landsverk, 1985). Social support is necessary to survive the ordeal of this disease (Yep, 1998). Thus, Cline and Boyd (1993) point out that,

> the dilemma faced by persons with HIV/AIDS is this: either risk becoming stigmatized by disclosing their condition, in order to take a chance on gaining the potential health benefits of social support, or avoid being stigmatized by engaging in information control and nondisclosure, thereby losing the potential health benefits of social support. (p. 132)

Fearing the loss of homes, jobs, and relationships, experiencing identity crises, and having to cope with the terror of knowing that AIDS is a death sentence makes telling others about their health status an unlikely prospect for those coping with HIV infection. Although there are real risks for telling, there are also risks in not revealing about this illness. The question is how individuals infected with the HIV virus may overcome these risks so that they might be able to benefit from disclosure.

Pennebaker's (1990, 1995) research clearly shows there are many negative physical and psychological consequences for those people facing the trauma of HIV/AIDS who are unable to talk about their situation. Yet, silence also has potential harm for others (Greene & Serovich, 1996). The most dramatic danger is in HIV-positive individuals not telling sexual partners about their status. For example, 29% of gay men in a study by Perry et al. (1994) did not disclose their HIV status to any present partner.

The consequences of the partner keeping this information private are obvious. In addition, concealing the knowledge of this health condition from family members may make it difficult for them to understand actions of loved ones with the AIDS virus. For both the HIV-positive individual and those close to him or her, understanding how decisions are made to disclose HIV status is critically important. To pursue this question, researchers have employed Communication Privacy Management Theory (Petronio, 1991) as an explanatory tool.

Yep (2000) argues that the transactional nature of CPM is significant in understanding the interface between HIV/AIDS disclosers and their confidants. Through examining the interaction between disclosers and recipients, a more complete picture may be learned about the nature of this process. CPM theory points out ways to take into account expectations and reactions of the confidant in conjunction with those of the discloser.

In disclosure of HIV/AIDS status, privacy rules are used and the individuals involved coordinate them depending on how others respond to the disclosure. The way that decisions to disclose and subsequent reactions to those disclosures fit together provides a whole picture of the event. Given the reluctance of those infected with the HIV virus to reveal their health status, examining boundary access rules to privacy is a first step in locating ways to encourage others to disclose.

The privacy access rules depend on a number of reasons to disclose. For example, after an initial adjustment period to learning about their HIV status, individuals may wish to tell others so that they can be educated about the disease (Cline & Boyd, 1993; Lewis, 1988; Yep, 2000). "Going public" may be done on a limited basis, with only friends and family members, or to a wider audience, depending on how comfortable the infected person feels. Besides educating others, sometimes HIV-positive individuals tell in order to gain a perspective on their disease or make it real in the early phases (Yep, 2000). For example, one person stated "it wasn't so much because I didn't know what AIDS meant to others but I wasn't sure what AIDS meant to me at the time" (Cline & Boyd, 1993, p. 136).

In addition to these reasons for telling, research by Serovich et al. (1992) suggests that people who are HIV-positive make judgments about the appropriateness of disclosure recipients. In other words, they generally have rules for who is most and least likely to hear about their medical condition. The linkage of boundaries between people with the HIV virus and their confidants depends on a hierarchy of access rules.

Overall, information about HIV-positive status is protected the most from the general public. Community leaders, employers and coworkers, teachers, and potential employers are the least likely to be told about the outcome of HIV testing. Next in line as more probable confidants are extended family members, such as aunts, uncles, and in-laws. Privacy access rules determined in this study that disclosure would most likely focus on the immediate family of the infected individual (Serovich et al., 1992). Thus, spouses, lovers, sons, daughters, mothers, and fathers tend to be first on the list of people to tell. This selectivity, found in other research on disclosure of HIV-positive individuals (Marks et al., 1992), speaks to the way boundaries are managed for people infected with this disease. Clearly, this hierarchical rule structure gives a sense of those whom HIV-positive individuals consider appropriate confidants and those whom they least prefer.

Because family members tend to be the most favored confidants, Greene and Serovich (1996) focus additional research to determine if there is any variation within the family system. In fact, intimate or marital couples tend to select each other as the most desired disclosure recipients, followed by mothers and fathers. In this scheme, the least desirable confidants, by comparison, are the extended family members such as aunts and uncles. Consequently, the hierarchy of privacy access rules becomes more fine-tuned with this second study.

In their initial research, Greene and Serovich (1996; Serovich & Greene, 1993) asked participants to respond to normative statements. Hence, their locus was on the degree of agreement for statements such as "spouses should have access to information about results of AIDS tests" (p. 5). In considering who "should" have privacy access, clearly spouses and lovers are the most likely to know about a person's HIV-positive status. However, focusing on the appropriateness of a target confidant may be different from who actually is told. As Greene and Serovich (1998) point out, using this method leads to some validity concerns.

The question, therefore, is whether the participants are responding to what people "ought" to do, or what they "would" do in this situation. Greene and Serovich (1996) test this premise and find that there is a close relationship between personal boundary access rules and normative expectations about disclosure for people living with the HIV virus. In this study, people infected seemed to perceive the "should" and "would" in a similar vein. They did not seem to draw a distinction between what the general population "should" do if they were faced with this disease and what they themselves "would" do as infected individuals.

The difficulty is in determining whether HIV-infected individuals fulfill their own expectations for disclosure. When comparing current research with earlier studies, there may be a changing trend toward opening the privacy boundaries around HIV-positive status (Greene & Serovich, 1998). Reported rates of disclosure appear lower in the late 1980s and higher in research that is more recent. For example, earlier studies reported that only 31% of the HIV-positive gay men (Stempel, Moulton, Bachetti, & Moss, 1989) and 48% of the HIV-positive Hispanic men participating in this research disclosed to their partners (Marks et al., 1992).

Studies that are more recent attest to a possible trend in heightened levels of disclosure of HIV infection. For example, Greene and Serovich (1996) reported 78% of their participants had disclosed to their partners. In another study, 87% of HIV-positive women had disclosed (Simoni et al., 1995), and 89% in a third study had disclosed (Mansergh, Marks, & Simoni, 1995). Although it is impossible to confirm this observation by simply charting the increase in numbers of individuals reporting disclosure, this suggests an important research question to consider.

One way to approach the puzzle over disclosure to partners and family members may be to consider several factors that determine when the rules for privacy access become salient. For example, research shows that when the severity of the disease increases, new privacy rules for disclosure are triggered (Marks et al., 1992). As the symptoms become more pronounced, earlier privacy rules may no longer apply or function in a productive way for HIV-positive people. Early in the disease, people may develop access rules that protect rather than reveal their health status. However, as the symptoms become more obvious and the need for support from others grows more intense, the old privacy rules do not help their situation.

Consequently, HIV-positive people change the rules to meet a new need. Marks et al. (1992) find that when overt physical symptoms are manifested for people with AIDS, they tended to be more likely than individuals who are asymptomatic to reveal their health status to close relatives, employers, and coworkers. Hence, the privacy rules may change because their need for support increases and keeping their status concealed is likely more difficult. Though the research did not suggest this, perhaps they see no logic in keeping obvious symptoms private, when there is a possibility of reaping the benefits of others knowing.

On the other hand, HIV/AIDS is progressing toward being considered a chronic disease (Siegel & Krauss, 1991; Yep, 2000). Siegel and Krauss (1991) indicate that because people may live with this disease for years, as with other chronic illnesses, individuals must face decisions about achieving life goals, investing in the future, and considering how they will live with this disease. Because people who are HIV-positive must deal with the difficulties of the disease, maintaining an optimal sense of well-being may be a challenge.

It would be interesting to know if hierarchical privacy rules about the targets of disclosure become routinized as a person lives with the disease. Perhaps those infected with the HIV virus come to depend on routinized access rules for some of their disclosure choices. By using routinized privacy rules, some stability for disclosure decisions may be achieved. These rules become dependable because they work to manage decisions about revealing and concealing.

In addition, people living with the HIV infection must also cope with other individuals' reactions to their health status in any given phase. Thus, privacy rules may evolve out of encountering these adaptive challenges. Taking the chance on revealing is often associated with predicting the ramifications of telling someone (Petronio, 1991; Petronio & Martin, 1986; Petronio et al., 1997). Being symptomatic reduces some of the decision-making issues, and living with a chronic illness may affect the nature of these issues. However, the response of the confidant is still considered in the disclosure equation.

Kimberly, Serovich, and Greene (1995) report that the HIV-positive women in their study cite expected responses from a confidant as a reason for revealing or not revealing this health-status information. In a follow-up study, Serovich, Kimberly, and Greene (1998) report that when HIV-positive individuals anticipate negative responses or even neutral reactions to the disclosure, they are more likely to conceal their health status. Finally, Greene and Serovich (1998) show that when HIV-positive people anticipate a positive response to disclosing their health status, they are more willing to disclose.

Evidently, the anticipated reactions of the confidant are an important factor in whether a person who is HIV-positive will tell others about his or her health status. The response to hearing about the disease may be so salient because the risk of telling is so high for people infected with the HIV virus.

The way others evaluate people who are HIV-positive has importance in maintaining relational ties, keeping their jobs, maintaining respect, receiving decent health care, and continuing to live in their home or apartment. Many remember the sensational AIDS cases of Ryan White, Arthur Ashe, and Rock Hudson. Although these individuals charted the course of AIDS early in U.S. awareness of the disease, reactions to people infected with the HIV virus have not varied greatly over time.

Even currently, newspaper headlines attest to the continual problems people living with AIDS face everyday. For example, in Phoenix, Arizona, a boy with AIDS has been barred from attending a charter school for children with special needs (Creno, 1998). The school does not have wheelchair access, but his mother believes her child is being turned away not because he uses a wheelchair, but because of his disease. The school officials deny that his disease is a factor; however, the issues are not clear. As CPM theory predicts, because the risks are real for people infected with the HIV virus, the anticipated reactions of potential confidants function as privacy access rules and are critical to the decision to disclose. However, other factors may mitigate certain outcomes.

Anticipated reactions may depend, in part, on previous discussions about AIDS. In one study, Greene and Serovich (1998) found that past discussions about AIDS with their mothers and fathers result in increased likelihood that HIV-positive individuals will disclose to their parents. Curiously, this study finds the reverse is true for discussions with sons and daughters. Perhaps it may be more difficult for parents to talk to their children about their own HIV/AIDS status. Thus, when it comes to anticipating the possibility of revealing their own HIV-positive status, infected individuals take into account their past interactions.

Relational quality is also a factor for access rules (Greene & Serovich, 1998). When the participants in the study by Greene and Serovich (1998) perceived a good relationship with the confidant, they were more likely to disclose. The perception of a good relationship, which leads to disclosure of one's health status, may work to reinforce intimacy. As Yep (2000) points out, many HIV-diagnosed individuals desire a serious relationship. Not all those who take the risk of disclosure lose. In a six-month follow-up, Schnell et al. (1992) found that 82% of the seropositive gay men who participated in their study reported no relational disruption after disclosing their health status to their partners.

Although we can see several pieces of the puzzle, locating the complete set of predictor variables that contribute to how an HIV-positive person decides to disclose is still a challenge. At this point, the research confirms that privacy boundaries protecting disclosures of HIV-positive status depend on certain privacy access rules. In addition, there is information to suggest that routinized privacy rules may change as they are triggered by increased severity of the disease. Confidants play an important role in the judgment to reveal HIV status, in terms of appropriateness, anticipated reactions, previous conversations, and an assessment of the relationship.

However, as Greene and Serovich (1998) point out, it is still unclear how this kind of revelation is made to a partner. The stakes are high either way. Thus, telling about health status risks losing the relationship, and not telling may risk the partner's life. There may be a certain amount of embarrassment involved in disclosing the health status of an HIV-positive individual. Because other private information (e.g., explaining how one contracted the disease) may also have to be revealed, the disclosure may be more problematic.

The pragmatics of coping with newly discovered HIV-positive status may make people retreat from others until they are able to handle the situation. The partner may feel rejected if there have been long stretches with no sexual activity. The resentment or sadness harbored by the partner, therefore, may close off the privacy boundaries of the recipient.

CPM argues that when boundaries become linked, there are expectations for sharing feelings of private information relevant to the relationship. If there are cues suggesting the privacy boundary walls have contracted, reducing permeability, it may be more difficult to bring up a serious problem like HIV/AIDS status. Likewise, the partner may not be altogether receptive to hearing the information. If privacy boundaries are changing, making the partners feel more isolated rather than connected, they may act in ways that signal the lack of receptiveness to high-risk disclosures.

In addition to coping with the pragmatics of relationships on top of dealing with this disease, some individuals also have cultural issues that intervene. As Yep (2000) points out, the HIV/AIDS epidemic has disproportionately affected minorities. Cultural beliefs about sexuality and relationships influence the value placed on private information (Michal-Johnson & Bowen, 1992; Yep, 1992, 1993b, 1995, 1998). Latino men tend to disclose less than European-Americans (Marks et al., 1992). Asians and Pacific Islanders generally have difficulty discussing issues of sexuality and terminal illness (Yep, 1993b). Thus, privacy management for these groups is influenced by their cultural expectations about disclosure. As CPM theory argues, culture is a basic criterion for privacy rule making. People identifying with different ethnic or cultural groups may vary greatly in their values and, therefore, the applications of rules they use for disclosure may differ.

Using CPM theory gives some direction to those studying disclosure practices of individuals infected with the HIV/AIDS virus. Yep (2000) points out that the "theory appears to be particularly relevant to the examination of disclosure of HIV infection in interpersonal relationships for several reasons" (p. 86). Among those reasons, Yep suggests the theory frames the parameters for understanding unsolicited disclosure, a primary type mode of revealing for HIV-infected people. In addition, CPM has the ability to explain high-risk disclosures as well as a management system that clearly lays the foundation for examining a transactional view of privacy. These dimensions seem to be fundamental to grasping the dilemma those infected with HIV/AIDS face when they decide to either keep their status secret or tell others.

## CONCLUSION AND FUTURE ISSUES

This chapter offers three instances in which CPM is instrumental in explaining the revealing and concealing of private information. Our knowledge of many other issues can benefit from using the explanatory power of this theory. Indeed, people are concerned about their privacy. Since the 1980s, people's anxieties about privacy and privacy invasion have increased dramatically (Katz & Tassone, 1990). In a 1990 survey, it was clear that people thought they would have less privacy in the future (Katz & Tassone, 1990). In fact, with the increasing technological advances, this is a reality:

> The idea that there exists in technology a potential capable of radically modifying the conditions of human existence has made prophecy a matter of common concern. In former times, when life and death were the only great changes noticeable or conceivable, the future was a drama to be played out in the next world. Prediction, accordingly, was the proper function of priests. (Fleisher, 1966, p. 37)

"Prophecy no longer has an ecclesiastical quality but is a concern of everyday life" (Sawhney, 1995, p. 1). Everywhere we look, there are technological issues that impact privacy. It is difficult to separate the two concepts. In our world today we are concerned about medical records, for instance, because we have used technology to ease the burden of tracking large volumes of private information. Privacy violations are bountiful, and although some are random, whereas others are intentional, their outcomes are difficult to absorb. For example,

> A database created by the state of Maryland in 1993 to keep the medical records of all its residents for cost containment purposes was used illegally by state employees to sell confidential information on Medicaid recipients to sales representatives of health maintenance originations. (Etzioni, 1999, p. 140)

The difficulty of keeping medical information confidential is becoming so pervasive that the Office of Technology Assessment has issued the following statement:

> Because of the linkage of computers, patient information will no longer be maintained, be accessed, or even necessarily originate with a single institution, but will instead travel among a myriad of facilities. As a result, the limited protection to privacy of health care information now in place will be further strained. (U.S. Congress, Office of Technology Assessment, 1991, p. 6)

The paradox is that for every technological advance, we both gain and lose. Ultimately, as with medical records, we need to judge when privacy violations really are problematic and when they can be accommodated even if they are annoying. The trade-offs of gain and loss figure prominently in medical research on DNA.

Genetic testing is fast becoming a central issue. The prospects for privacy violations and infractions are endless. However, the benefits of knowing predispositions to certain life-threatening diseases are also exciting. The question seems to center on the boundary ownership of the information.

Learning that a person has predispositions toward colon cancer is important for that individual to know. The information belongs to him or her because it has life-threatening consequences. Such is the case with recent research that has isolated the fact that approximately 6% of those individuals who are Ashkenazi Jews have a high probability of contracting colon cancer (Wade, 1997). However, if other people learn about this information it poses certain risks. People's ownership of the information can be compromised and used against them, as we have seen in history.

For example, "reports emerged last month that until the 1970s some 60,000 people had been sterilized in Sweden, and 11,000 in Finland, under government policies designed to weed out properties like poor eyesight and Gypsy features" (Wade, 1997, p. 5). Clearly, government appropriation of "personally" private information for eliminating whimsically selected human differentiations is the ultimate in privacy violations.

As this book illustrates, the theory of Communication Privacy Management offers a map to determine how privacy is managed by people. The more we consider the privacy issues facing us, the more imperative it becomes for us to seek a definitive understanding of where privacy boundary lines can and should be drawn, a clear insight into how to protect and solve ownership issues, and a firm handle on the way people manage their private information.

# References

Abelman, A. K. (1975). The relationship between family self-disclosure, adolescent adjustment, family satisfaction, and family congruence. *Dissertation Abstracts International, 36,* 4248A.

Afifi, W. A., & Guerrero, L. K. (1998). Some things are better left unsaid: II. Topic avoidance in friendships. *Communication Quarterly, 36,* 231–249.

Afifi, W. A., & Guerrero, L. K. (2000). Motivations underlying topic avoidance in close relationships. In S. Petronio (Ed.), *Balancing the secrets of private disclosures* (pp. 165–179). Mahwah, NJ: LEA Publishers.

Alderman, E., & Kennedy, C. (1995). *The right to privacy.* New York: Knopf.

Allman, J. (1995). *Bearing the burden or baring the soul: Physicians' self-disclosure and boundary management regarding medical mistakes.* Unpublished doctoral dissertation, University of Oklahoma, Norman.

Allman, J. (1998). Bearing the burden or baring the soul: Physicians' self-disclosure and boundary management regarding medical mistakes. *Health Communication, 10,* 175–197.

Alsbrook, L. (1976). Marital communication and sexism. *Social Casework, 57,* 195–198.

Altman, I. (1973). Reciprocity of interpersonal exchange. *Journal for the Theory of Social Behavior, 3,* 249–261.

Altman, I. (1974). The communication of interpersonal attitudes. In E. T. Huston (Ed.), *Foundations of interpersonal attraction* (pp. 121–142). New York: Academic Press.

Altman, I. (1975). *Environment and social behavior: Privacy, personal space, territory, and crowding.* Belmont, CA: Wadsworth Publishing.

Altman, I. (1977). Privacy regulation: Culturally universal or culturally specific? *Journal of Social Issues, 33*(3), 66–84.

Altman, I. (1993). Dialectics, physical environments, and personal relationships. *Communication Monographs, 60,* 26–34.

Altman, I., & Taylor, D. A. (1973). *Social penetration: The development of interpersonal relationships.* New York: Holt, Rinehart, & Winston.

Altman, I., Vinsel, A., & Brown, B. (1981). Dialectic conceptions in social psychology: An application to social penetration and privacy regulation. In L. Berkowitz (Ed.), *Advances in experimental social psychology* (Vol. 14, pp. 107–160). New York: Academic Press.

Americans guard privacy, poll finds. (1993, January 25). *Tempe Tribune*, p. A5.

Annicchiarico, L. K. B. (1973). Sex differences in self-disclosure as related to sex and status of the interviewer. *Dissertation Abstracts International, 34,* 2296B.

Archer, R. L., & Berg, J. H. (1978). Disclosure reciprocity and its limits: A reactance analysis. *Journal of Experimental Social Psychology, 16,* 527–540.

Archer, R. L., & Burleson, J. A. (1980). The effects of timing and responsibility of self-disclosure on attraction. *Journal of Personality and Social Psychology, 38,* 120–130.

Aries, E. J., & Johnson, F. L. (1983). Close friendship in adulthood: Conversational content between same-sex friends. *Sex Roles, 9,* 1183–1196.

Ashworth, C., Furnman, G., Chaikin, A.L., & Derlega, V.J. (1976). Physiological response to self-disclosure. *Journal of Humanistic Psychology, 16,* 71–80.

Atkeson, B. M., Calhoun, K. S., Resnick, P. A., & Ellis, E. M. (1982). Victims of rape: Repeated assessment of depressive symptoms. *Journal of Consulting and Clinical Psychology, 50,* 96–102.

Baird, J. (1977). *The dynamics of organizational communication.* New York: Harper & Row

Barbee, A. (1990). Interactive coping: The cheering up process in close relationships. In S. W. Duck (Ed.), *Personal relationships and social support.* Newbury Park, CA: Sage.

Bardwick, J. (1971). *Psychology of women.* New York: Harper & Row.

Barnlund, D. (1962). Toward a meaning-centered philosophy of communication. *Journal of Communication, 12,* 198–202.

Barrell, J., & Jourard, S. (1976). Being honest with persons we like. *Journal of Individual Psychology, 32,* 185–193.

Barrera, M., & Baca, L. M. (1990). Recipient reactions to social support: Contributions of enacted support, conflicted support, and network orientation. *Journal of Social and Personal Relationships, 7,* 541–551.

Basecu, S. (1990). Show and tell: Reflections on the analyst's self-disclosure. In G. Stricker & M. Fisher (Eds.), *Self-disclosure in the therapeutic relationship* (pp. 47–60). New York: Plenum Press.

Bath, K. E., & Daly, D. L. (1972). Self-disclosure: Relationships to self-described personality and sex differences. *Psychological Reports, 31,* 623–628.

Bavelas, J. B., Black, A., Chovil, N., & Mullett, J. (1990). *Equivocal communication.* Newbury Park, CA: Sage.

Baxter, L. A. (1979). Self-disclosure as a disengagement strategy. *Human Communication Research, 5,* 215–222.

Baxter, L. A. (1987). Self-disclosure and relationship disengagement. In V. Derlega & J. H. Berg (Eds.), *Self-disclosure: Theory, research, and therapy* (pp. 155–174). New York: Plenum Press.

Baxter, L. A. (1988). A dialectical perspective on communication strategies in relationship development. In S. Duck (Ed.), *Handbook of personal relationships* (pp. 257–273). New York: Wiley.

Baxter, L. A. (1990). Dialectical contradictions in relationship development. *Journal of Social and Personal Relationships, 7,* 69–88.

Baxter, L. A. (1993). The social side of personal relationships: A dialectic perspective. In S. W. Duck (Ed.), *Social contexts and relationships: Understanding relationship processes* (Vol. 3, pp. 139–169). Newbury Park, CA: Sage.

Baxter, L. A. (1994). A dialogic approach to relationship maintenance. In D. J. Canary & L. Stafford (Eds.), *Communication and relational maintenance* (pp. 233–254). San Diego, CA: Academic Press.

Baxter, L. A., & Montgomery, B. M. (1996). *Relating: Dialogues and dialectics.* New York: Guilford.

Baxter, L. A., & Simon, E. P. (1993). Relationship maintenance strategies and dialectical contradiction in personal relationships. *Journal of Social and Personal Relationships, 10,* 321–338.

Baxter, L. A., & Widenmann, S. (1993). Revealing and not revealing the status of romantic relationships to social networks. *Journal of Social and Personal Relationships, 10,* 331–338.

Baxter, L. A., & Wilmot, W. (1984). "Secret tests": Social strategies for acquiring information about the state of the relationship. *Human Communication Research, 11,* 171–201.

Baxter, L. A., & Wilmot, W. W. (1985). Taboo topics in close relationships. *Journal of Social and Personal Relationships, 2,* 253–269.

Bem, S. L. (1974). The measurement of psychological androgyny. *Journal of Consulting and Clinical Psychology, 42,* 155–162.

Bem, S. L. (1977). On the utility of alternative procedures for assessing psychological androgyny. *Journal of Consulting and Clinical Psychology, 45,* 196–205.

Bem, S. L. (1979). Theory and measurement of androgyny: A reply to the Pedhazur-Telenbaum and Locksley-Colten critiques. *Journal of Personality and Social Psychology, 37,* 1047–1054.

Bem, S. L. (1981). Gender schema theory: A cognitive account of sex typing. *Psychological Review, 88,* 354–364.

Benn, S. I., & Gaus, G. F. (1983). The public and the private: Concepts and action. In S. I. Benn & G. F. Gaus (Eds.), *Public and private in social life.* New York: St. Martin's Press.

Berardo, F. M. (1974). Family invisibility and family privacy. In S. T. Margulis (Ed.), *Privacy* (pp. 55–72). Stony Brook, NY: Environmental Design Research Association.

Berg, J. H. (1987). Responsiveness and self-disclosure. In V. J. Derlega & J. H. Berg (Eds.), *Self-disclosure: Theory, research, and therapy* (pp. 101–130). New York: Plenum Press.

Berg, J. H., & Archer, R. L.(1983). The disclosure-liking relationship: Effects on self-perception, order of disclosure, and topical similarity. *Human Communication Research, 10,* 269–281.

Berg, J. H., & Derlega, V. J. (1987). Themes in the study of self-disclosure. In V. J. Derlega & J. H. Berg (Eds.), *Self-disclosure: Theory, research, and therapy* (pp. 1–8). New York: Plenum Press.

Berg, J. H., & Peplau, L. A. (1982). Loneliness: The relationship of self-disclosure and androgyny. *Personality and Social Psychology Bulletin, 8,* 624–630.

Bergmann, J. R. (1993). *Discreet indiscretions: The social organization of gossip.* New York: Aldine de Gruyter.

Berzon, B. (1979). Developing a positive gay identity. In B. Berzon & R. Leighton (Eds.), *Positively gay* (pp. 3–17). Milrose, CA: Celestial Arts.

Bettelheim, B. (1960). *The informed heart.* New York: Avon Books.

Blaker, K. L. (1974). Self-disclosure and depression during the antepartum and postpartum periods among primiparous spouses. *Dissertation Abstracts International, 34,* 6190B.

Bohannan, P. (1970). *Divorce and after.* Garden City, NY: Doubleday.

Bok, S. (1982). *Secrets: On the ethics of concealment and revelation.* New York: Pantheon.

Bradac, J., Hosman, L. A., & Tardy, C. H. (1978). Reciprocal disclosures and language intensity: Attributional consequences. *Communication Monographs, 45,* 1–17.

Braiker, H. G., & Kelley, H. H. (1979). Conflict in the development of close relationships. In R. L. Burgess & T. L. Huston (Eds.), *Social exchange in developing relationships* (pp. 135–168). New York: Academic Press.

Braithwaite, D. O. (1991). "Just how much did that wheelchair cost?": Management of privacy boundaries by persons with disabilities. *Western Journal of Speech Communication, 55,* 254–274.

Branscomb, A. W. (1994). *Who owns information? From privacy to public access.* New York: Basic Books.

Braudy, L. (1986). *The frenzy of renown: Fame and its history*. New York: Oxford University Press.

Brems, C., Fromme, D. K., & Johnson, M. E. (1992). Group modification of empathic verbalizations and self-disclosure. *Journal of Social Psychology,2*, 189–200.

Brewer, M. B., & Mittelman, J. (1980). Effects of normative control of self-disclosure on reciprocity. *Journal of Personality, 48*, 89–102.

Brooks, E. (1997, July). Former exec prevails in *Seinfeld* case. *The Tribune*, p. A8.

Brooks, L. (1974). Interactive effects of sex and status on self-disclosure. *Journal of Counseling Psychology, 21*, 469–474.

Brown, E. C., & Guy, R. F. (1983). The effects of sex and Machiavellianism on self-disclosure patterns. *Social Behaviour and Personality, 11*, 93–96.

Brown, G. W., & Harris, T. (1978). *Social origins of depression*. London: Tavistock Publications.

Burgoon, J. K. (1982). Privacy and communication. In M. Burgoon (Ed.), *Communication yearbook 6*, (pp. 206–288). Beverly Hills, CA: Sage.

Burke, R. J. (1982). Disclosure of problems and informal helping in work settings. *Psychological Reports, 50*, 811–817.

Burke, R. J., Weir, T., & Harrison, D. (1976). Disclosure problems and tensions experienced by marital partners. *Psychological Reports, 38*, 531–542.

Burleson, B. R. (1985). The production of comforting messages: Social-cognitive foundation. *Journal of Language and Social Psychology, 4*, 253–273.

Caldwell, M. A., & Peplau, L. A. (1982). Sex differences in same-sex friendship. *Sex Roles, 8*, 21–32.

Canary, D. J., & Emmers-Sommer, T. M., with Faulkner, S. (1997). *Sex and gender differences in personal relationships*. New York: Guildford Press.

Carpenter, B. N. (1997). The relationship between psychopathology and self-disclosure: An interference/competence model. In V. J. Derlega & J. H. Berg (Eds.), *Self-disclosure: Theory, research, and therapy* (pp. 203–227). New York: Plenum Press.

Cash, T. F. (1975). Self-disclosure in the acquaintance process: Effects of sex, physical attractiveness, and approval motivation. *Dissertation Abstracts International, 35*, 3572B.

Cash, T. F., & Soloway, D. (1975). Self-disclosure correlates of physical attractiveness: An exploratory study. *Psychological Reports, 36*, 579–586.

Caughlin, J. P., Golish, T. D., Olson, L. N., Sargent, J. E., Cook, J. S., & Petronio, S. (2000). Intrafamily secrets in various family configurations: A communication boundary management perspective. *Communication Studies, 51*,116–134.

Certner, B. C. (1973). The exchange of self-disclosures in same-sexed groups of strangers. *Journal of Consulting and Clinical Psychology, 40*, 292–297.

Chaikin, A. L., & Derlega, V. J. (1974a). Liking for the norm-breaker in self-disclosure. *Journal of Personality, 42*, 117–129.

Chaikin, A. L., & Derlega, V. J. (1974b). Variables affecting the appropriateness of self-disclosure. *Journal of Consulting and Clinical Psychology, 42*, 588–593.

Chaikin, A. L., Derlega, V. J., Bayma, B., & Shaw, J. (1975). Neuroticism and disclosure reciprocity. *Journal of Consulting and Clinical Psychology, 1*, 359–369.

Chelune, G. J. (1975a). Self-disclosure: An elaboration of its basic dimensions. *Psychological Reports, 36*, 79–85.

Chelune, G. J. (1975b). Sex differences and relationship between repression-sensitization and self-disclosure. *Psychological Reports, 37*, 920.

Chelune, G. J. (1976). A multidimensional look at sex and target differences in disclosure. *Psychological Reports, 39*, 259–263.

Chelune, G. J. (1979). Measuring openness in interpersonal communication. In G. J. Chelune (Ed.), *Self-disclosure: Origins, patterns, and implications of openness in interpersonal relationships* (pp. 1–27). San Francisco: Jossey-Bass.

Chelune, G. J., Sultan, F. E., & Williams, C. L. (1980). Loneliness, self-disclosure, and interpersonal effectiveness. *Journal of Counseling Psychology, 27*, 462–468.

Chelune, G. J., Waring, E. M., Vosk, B. N., Sultan, F. E., & Ogden, J. K. (1984). *Journal of Clinical Psychology, 40*, 216–219.

Cherbosque, J. (1987). Differential effects of counselor self-disclosure statements of perception of the counselor and willingness to disclose: A cross-cultural study. *Psychotherapy, 24*, 434–437.

Cline, R. J. (1982, May). *Revealing and relating: A review of self-disclosure theory and research.* Paper presented at the annual meeting of the International Communication Association, Boston, MA.

Cline, R. J. W., & Boyd, M. F. (1993). Communication as threat and therapy: Stigma, social support, and coping with HIV infection. In E. B. Ray (Ed.), *Case studies in health communication* (pp. 131–147). Hillsdale, NJ: LEA.

Cline, R. J. W., & Musolf, K. E. (1985). Disclosure as social exchange: Anticipated length of relationship, sex roles, and disclosure intimacy. *Western Journal of Speech Communication, 49*, 43–56.

Coates, D., & Winston, T. (1987). The dilemma of distress disclosure. In V. J. Derlega & J. H. Berg (Eds.), *Self-disclosure: Theory, research, and therapy* (pp. 229–256). New York: Plenum Press.

Cohen, S., & Willis, T. A. (1985). Stress, social support and the buffering hypothesis. *Psychological Bulletin, 98,* 319–357.

Cohn, N. B., & Strassberg, D. S. (1983). Self-disclosure reciprocity among preadolescents. *Personality and Social Psychology Bulletin, 9,* 97–102.

Collett, P. (1977). Rules of conduct. In P. Collett (Ed.), *Social rules and social behaviour* (pp. 1–27). Totowa, NJ: Rowman and Littlefield.

Collins, N. L., & Miller, L. C. (1994) The disclosure-liking link: From meta-analysis toward a dynamic reconceptualization, *Psychological Bulletin, 116,* 457–475.

Colwill, N. L., & Perlman, D. (1977). Effects of sex and relationship on self-disclosure. *JSAS Catalog of Selected Documents in Psychology, 7,* 40.

Cooper, C. L. (1984). The social-psychological precursors to cancer. *Journal of Human Stress, 2,* 4–11.

Coupland, N., Giles, H., & Wiemann, J. M. (Eds.) (1991). *"Miscommunication" and problematic talk.* Newbury Park, CA: Sage.

Courtois, C. A. (1988). *Healing the incest wound: Adult survivors in therapy.* New York: W. W. Norton.

Coyne, J. C. (1976a). Toward an interactional description of depression. *Psychiatry, 39,* 28–40.

Coyne, J. C. (1976b). Depression and the response of others. *Journal of Abnormal Psychology, 853,* 186–193.

Coyne, J.C., Kessler, R.C., Tal, M., Turnbull, J., Wortman, C.B., & Greden, J.F. (1987). Living with a depressed person. *Journal of Consulting and Clinical Psychology, 55,* 347–352.

Cozby, P. C. (1973). Self-disclosure: A literature review. *Psychological Bulletin, 79*(2), 73–91.

Creno, C. (1998, June). Suit: Charter closed to boy with AIDS. *The Arizona Republic,* pp. A1, A10.

Cronen, V. E., Chen, V., & Pearce, W. B. (1988). Coordinated management of meaning: A critical theory. In Y. Y. Kim & W. B. Gudykunst (Eds.), *Theories in intercultural communication* (pp. 69–98). Newbury Park, CA: Sage.

Culbert, S. A. (1967). *Interpersonal process of self-disclosure: It takes two to see one.* Washington: N. T. L. Institute for Applied Behavioral Science.

Cunningham, J. A. (1981). Effects of intimacy and sex-role congruency of self-disclosure. *Dissertation Abstracts International, 42,* 2597.

Cupach, W. R., & Metts, S. (1994). *Facework.* Thousand Oaks, CA: Sage.

Cutler, B. R., & Dyer, W. G. (1965). Initial adjustment processes in young married couples. *Social Forces, 2,* 195–201.

Cutrona, C. E. (1996). *Social support in couples.* Thousand Oaks, CA: Sage.

Cutrona, C. E., Suhr, J. A., & MacFarlane, R. (1990). Interpersonal transactions and the psychological sense of support. In S. W. Duck (Ed.), *Personal relationships and social support* (pp. 30–45). London: Sage.

Daluiso, V. E. (1972). Self-disclosure and perception of that self-disclosure between parents and their teen-age children. *Dissertation Abstracts International, 33,* 420B.

Danieli, Y. (1984). Psychotherapist participation in the conspiracy of silence about the Holocaust. *Psychoanal Psychology, 1,* 23–42.

Daniels, A. K. (1970). Development of the scapegoat in sensitivity training sessions. In T. Shibutani (Ed.), *Human nature and collective behavior* (pp. 234–249). Englewood Cliffs, NJ: Prentice-Hall.

Davidson, B., Balswick, J., & Halverson, C. (1983). Affective self-disclosure and marital adjustment: A test of equity theory. *Journal of Marriage and the Family, 45,* 93–102.

Davis, D., & Holtgraves, T. (1984). Perceptions of unresponsive others: Attributions, attraction, understandability, and memory of their utterances. *Journal of Experimental Social Psychology, 20,* 383–408.

Davis, D., & Perkowitz, W. T. (1979). Consequences of responsiveness in dyadic interactions: Effects of probability of response and proportion of content related responses. *Journal of Personality and Social Psychology, 37,* 534–550.

Davis, J. D. (1977). Effects of communication about interpersonal process on the evolution of self-disclosure in dyads. *Journal of Personality and Social Psychology, 35,* 31–37.

Davis, J. D. (1978). When boy meets girl: Sex roles and the negotiation of intimacy in an acquaintance exercise. *Journal of Personality and Social Psychology, 36,* 684–692.

Davis, M. H., & Franzoi, S. (1987). Private self-consciousness and self-disclosure. In V. J. Derlega & J. H. Berg (Eds.), *Self-disclosure: Theory, research, and therapy* (pp. 60–80). New York: Plenum Press.

Dawson, C., Schirmer, M., & Beck, L. (1984). A patient self-disclosure instrument. *Research in Nursing and Health, 7,* 135–147.

DeCew J. W. (1997). *In pursuit of privacy: Law, ethics, and the rise of technology.* Ithaca, NY: Cornell University Press.

Deevey, S. (1993). Lesbian self-disclosure: Strategies for success. *Journal of Psychosocial Nursing, 31*(4), 21–26.

Denholm-Carey, J., & Chabassol, D. J. (1987). Adolescents' self-disclosure of potentially embarrassing events. *Psychological Reports, 60,* 45–46.

Derlega, V. J., & Barbee, A. P. (Eds.). (1998*). HIV and social interaction.* Thousand Oaks, CA: Sage

Derlega, V. J., & Chaikin, A. (1975). *Sharing intimacy: What we reveal to others and why.* Englewood Cliffs, NJ: Prentice-Hall.

Derlega, V. J., & Chaikin, A. (1976). Norms affecting self-disclosure in men and women. *Journal of Counseling and Clinical Psychology, 44,* 376–380.

Derlega, V. J., & Chaikin, A. L. (1977). Privacy and self-disclosure in social relationships. *Journal of Social Issues, 33,* 102–115.

Derlega, V. J., Durham, B., Gockel, B., & Sholis, D. (1981). Sex differences in self-disclosure: Effects of topic content, friendship, and partner's sex. *Sex Roles, 7,* 433–447.

Derlega, V. J., & Grzelak, J. (1979). Appropriateness of self-disclosure. In G. J. Chelune (Ed.), *Self-disclosure: Origins, patterns, and implications of openness in interpersonal relationships* (pp. 151–176). San Francisco: Jossey-Bass.

Derlega, V. J., Harris, M. S., & Chaikin, A. L. (1973). Self-disclosure reciprocity, liking, and the deviant. *Journal of Experimental Social Psychology, 9,* 277–284.

Derlega, V. J., & Margulis, S. J. (1982). Why loneliness occurs: The interrelationship of social psychological and privacy concepts. In L. A. Peplau & D. Perlman (Eds.), *Loneliness: A sourcebook of current theory, research and therapy* (pp. 183–205). New York: Wiley.

Derlega, V. J., Margulis, S. J., & Winstead, B. A. (1987). A social-psychological analysis of self-disclosure in psychotherapy. *Journal of Counseling and Clinical Psychology, 5,* 205–215.

Derlega, V. J., Metts, S., Petronio, S., & Margulis, S. J. (1993). *Self-disclosure.* Newbury Park, CA: Sage.

Derlega, V. J., Sherburne, S. & Lewis, R. J. (1998). Reactions to an HIV-positive man: Impact of his sexual orientation, cause of infection, and research participants' gender. *AIDS and Behavior, 2,* 339–348.

Derlega, V. J., Winstead, B. A., Wong, P. T. P., & Hunter, S. (1985). Gender effects in an initial encounter: A case where men exceed women in disclosure. *Journal of Personal and Social Relationships, 2,* 25–44.

Derogatis, L. R., Abeloff, M. D., & Melisaratos, N. (1979). Psychological coping mechanisms and survival time in metastatic breast cancer. *Journal of the American Medical Association, 242,* 1504–1508.

Diamond, J. (1998, January 27). Navy's outing wrong, judge rules. *The Arizona Republic,* p. A3.

Dindia, K. (1982). Reciprocity of self-disclosure: A sequential analysis. In M. Burgoon (Ed.), *Communication yearbook 6* (pp. 506–530). Beverly Hills, CA: Sage.

Dindia, K. (1988). A comparison of several statistical tests of reciprocity of self-disclosure. *Communication Research, 15,* 726–752.

Dindia, K. (1994). The intrapersonal-interpersonal dialectical process of self-disclosure. In S. W. Duck (Ed.), *Dynamics of relationships* (pp. 27–57). Thousand Oaks, CA: Sage.

Dindia, K. (1998). "Going into and coming out of the closet": The dialectics of stigma disclosure. In B. M. Montgomery & L. A. Baxter (Eds.), *Dialectical approaches to studying personal relationships* (pp. 83–108). Mahwah, NJ: LEA.

Dindia, K. (2000). Sex differences in self-disclosure, reciprocity of self-disclosure, and self-disclosure and liking: Three meta-analyses reviewed. In S. Petronio (Ed.), *Balancing the secrets of private disclosures* (pp. 21–36). Mahwah, NJ: LEA.

Dindia, K., & Allen, M. (1992). Sex differences in self-disclosure: A meta-analysis. *Psychological Bulletin, 112,* 106–128.

Dinger-Duhon, M., & Brown, B. B. (1987). Self-disclosure as an influence strategy: Effects of Machiavellianism, androgyny, and sex. *Sex Roles, 16,* 109–123.

Dolgin, K. G., Meyer, L., & Schwartz, J. (1991). Effects of gender, target's gender, topic, and self-esteem on disclosure to best and middling friends. *Sex Roles, 25,* 311–329.

Donlou, J. N., Wolcott, D. L., Gottlieb, M. S., & Landsverk, J. (1985). Psychological aspects of AIDS and AIDS-related complex: A pilot study. *Journal of Psychosocial Oncology, 3,* 39–55.

Doster, J. A. (1976). Sex learning and interview communication. *Journal of Counseling Psychology, 23,* 482–485.

Doster, J. A., & Nesbitt, J. G. (1979). Psychotherapy and self-disclosure. In G. Chelune (Ed.), *Self-disclosure: Origins, patterns, and implications of openness in interpersonal relationships* (pp. 177–224). San Francisco: Jossey-Bass.

Doster, J. A., & Strickland, B. R. (1969). Disclosing of verbal material as a function of information requested, information about the reviewer, and interviewee differences. *Journal of Consulting and Clinical Psychology, 37,* 187–194.

Eckenrode, J. & Wethington, E. (1990). The process and outcome of mobilizing social support. In S. W. Duck (Ed.), *Personal relationships and social support* (pp. 83–103). London: Sage.

Egan, G. (1970). *Encounter: Group processes for interpersonal growth.* Belmont, CA: Brooks/Cole.

Eisenberg, E. M., & Witten, M. G. (1987). Reconsidering openness in organizational communication. *Academy of Management Review, 12,* 418–426.

Electrionic Spying by Boss. (1995, November 16). *The Arizona Republic,* pp. A1, A14.

Ellenberger, H. F. (1966). The pathogenic secret and its therapeutics. *Journal of the History of Behavioral Sciences, 2,* 29–42.

Etzioni, A. (1999). *The limits of privacy.* New York: Basic Books.

Falk, D. R., & Wagner, P. N. (1985). Intimacy of self-disclosure and response processes as factors affecting the development of interpersonal relationships. *Journal of Social Psychology, 125,* 557–570.

Feldstein, J. C. (1979). Effects of counselor sex, and sex-role and client sex on clients' perceptions and self-disclosure in a counseling analogue study. *Journal of Counseling Psychology, 26,* 437–443.

Fisher, D. (1986). Decision-making and self-disclosure. *Journal of Social and Personal Relationships, 3,* 323–336.

Fitzpatrick, M. A. (1987). Marriage and verbal intimacy. In V. J. Derlega & J. H. Berg (Eds.), *Self-disclosure: Theory, research, and therapy.* New York: Plenum Press.

Fleisher, A. (1966). Technology and urban form. In M. Whiffen (Ed.), *The architect and the city* (pp. 37–52). Cambridge, MA: M.I.T. Press.

Frank, J. D., & Frank, J. B. (1991). *Persuasion and Healing* (3rd ed.). Baltimore: Johns Hopkins University Press.

Franzoi, S. L., & Davis, M. H. (1985). Adolescent self-disclosure and loneliness: Private self-consciousness and parental influences. *Journal of Personality and Social Psychology, 48,* 768–780.

Frawley, M. G. (1990). From secrecy to self-disclosure: Healing the scars of incest. In G. Stricker & M. Fisher (Eds.), *Self-disclosure in the therapeutic relationship* (pp. 247–260). New York: Plenum Press.

Friedland, B. (1994). Physician-patient confidentiality: Time to re-examine a venerable concept in light of contemporary society and advances in medicine. *Journal of Legal Medicine, 15,* 249–277.

Funabiki, D., Bologna, N. C., Pepping, M., & Fitzgerald, K. C. (1980). Revisiting sex differences in the expression of depression. *Journal of Abnormal Psychology, 89,* 194–202.

Gamson, J. (1992). The assembly line of greatness: Celebrity in twentieth century America. *Critical Studies in Mass Communication, 9,* 1–24.

Garai, J. E. (1970). Sex differences in mental health. *Genetic Psychology Monographs, 81,* 123–142.

Garamone, J. (2000, February). DoD approves "don't ask, don't tell, don't harass plans. http://www.defenselink.mil/news/Feb2000.html.

Garbarino, J. (1986). Can we measure success in preventing child abuse? *Child Abuse and Neglect, 10,* 143–156.

Garcia, P. A., & Geisler, J. S. (1988). Sex and age/grade differences in adolescents' self-disclosure. *Perceptual and Motor Skills, 67,* 427–432.

Gavison, R. (1984). Privacy and the limits of the law. In F. D. Schoeman (Ed.), *Philosophical dimensions of privacy: An anthology* (pp. 346–402). Cambridge, England: Cambridge University Press.

Gilbert, S. J. (1976). Self-disclosure, intimacy and communication in families. *Family Coordinator, 25,* 221–230.

Gilbert, S. J. (1977). Effects of unanticipated self-disclosure on recipients of varying levels of self-esteem: A research note. *Human Communication Research, 3,* 368–371.

Gilbert, S. J., & Whiteneck, G. G. (1976). Toward a multidimensional approach to the study of self-disclosure. *Human Communication Research, 2,* 347–356.

Giles, H., Coupland, N., Coupland, J., Williams, A. M., & Nussbaum, J. F. (1992). Integenerational talk and communication with older people. *International Journal of Aging and Human Development, 34,* 271–297.

Glaser, B. G., & Strauss, A. L. (1967). Awareness contexts and social interaction. *American Sociological Review, 19,* 669–679.

Goffman, E. (1967). *Interaction ritual.* New York: Pantheon Books.

Goffman, E. (1971). *Relations in public.* New York: Harper Colophon.

Goodstein, L., & Reinecker, V. (1974). Factors affecting self-disclosure: A review of the literature. *Progress in Experimental Personality Research, 7,* 49–77.

Gordon, A. C. (1990). Self-disclosure in Holocaust survivors: Effects on the next generation. In G. Stricker & M. Fisher (Eds.), *Self-disclosure in the therapeutic relationship* (pp. 227–260). New York: Plenum Press.

Gordon, M. (1995, November). Patient's medical records lose privacy aura, are sold. *The Arizona Republic,* p. A 14.

Gouldner, A. W. (1960). The norm of reciprocity: A preliminary statement. *American Sociological Review, 25,* 161–178.

Gouran, D., Hirokawa, R. Y., Julian, K. M. & Leatham, G. B. (1993). The evolution and current status of the functional perspective on communication in decision-making and problem-solving groups. In S. A. Deetz (Ed.), *Communication yearbook 16* (pp. 573–600). Newbury Park, CA: Sage.

Graham, B. (1998, June 13). Sailor accepts early retirement in privacy case. *The Tempe Tribune,* p. A11.

Green, S. K., & Sandos, P. (1983). Perceptions of male and female initiations of relationships. *Sex Roles, 9,* 849–852.

Greene, K. (2000). Disclosure of chronic illness varies by topic and target: The role of stigma and boundaries in willingness to disclose. In S. Petronio (Ed.), *Balancing the secrets of private disclosures* (pp. 123–135). Mahwah, NJ: LEA.

Greene, K. L., Parrott, R., & Serovich, J. M. (1993). Privacy, HIV testing, and AIDS: College students' versus parents' perspectives. *Health Communication, 5,* 59–74.

Greene, K. L., & Serovich, J. M. (1996). Appropriateness of disclosure of HIV-testing information: The perspective of PLWAs. *Journal of Applied Communication Research, 24,* 50–65.

Greene, K. L., & Serovich, J. M. (1998). Epilogue. In V. J. Derlega & A. P. Barbee (Eds.), *HIV and social interaction* (pp. 369–384). Newbury Park, CA: Sage.

Grigsby, J. P., & Weatherley, D. (1983). Gender and sex-role differences in intimacy of self-disclosure. *Psychological Reports, 53,* 891–897.

Haas, A. (1979). Male and female spoken language differences: Stereotypes and evidence. *Psychological Bulletin, 86,* 616–626.

Hacker, H. M. (1981). Blabbermouths and clams: Sex differences in disclosure in same-sex and cross-sex friendship dyads. *Psychology of Women Quarterly, 5,* 385–401.

Hales, D. (1991, August). Patient or victim? How to fight for your medical rights. *Family Circle,* p. 52.

Halverson, C. F., & Shore, R. E. (1969). Self-disclosure and interpersonal functioning. *Journal of Consulting and Clinical Psychology, 33,* 213–217.

Hames, J., & Waring, E. M. (1979). Marital intimacy and non-psychotic emotional illness. *Psychiatric Forum, 9,* 13–19.

Harber, K. D., & Pennebaker, J. W. (1992). Overcoming traumatic memories. In S. A. Christianson (Ed.), *The handbook of emotion and memory* (pp. 359–387). Hillsdale, NJ: Erlbaum.

Harden, J. (1986, May). *Response differences to intimate disclosures.* Paper presented at the annual meeting of the International Communication Association, Chicago, IL.

Harré, R. (1977). Rules and explanation of social behaviour. In P. Collett (Ed.), *Social rules and social behaviour* (pp. 28–41). Totowa, NJ: Rowman and Littlefield.

Harris, L. (1980). Analysis of a paradoxical logic: A case study. *Family Processes, 19,* 19–33.

Harris, L., & Cronen, V. E. (1979). A rules-based model for the analysis and evaluation of organizational communication. *Communication Quarterly, 27*(1), 12–29.

Hecht, M., Shepard, T., & Hall, M. J. (1979). Multivariate indices of the effects of self-disclosure. *Western Journal of Speech Communication, 43,* 235–245.

Hendrick, S. S. (1981). Self-disclosure and marital satisfaction. *Journal of Personality and Social Psychology, 40,* 1150–1159.

Hendrick, S. S. (1987). Counseling and self-disclosure. In V. J. Derlega & J. H. Berg (Eds.), *Self-disclosure: Theory, research, and therapy* (pp. 303–324). New York: Plenum Press.

Henwood, K., Giles, H., Coupland, J., & Coupland, N. (1993). Stereotyping and affect in discourse: Interpreting the meaning of elderly, painful self-disclosure. In D. M. Mackie & D L. Hamilton (Eds.), *Affect, cognition and stereotyping: Interactive processes in group perception* (pp. 269–296). San Diego, CA: Academic Press.

Herman, J. (1981). *Father-daughter incest.* Cambridge, MA: Harvard University Press.

Higbee, K. L. (1973). Group influence on self-disclosure. *Psychological Reports, 32,* 903–909.

Hilfiker, D. (1984). Sounding board: Facing our mistakes. *New England Journal of Medicine, 310,* 118–122.

Hill, C. T., Rubin, Z., & Peplau, L. A. (1976). Breakups before marriage: The end of 103 affairs. *Journal of Social Issues, 32,* 147–168.

Hill, C. T., & Stull, D. (1987). Gender and self-disclosure: Strategies for exploring the issues. In V. J. Derlega & J. H. Berg (Eds.), *Self-disclosure: Theory, research, and therapy* (pp. 81–96). New York: Plenum Press.

Hilts, P. (1997, August 10). University forced to pay $1.6 million to researcher. *The New York Times,* p. A13.

Hobfoll, S. E. & Stokes, J. P. (1988). The process and mechanics of social support. In S. W. Duck (Ed.), *Handbook of personal relationships* (pp. 497–517). New York: Wiley.

Hoffman-Graff, M. A. (1977). Interviewer use of positive and negative self-disclosure and interviewer-subject sex pairing. *Journal of Counseling Psychology, 24,* 184–190.

Holtgraves, T. (1990). The language of self-disclosure. In H. Giles & W. P. Robinson (Eds.), *Handbook of language and social psychology* (pp. 191–207). New York: Wiley.

Homans, G. C. (1950). *The human group.* New York: Harcourt, Brace, Jovanovich.

Homans, G. C. (1956). Social behavior as exchange. *American Journal of Sociology, 63,* 597–606.

Homans, G. C. (1961). *Social behavior: Its elementary forms.* New York: Harcourt, Brace, Jovanovich.

Hornstein, G. A. (1985). Intimacy in conversational style as a function of the degree of closeness between members of a dyad. *Journal of Personality and Social Psychology, 49,* 671–681.

Horowitz, L. M., French, R., & Anderson, C. A. (1982). The prototype of a lonely person. In L. A. Peplau & D. Perlman (Eds.), *Loneliness: A sourcebook of current theory, research and therapy* (pp. 183–205). New York: Wiley.

Hosman, L. A., & Siltanen, S. A. (1995). Relationship intimacy, need for privacy, and privacy restoration behaviors. *Communication Quarterly, 43,* 64–74.

Hubbartt, W. S. (1998). *The new battle over workplace privacy.* New York: Amacom.

Huber, G. P., & Daft, R. L. (1987). The information environments of organizations. In F. M. Jablin, L. L. Putnam, & L. W. Porte (Eds.), *Handbook of organizational communication: An interdisciplinary perspective* (pp. 389–419), Newbury Park, CA: Sage.

Hunter, J. D. (1991). *Culture wars: The struggle to define America.* New York: Basic Books.

Huston, T. L., & Ashmore, R. D. (1986). Women and men in personal relationships. In R. D. Ashmore & F. K. Del Boca (Eds.), *The social psychology of female-male relations: A critical analysis of central topics* (pp. 167–209). New York: Academic Press.

Hyink, P. W. (1975). The influence of client ego strength, client sex, and therapist sex on the frequency, depth, and focus of client self-disclosure. *Dissertation Abstracts International, 38,* 3398B.

Imber-Black, E. (Ed.). (1993). *Secrets in families and family therapy.* New York: W. W. Norton.

Inman, D. J. (1978). Self-disclosure and interview reciprocity *Dissertation Abstracts International, 38,* 3398B.

Jablin, F. M. (1982). Organizational communication: An assimilation approach. In M. E. Roloff & C. R. Berger (Eds.), *Social cognition and communication* (pp. 255–286). Newbury Park, CA: Sage.

Johnson, C. (1974). Privacy as personal control. In S. T. Margulis (Ed.), *Privacy* (pp. 83–100). Stony Brook, NY: Environmental Design Research Association.

Jones, E. E., & Archer, R. L. (1976). Are there special effects of personalistic self-disclosure? *Journal of Experimental Social Psychology, 12,* 180–193.

Jones, E. E., & Gordon, E. M. (1972). Timing of self-disclosure and its effects on personal attraction. *Journal of Personality and Social Psychology, 24,* 358–365.

Jones, W. H., Freemon, J. E., & Goswick, R. A. (1981). The persistence of loneliness: Self and other determinants. *Journal of Personality, 49,* 27–48.

Jorgensen, S. R., & Gaudy, J. C. (1980). Self-disclosure and satisfaction in marriage: The relation examined. *Family Relations, 29,* 281–287.

Jourard, S. M. (1971). *The transparent self.* New York: Van Nostrand Reinhold.

Kalichman, S.C. (1995). *Understanding AIDS: A guide for mental health professionals.* Washington, DC: American Psychological Association.

Karpel, M. A. (1980). Family Secrets: I. Conceptual and ethical issues in the relational context, II. Ethical and practical considerations in therapeutic management. *Family Processes, 19,* 295–306.

Katz, J. E., & Tassone A. R. (1990). Poll report: Privacy and information technology. *Public Opinion Quarterly, 54,* 125–143.

Kelly, A. E., & McKillop, K. J. (1996). Consequences of revealing personal secrets. *Psychological Bulletin, 120,* 450–465.

Kelvin, P. (1977). Predictability, power and vulnerability in interpersonal attraction. In S. W. Duck (Ed.), *Theory and practice in interpersonal attraction* (pp. 339–354) London: Academic Press.

Kessler, R. C., Price, R. H., & Wortman, C. B.(1985). Social factors in psychopathology: Stress, social support, and coping processes. *Annual Review of Psychology, 36,* 531–572.

Kimberly, J. A., Serovich, J. M., & Greene, K. (1995). Disclosure of HIV-positive status: Five women's stories. *Family Relations, 44,* 316–322.

Kleinke, C. L. (1979). Effects of personal evaluations. In G. J. Chelune (Ed.), *Self-disclosure: Origins, patterns, and implications of openness in interpersonal relationships* (pp. 59–79). San Francisco: Jossey-Bass.

Knapp, M. L., & Vangelisti, A. L. (1991). *Interpersonal communication and human relationships* (2nd ed.). Boston: Allyn & Bacon.

Kohen, J. A. (1975). Liking and self-disclosure in opposite sex dyads. *Psychological Reports, 36,* 695–698.

Komarovsky, M. (1967). *Blue-collar marriage.* New York: Vintage Books.

Komarovsky, M. (1974). Patterns of self-disclosure of male undergraduates. *Journal of Marriage and the Family, 36,* 677–686.

Kopfstein, J. H., & Kopfstein, D. (1973). Correlates of self-disclosure in college students. *Journal of Consulting and Clinical Psychology, 41,* 163.

LaGaipa, J. J. (1990). The negative effects of informal support systems. In S. W. Duck (Ed.), *Personal relationships and social support* (pp. 122–139). Newbury Park, CA: Sage.

Lako, C. J., & Lindenthal, J. J. (1991). The management of confidentiality in general medical practice: A comparative study in the U.S.A. and the Netherlands. *Social Science Medicine, 32,* 153–157.

Lane, J. D., & Wegner, D. M. (1995). The cognitive consequences of secrecy. *Journal of Personality and Social Psychology, 69,* 237–253.

Lane, R. C., & Hull, J. W. (1990). Self-disclosure and classical psychoanalysis. In G. Stricker & M. Fisher (Eds.), *Self-disclosure in the therapeutic relationship* (pp. 31–46). New York: Plenum Press.

Laufer, R. S., Proshansky, H. M., & Wolfe, M. (1974). Some analytic dimensions of privacy. In R. Kuller (Ed.), *Architectural psychology* (pp. 1–21). Stroudsberg, PA: Dowden, Hutchinson, & Ross.

Leape, L. L. (1994a). Error in medicine. *Journal of the American Medical Association, 272,* 1851–1857.

Leape, L. L. (1994b). The preventability of medical injury. In M. S. Bogner (Ed.), *Human error in medicine* (pp. 13–25). Hillsdale, NJ: LEA.

Leets, L., deBecker, G., & Giles, H. (1995). Fans: Exploring expressed motivations for contacting celebrities. *Journal of Language and Social Psychology, 14,* 102–123.

LePoire, B. A., Burgoon, J. K., & Parrott, R. (1992). Status and privacy restoring communication in the workplace. *Journal of Applied Communication Research, 20,* 419–436.

Levinger, G., & Senn, D. J. (1967). Disclosure of feelings in marriage. *Merrill Palmer Quarterly, 13,* 237–249.

Lewis, A. (1988). Development of AIDS awareness: A personal history. *Death Studies, 12,* 371–379.

Littlefield, R. P. (1974). Self-disclosure among some Negro, White, and Mexican-American adolescents. *Journal of Counseling Psychology, 21,* 133–136.

Locke, S., & Colligan, D. (1986). *The new medicine of mind and body.* New York: Dutton.

Lord, C. G., & Velicer, W. F. (1975). Effects of sex, birth order, target's relationship, and target's sex on self-disclosure by college students. *Psychological Reports, 37,* 1167–1170.

Lorentz, M., & Cobbs, S. (1953). Language behavior in psychoneurotic patients. *A. M. A. Archives of Neurology & Psychiatry, 69,* 684–694.

Ludwig, D., Franco, J. N., & Malloy, T. E. (1986). Effects of reciprocity and self-monitoring on self-disclosure with a new acquaintance. *Journal of Personality and Social Psychology, 50,* 1077–1082.

Luhrman, T. M. (1989). The magic of secrecy. *Ethos, 17,* 131–165.

Lynn, S. J. (1978). Three theories of self-disclosure exchange. *Journal of Experimental Social Psychology, 14,* 466–479.

Maltz, D. N., & Borker, R. A. (1982). A cultural approach to male-female miscommunication. In J. J. Gumperz (Ed.), *Language and social identity* (pp. 195–216). Cambridge, England: Cambridge University Press.

Mansergh, G., Marks, G., & Simoni, J. M. (1995). Self-disclosure of HIV-infection among men who vary in time since seropositive diagnosis and symptomatic status. *AIDS, 9,* 639–644.

Marks, G., Bundek, N. I., Richardson, J. L., Ruiz, M. S., Maldonado, N., & Mason, H. R. (1992). Self-disclosure of HIV-infection: Preliminary results from a sample of Hispanic men. *Health Psychology, 11,* 300–306.

Martin, M. M., & Anderson, C. M. (1995). The father-young adult relationship: Interpersonal motives, self-disclosure and satisfaction. *Communication Quarterly, 43,* 119–130.

McAllister, H. A., & Bregman, N. J. (1985). Reciprocity effects with intimate and non-intimate disclosure: The importance of establishing baseline. *Journal of Social Psychology, 125,* 775–776.

McCall, G. J., & Simmons, J. L. (1966). *Identities and interactions.* New York: Free Press.

McCarthy, A. (1972). *Private faces/public places.* Garden City, NY: Doubleday.

McDaniel, S. H., Stiles, W. B., & McGaughey, K. J. (1981). Correlations of male college students' verbal response mode use in psychotherapy with measures of psychological disturbance and psychotherapy outcome. *Journal of Consulting and Clinical Psychotherapy, 49,* 571–582.

McGarity, T. O., & Shapiro, S. A. (1980). The trade secret status of health and safety testing information: Reforming agency disclosure policies. *Harvard Law Review, 93,* 837–888.

McGuire, J. M., Graves, S., & Blau, B. (1985). Depth of self-disclosure as a function of assured confidentiality and videotape recording. *Journal of Counseling and Development, 64,* 259–263.

McLaughlin, M., Cody, M., & Robey, C. (1980). Situational influences on the selection of strategies to resist compliance-gaining attempts. *Human Communication Research, 7,* 14–36.

McVeigh v. Civil Action, 98–116 (U.S. District Court, District of Columbia, 1998) [On-line]. Available: www.Proskauer.com/pressroom/briefs/mcveigh/sporkin.html.

Metts, S., Cupach, W. R., & Imahori, T. T. (1992). Perceptions of sexual compliance-resisting messages in three types of cross-sex relationships. *Western Journal of Communication, 56,* 1–17.

Meyer, C. F., & Taylor, S. E. (1986). Adjustment to rape. *Journal of Personality and Social Psychology, 50,*1226–1234.

Michal-Johnson, P., & Bowen, S. P. (1992). The place of culture in HIV education. In T. Edgar, M. A. Fitzpatrick, & V. S. Freimuth (Eds.), *AIDS: A communication perspective* (pp. 147–172). Hillsdale, NJ: Lawrence Erlbaum Associates.

Mikulincer, M., & Nachshon, O. (1991). Attachment styles and patterns of self-disclosure. *Journal of Personality and Social Psychology, 61,* 321–331.

Miller, L. C., & Berg, J. H. (1984). Selectivity and urgency in interpersonal exchange. In V. J. Derlega (Ed.), *Communication, intimacy, and close relationships* (pp. 161–206). New York: Academic Press.

Miller, L. C., Berg, J. H., & Archer, R. L. (1983). Openers: Individuals who elicit intimate self-disclosure. *Journal of Personality and Social Psychology, 44,* 1234–1244.

Miller, L. C., & Kenny, D. A. (1986). Reciprocity of self-disclosure at the individual and dyadic levels: A social relations analysis. *Journal of Personality and Social Psychology, 50,* 713–719.

Miller, L. C., & Read, S. (1987). Why am I telling you this? Self-disclosure in a goal-based model of personality. In V. Derlega & J. Berg (Eds.),

*Self-disclosure: Theory, research, and therapy* (pp. 35–58). New York: Plenum Press.

Millman, M. (1977). *The unkindest cur: Life in the backrooms of medicine.* New York: Morrow.

Moore, B. (1984). *Privacy: Studies in Social and Cultural History.* Armank, NY: M. E. Sharpe.

Montgomery, B. M., & Baxter, L. A. (Eds.). (1998). *Dialectical approaches to studying personal relationships.* Mahwah, NJ: Lawrence Erlbaum Associates.

Morgan, B. S. (1976). Intimacy of disclosure topics and sex differences in self-disclosure. *Sex Roles, 2,* 161–166.

Morin, S. F., Charles, K. A., & Malyon, A. K. (1984). The psychological impact of AIDS on gay men. *American Psychologist, 39,* 1288–1293.

Morton, T. L. (1978). Intimacy and reciprocity of exchange: A comparison of spouses and strangers. *Journal of Personality and Social Psychology, 36,* 72–81.

Mulcahy, G. A. (1973). Sex differences in patterns of self-disclosure among adolescents: A developmental perspective. *Journal of Youth and Adolescence, 2,* 343–356.

Neufeldt, V. (Ed.). (1995). *Webster's new world dictionary.* New York: Pocket Books.

Norton, R. (1982). Style, content, and target components of openness. *Communication Research, 9,* 399–431.

Notarius, C.I., & Herrick, L.R. (1988). Listener response strategies to a distressed other. *Journal of Social and Personal Relationships, 5,* 97–108.

Olson, D. H., Russell, C. S. & Sprenkel, D. H. (1984). Circumplex model of marital and family systems: VI. Theoretical update. In D. H. Olson & B. C. Miller (Eds.), *Family studies review yearbook* (Vol. 2, pp. 59–74). Beverly Hills, CA: Sage.

O'Neill, S., Fein, D., Velit, K. M., & Frank, C. (1976). Sex differences in preadolescent self-disclosure. *Sex Roles, 2,* 85–88.

*Ordinary People* (1980). CA: Paramount Films.

Orfali, K., Saracenco, C., Weber-Kellermann, I., & May, E. T. (1991). Nations of families. In A. Prost & G. Vincent (Eds.), *A history of private lives* (pp. 415–539). Cambridge, MA: Belknap Press of Harvard University Press.

Palombo, J. (1987). Spontaneous self-disclosures in psychotherapy. *Clinical Social Work Journal, 15,* 107–120.

Papini, D. R., Farmer, F. F., Clark, S. M., Micka, J. C., & Barnett, J. K. (1990). Early adolescent age and gender differences in patterns of emotional self-disclosure to parents and friends. *Adolescence, 25,* 959–976.

Pardo, S. (1998, January 7). Patient says Arbor divulged his AIDS. *Detroit News*, pp. D1, D6.

Parke, R. D., & Sawin, D. B. (1979). Children's privacy in the home: Developmental, ecological, and child-rearing determinants. *Environment and Behavior, 11*, 87–104.

Parker, G. B., & Brown, L. B. (1982). Coping behaviors that mediate between life events and depression. *Archives of General Psychiatry, 39*, 1386–1391

Parker, K. (1998, January 26). With friends like this . . . Monica Lewinsky was betrayed by tape-recording pal. *The Tribune*, p. A15.

Parks, M. R. (1982). Ideology of interpersonal communication: Off the couch and into the world. In M. Burgoon (Ed.), *Communication yearbook 5* (pp. 79–108). New Brunswick, NJ: Transaction Books.

Parks, M. R. (1995). Ideology in interpersonal communication: Beyond the couches, talk shows, and bunkers. In B. R. Burleson (Ed.), *Communication yearbook 18* (pp. 480–497). Thousand Oaks, CA: Sage.

Pearce, W. B. (1976). The coordinated management of meaning: A rule-based theory of interpersonal communication. In G. R. Miller (Ed.), *Explorations in human communication* (pp. 9–16). Beverly Hills, CA: Sage.

Pearce, W. B., & Cronen, V. E. (1980). *Communication, action, and meaning: The creation of social realities.* New York: Praeger.

Pearce, W. B., & Sharp, S. M. (1973). Self-disclosing communication. *Journal of Communication, 23*, 409–425.

Pearlin, L. I., Lieberman, M. A., Menaghan, E. G., & Mullen, J. T. (1981). The stress process. *Journal of Health and Social Behavior, 22*, 337–356.

Pearson, J. C. (1980). Sex role and self-disclosure. *Psychological Reports, 47*, 640.

Pennebaker, J. W. (1989). Confession, inhibition, and disease. In L. Berkowitz (Ed.), *Advances in experimental social psychology* (Vol. 22, pp. 211–244) New York: Academic Press.

Pennebaker, J. W. (1990). *Opening up: The healing power of confiding in others.* New York: Avon Books.

Pennebaker, J. W. (1993). Putting stress into words: Health, linguistic, and therapeutic implications. *Behaviour Research and Therapy, 31*, 539–548.

Pennebaker, J. W. (1995). Emotion, disclosure, and health: An overview. In J. W. Pennebaker (Ed.), *Emotion, disclosure, and health* (pp. 3–10). Washington, DC: American Psychological Association.

Pennebaker, J. W., Barger, S. D., & Tiebout, J. (1989). Disclosure of traumas and health among holocaust survivors. *Psychosomatic Medicine, 51*, 577–589.

Peplau, L. A., Rubin, Z., & Hill, C. (1977). Sexual intimacy in dating relationships. *Journal of Social Issues, 33*, 86–109.

Perls, F. S. (1969). *Gestalt therapy verbatim.* La Fayette, CA: Real People Press.

Perrine, R. M. (1993). On being supportive: The emotional consequences of listening to another's distress. *Journal of Social and Personal Relationships, 10*, 371–384.

Perry, S., Card, C., Moffatt, M., Ashman, T., Fishman, B., & Jacobsberg, L. (1994). Self-disclosure of HIV infection to sexual partners after repeated counseling. *AIDS Education and Prevention, 6*, 403–411

Persons, R. W., & Marks, P. A. (1970). Self-disclosure with recidivists: Optimum interviewer-interviewee matching. *Journal of Abnormal Psychology, 76*, 387–391.

Petrie, K. J., Booth, R. J., & Davison, K. P. (1995). Repression, disclosure, and immune function: Recent findings and methodological issues. In J. W. Pennebaker (Ed.), *Emotion, disclosure, and health* (pp. 223–240). Washington, DC: American Psychological Association.

Petronio, S. (1982). The effect of interpersonal communication on women's family role satisfaction. *Western Journal of Speech Communication, 46*, 208–222.

Petronio, S. (1991). Communication boundary management: A theoretical model of managing disclosure of private information between marital couples. *Communication Theory, 1*, 311–335.

Petronio, S. (1994). Privacy binds in family interactions: The case of parental privacy invasion. In W. R. Cupach & B. H. Spitzberg (Eds.), *The dark side of interpersonal communication.* Hillsdale, NJ: Lawrence Erlbaum Associates.

Petronio, S. (2000a). The boundaries of privacy: Praxis of everyday life. In S. Petronio (Ed.), *Balancing the secrets of private disclosures* (pp. 37–50). Mahwah, NJ: LEA.

Petronio, S. (2000b). The meaning of balance. In S. Petronio (Ed.), *Balancing the secrets of private disclosures* (pp. xiii–xvi). Mahwah, NJ: LEA.

Petronio, S. (2000c). The ramifications of a reluctant confidant. In A. C. Richards & T. Schumrum (Eds.), *Invitations to dialogue: The legacy of Sidney Jourard* (pp. 113–132). Dubuque, IA: Kendall/Hunt Publishers.

Petronio, S. (2000d). The embarrassment of private disclosures: A case study of newly married couples. In D. O Braithwaite & J. T. Wood (Eds.), *Case studies in interpersonal communication: Processes and problems* (pp. 131–144). Belmont, CA: Wadsworth.

Petronio, S. (2000e). [Couples privacy]. Unpublished raw data.

Petronio, S. & Bantz, C. (1991). Controlling the ramifications of disclosure: "Don't tell anybody but. . . ." *Journal of Language and Social Psychology, 10*, 263–269.

Petronio, S., & Braithwaite, D. (1987). I'd rather not say: The role of personal privacy in small groups. In M. Mayer & N. Dollar (Eds.), *Issues in group communication* (pp. 67–69). Scottsdale, AZ: Gorsuch Scarisbrick.

Petronio, S., & Chayer, J. (1988). Communicating privacy norms in a corporation: A case study. Paper presented at International Communication Association Convention, New Orleans, LA.

Petronio, S., Ellermers, N., Giles, H., & Gallois, C. (1998). (Mis)communicating across boundaries: Interpersonal and intergroup considerations. *Communication Research, 25*, 571–595.

Petronio, S., Flores, L., & Hecht, M. (1997). Locating the voice of logic: Disclosure of sexual abuse. *Western Journal of Communication, 61*, 101–113.

Petronio, S., & Jones, S. S. (2001). *When "friendly advice" becomes privacy invasion: A case of pregnant couples.* Paper presented at the International Communication Association Convention, Washington, DC.

Petronio, S., Jones, S. S., & Morr, M. (in press). Family privacy dilemmas: A communication privacy management perspective. In L. Frey (Ed.), *Bona fide groups.* Mahwah, NJ: LEA.

Petronio, S., & Kovach, S. (1997). Managing privacy boundaries: Health providers' perceptions of resident care in Scottish nursing homes. Journal of Applied *Communication Research, 25*, 115–131.

Petronio, S., & Martin, J. (1986). Ramifications of revealing private information: A gender gap. *Journal of Clinical Psychology, 42*, 499–506.

Petronio, S., Martin, J., & Littlefield, R. (1984). Prerequisite conditions for self-disclosure: A gender issue. *Communication Monographs, 51*, 268–273.

Petronio, S., Reeder, H. M., Hecht, M. L., & Mon't Ros-Mendoza, T. (1996). Disclosure of sexual abuse by children and adolescents. *Journal of Applied Communication Research, 24*, 181–199.

Plasky, P., & Lorion, R. P. (1984). Demographic parameters of self-disclosure to psychotherapists and others. *Psychotherapy, 21*, 483–490.

Price, S. J., & McKenry, P. C. (1988). *Divorce.* Newbury Park, CA: Sage.

Prost, A. (1991). Public and private spheres in France. In A. Prost & G. Vincent (Eds.), *A history of private life* (pp. 3–103). Cambridge, MA: Belknap Press of Harvard University Press.

Putnam, L. L., & Stohl, C. (1990). Bona fide groups: A reconceptualization of groups in context. *Communication Studies, 41*, 248–265.

Rapaport, D. (1958). The theory of ego autonomy: A generalization. *Bulletin of the Menninger Clinic, 14,* 24–26.

Rawlins, W. K. (1983). Openness as problematic in ongoing friendships: Two conversational dilemmas. *Communication Monographs, 50,* 1–13.

Rawlins, W. K. (1991). On enacting friendship and interrogating discourse. In K. Tracy (Ed.), *Understanding face-to-face interaction: Issues linking goals and discourse* (pp. 101–115). Mahwah, NJ: LEA.

Rawlins, W. K. (1992). *Friendship matters: Communication, dialectics, and the life course.* New York: Academic Press.

Ray, E. B. (1996). When the protector is the abuser: Effects of incest on adult survivors. In E. B. Ray (Ed.), *Case studies in communication and disenfranchisement* (pp. 127–140). Mahwah, NJ: LEA.

Reis, H.T., & Shaver, P. (1988). Intimacy as an interpersonal process. In S. W. Duck (Ed.), *Handbook of personal relationships* (pp. 367–389). New York: Wiley.

Rickers-Ovsiankina, M. (1956). Social accessibility in three age groups. *Psychological Reports, 2,* 283–294.

Rippere, V. (1977). "What's the thing to do when you're feeling depressed?" A pilot study. *Behaviour Research and Therapy, 15,* 185–191.

Rivenbark, W. H. (1971). Self-disclosure patterns among adolescents. *Psychological Reports, 28,* 35–42.

Roberts, J. M., & Gregor, T. (1971). Privacy: A cultural view. In J. R. Pennock & J. W. Chapman (Eds.), *Privacy* (pp. 199–225). New York: Atherton Press.

Robinson, I. (1991). Confidentiality for whom? *Social Science of Medicine, 32,* 279–286.

Robinson, P. (1977). The rise of the rule: Mode or node? In P. Collett (Ed.), *Social rules and social behaviour* (pp. 70–87). Totowa, NJ: Rowman and Littlefield.

Rogers, C. R. (1961). *On becoming a person.* Boston: Houghton Mifflin.

Roloff, M. E., & Campion, D. E. (1985). Conversational profit-seeking interaction as social exchange. In R. L. Street & J. N. Cappella (Eds.), *Sequence and pattern in communication behaviour* (pp. 161–189). London: Edward Arnold.

Roloff, M. E., & Ifert, D. E. (2000). Conflict management through avoidance: Withholding complaints, suppressing arguments, and declaring topics taboo. In S. Petronio (Ed.), *Balancing the secrets of private disclosures* (pp. 151–163). Mahwah, NJ: LEA Publishers.

Roloff, M., Janiszewski, C., McGrath, M., Burns, C., & Manrai, L. (1988). Acquiring resources from intimates: When obligation substitutes for persuasion. *Human Communication Research, 14,* 364–396.

Rosenfeld, L. B. (1979). Self-disclosure avoidance: Why am I afraid to tell you who I am? *Communication Monographs, 46,* 63–74.

Rosenfeld, L. B. (2000). Overview of the ways privacy, secrecy, and disclosure are balanced in today' s society. In S. Petronio (Ed.). *Balancing the secrets of private disclosures* (pp. 3–17). Mahwah, NJ: LEA.

Rosenfeld, L. B., Civikly, J. M., & Herron, J. R. (1979). Anatomical and psychological sex differences. In G. J. Chelune (Ed.), *Self-disclosure: Origins, patterns, and implications of openness in interpersonal relationships* (pp. 80–109). San Francisco: Jossey-Bass.

Ross, M., & Sicoly, F. (1979). Egocentric biases in availability and attribution. *Journal of Personality and Social Psychology, 37,* 322–336.

Roth, N. L. (1991, February). *Secrets in organizations: Addressing taboo topics at work.* Paper presented at the annual meeting of the Western States Communication Association, Phoenix, AZ.

Rothenberg, K. J. (1995). Development of children's restrictive disclosure to friends. *Journal of Genetic Psychology, 156,* 279–292.

Rubin, Z. (1973). *Liking and loving: An invitation to social psychology.* New York: Holt, Rinehart, & Winston.

Rubin, Z. (1974). Lovers and other strangers: The development of intimacy in encounters and relationships. *American Scientist, 62,* 182–190.

Rubin, Z. (1975). Disclosing oneself to a stranger: Reciprocity and its limits. *Journal of Experimental Social Psychology, 11,* 233–260.

Rubin, Z., Hill, C. T., Peplau, L. A., & Dunkel-Schetter, C. (1980). Self-disclosing in dating couples: Sex roles and the ethic of openness. *Journal of Marriage and the Family, 42,* 305–317.

Ryckman, R. M., Sherman, M. F., & Burgess, G. D. (1973). Locus of control and self-disclosure of public and private information by college men and women: Brief note. *Journal of Psychology, 84,* 317–318.

Sarason, S., Davidson, K., Lighthaas, F., Waite, R., & Ruebush, B. (1960). *Anxiety in elementary school children.* New York: Wiley.

Sawhney, H. S. (1995, May). *Information superhighway: Metaphors as midwives.* Paper presented at the 45th Annual Conference of the International Communication Association, Albuquerque, NM.

Scarp, M. (1998, February). Fleeting fame. *Tempe Tribune,* p. D5.

Schneider, C. D. (1992). *Shame, exposure, and privacy.* New York: W. W. Norton.

Schneider, D. J., & Eustis, A. C. (1972). Effects of ingratiation motivation, target positiveness, and revealingness on self-presentation. *Journal of Personality and Social Psychology, 22,* 149–155.

Schnell, D. J., Higgins, D. L., Wilson, R. M., Goldbaum, G., Cohn, D. L., & Wolitski, R. J. (1992). Men's disclosure of HIV test results to male primary sex partners. *American Journal of Public Health, 82,* 1675–1676.

Schoeman, F. D. (1984). Privacy: Philosophical dimensions of the literature. In F. D. Schoeman (Ed.), *Philosophical dimensions of privacy: An anthology* (pp. 1–33). Cambridge, England: Cambridge University Press.

Schoeman, F. D. (1992). *Privacy and social freedom.* Cambridge, England: Cambridge University Press.

Schumm, W. R., Barnes, H. L., Bollman, S. R., Jurich, A. P., & Bugaighis, M. A. (1986). Self-disclosure and marital satisfaction revisited. *Family Relations, 34,* 241–247.

Schwarzer, R. & Weiner, B. (1991). Stigma controllability and coping as predictors of emotions and social support. *Journal of Social and Personal Relationships, 8,* 133–140.

Serovich, J. M., & Greene, K. (1993). Perceptions of family boundaries: The case of disclosure of HIV testing information. *Family Relations, 42,* 193–197.

Serovich, J. M., Greene, K., & Parrott, R. (1992). Boundaries and AIDS testing: Privacy and the family system. *Family Relations, 41,* 104–109.

Serovich, J. M., Kimberly, J. A., & Greene, K. (1998). Perceived family member reaction to women's disclosure of HIV-positive information. *Family Relations, 47,* 15–22.

Shaffer, D. R., & Ogden, J. A. (1986). On sex differences and self-disclosure during the acquaintance process and the role of anticipated future interactions. *Journal of Personality and Social Psychology, 51,* 92–101.

Shaffer, D. R., Smith, J. E., & Tomarelli, M. T. (1982). Self-monitoring as a determinant of self-disclosure reciprocity during the acquaintance process. *Journal of Personality and Social Psychology, 45,* 163–175.

Shapiro, A., & Swensen, C. H. (1977). Self-disclosure as a function of self-concept and sex. *Journal of Personality Assessment, 41*(2), 144–149.

Shapiro, E. (1990, February). How Johnson Controls guarded its big secret. The *New York Times,* pp. D2, D5.

Shaver, P. R., & Hazan, C. (1988). A biased overview of the study of love. *Journal of Social and Personal Relationships, 5,* 473–501.

Shibutani, T. (1986). *Social processes: An introduction to sociology.* Berkeley, CA: University of California Press.

Shimanoff, S. B. (1985). Rules governing the verbal expression of emotions between married couples. *Western Journal of Speech Communication, 49,* 147–165.

Shimanoff, S. B. (1987). Types of emotional disclosures and request compliance between spouses. *Communication Monographs, 54,* 85–100.

Siegel, K., & Krauss, B. J. (1991). Living with HIV infection: Adaptive tasks of seropositive gay men. *Journal of Health and Social Behavior, 32*, 17–32.

Silver, R. L., & Wortman, C. B. (1980). Coping with undesirable life events. In J. Garber & M. E. P. Seligman (Eds.), *Human helplessness* (pp. 279–340). New York: Academic Press.

Simmel, G. (1964). The secret and the secret society. In K. Wolff (Ed.), *The sociology of George Simmel* (pp. 307–375). New York: Free Press.

Simon, J. C. (1990). Criteria for therapist self-disclosure. In G. Stricker & M. Fisher (Eds.), *Self-disclosure in the therapeutic relationship* (pp. 207–225). New York: Plenum Press.

Simoni, J. M., Mason, H. R. C., Marks, G., Ruiz, M. S., Reed, D., & Richardson, J. L. (1995). Women's self-disclosure of HIV-infection: Rates, reasons, and reactions. *Journal of Consulting and Clinical Psychology, 63*, 474–478.

Simonson, N. R. (1976). The impact of therapist disclosure on patient disclosure. *Journal of Counseling Psychology, 23*(1), 3–6.

Sinha, V. (1972). Age differences in self-disclosure. *Developmental Psychology, 7*(3), 257–258.

Snell, W. E., Belk, S. S., & Hawkins, R. C. II. (1986). The masculine and feminine self-disclosure scale: The politics of masculine and feminine self-presentation. *Sex Roles, 15*, 249–267.

Snoek, D. & Rothblum, E. (1979). Self-disclosure among adolescents in relation to parental affection and control patterns. *Adolescence, 54*, 333–339.

Snyder, D. K. (1979). Multidimensional assessment of marital satisfaction. *Journal of Marriage and the Family, 41*, 813–823.

Solano, C. H., Batten, P. G., & Parish, E. A. (1982). Loneliness and patterns of self-disclosure. *Journal of Personality and Social Psychology, 43*, 524–531.

Sollie, D. L., & Fischer, J. L. (1985). Sex-role orientation, intimacy of topic, and target person differences in self-disclosure among women. *Sex Roles, 12*, 917–929.

Sote, G. A., & Good, L. R. (1974). Similarity of self-disclosure and interpersonal attraction. *Psychological Reports, 34*, 491–494.

Spence, J. T., Helmreich, R. L., & Stapp, J. (1975). Ratings of self and peers on sex-role attributes and their relation to self-esteem and conceptions of masculinity and femininity. *Journal of Personality and Social Psychology, 32*, 29–39.

Spencer, T. (1991, June). *To come out or not to come out: A test of self-disclosure theories applied to adolescent-parent relationships.* Paper presented at the annual meeting of the International Network on Personal Relationships, Normal/Bloomington, IL.

Spencer, T., & Derlega, V. J. (1995, February). *Important self-disclosure decisions: Coming out to family and HIV-positive disclosures.* Paper presented at the annual meeting of the Western States Communication Association, Portland, OR.

Spiro, H. (1971). Privacy in comparative perspective. In J. R. Pennock & J. W. Chapman (Eds.), *Privacy* (pp. 121–148). New York: Atherton Press.

St. Lawrence, J. S., Husfeldt, B. A., Kelly, J. A., Hood, H. V, & Smith, S. (1990). The stigma of AIDS: Fear of disease and prejudice toward gay men. *Journal of Homosexuality, 19,* 85–99.

Steele, F. (1975). *The open organization: The impact of secrecy and disclosure on people and organizations.* Menlo Park, CA: Addison-Wesley.

Stempel, R., Moulton, J., Bachetti, P., & Moss, A. R. (1989, June*). Disclosure of HIV-antibody tests results and reactions of sexual partners, friends, family, and health professionals.* Paper presented at the fifth International Conference on AIDS, Montreal, Quebec.

Stiles, W. B. (1987). "I have to talk to somebody": A fever model of disclosure. In V. Derlega & J. Berg (Eds.), *Self-disclosure: Theory, research, and therapy* (pp. 257–277). New York: Plenum Press.

Stiles, W. B., Shuster, P. L., & Harrigan, J. A. (1992). Disclosure and anxiety: A test of the fever model. *Journal of Personality and Social Psychology, 63(6),* 980–988.

Stinson, M., & Hendrick, S. (1992). Reported childhood sexual abuse in university counseling center clients. *Journal of Counseling Psychology, 39,* 370–374.

Stokes, J. P. (1985). The relation of social network and individual difference variables to loneliness. *Journal of Personality and Social Psychology, 48,* 981–990.

Stokes, J. P., Fuehrer, A., & Childs, L. (1981). Gender and sex roles as predictors of self-disclosure. *Journal of Counseling Psychology, 28,* 510–514.

Stolberg, S. G. (1998, January 18). Quandary on donor eggs: What to tell the children. *New York Times,* p. A1.

Stricker, G., & Fisher, M. (1990). *Self-disclosure in the therapeutic relationship.* New York: Plenum Press.

Tannen, D. (1990). *You just don't understand: Women and men in conversation.* New York: Morrow.

Tardy, C. H. (2000). Self-disclosure and health: Revisiting Sidney Jourard's hypothesis. In S. Petronio (Ed.), *Balancing the secrets of private disclosures* (pp. 111–122). Mahwah, NJ: LEA.

Tardy, C. H., Hosman, L. A., & Bradac, J. J. (1981). Disclosing self to friends and family: A reexamination of initial questions. *Communication Quarterly, 29,* 263–268.

Taylor, D. A. (1979). Motivational bases. In G. J. Chelune (Ed.), *Self-disclosure* (pp. 110–150). San Francisco: Jossey-Bass.

Taylor, D. A., & Altman, I. (1975). Self-disclosure as a function of reward-cost outcomes. *Sociometry, 38*(1), 18–31.

Taylor, D. A., Altman, I., & Sorrentino, B. (1969). Interpersonal exchange as a function of rewards, and costs and situational factors: Expectancy confirmation-disconfirmation. *Journal of Experimental Social Psychology, 5,* 324–339.

Taylor, R. B., De Soto, C. B., & Lieb, R. (1979). Sharing secrets: Disclosure and discretion in dyads and triads. *Journal of Personality and Social Psychology, 37,* 1196–1203.

Thibaut, J. W., & Kelley, H. H. (1959). *The social psychology of groups.* New York: Wiley.

Thompson, C. (1997, November). Country doctor faced tough issue of HIV privacy. *The Arizona Republic*, p. A 23.

Tolstedt, B. E., & Stokes, J. P. (1984). Self-disclosure, intimacy, and the depenetration process. *Journal of Personality and Social Psychology, 46,* 84–90.

Turner, R. E., Edgely, C., & Olmstead, G. (1975). Information control in conversation: Honesty is not always the best policy. *Kansas Journal of Sociology, 11,* 69–89.

Ubel, P. A., Zell, M. M., Miller, D. J., Fischer, G. S., Peters-Stefani, D., & Arnold, R. M. (1995). Elevator talk: Observational study of inappropriate comments in a public space. *American Journal of Medicine, 99,* 190–194.

U.S. Congress, Office of Technology Assessment. (1991, October). Medical monitoring and screening in the workplace: Results of a survey. Washington DC: U.S. Government Printing Office.

Vachon, M. L. S., Rogers, J., Lyall, W. A., Lancee, W. J., Sheldon, A. R., & Freeman, S. J. J. (1982). Predictors and correlates of adaptation to conjugal bereavement. *American Journal of Psychiatry, 139,* 998–1002.

Van Buren, A. (1997, November 24). Sister's silence on aunt's death was cruel. *The Arizona Republic*, p. C6.

Vangelisti, A. L. (1994). Family secrets: Forms, functions, and correlates. *Journal of Social and Personal Relationships, 11,* 113–136.

Vangelisti, A. L., & Caughlin, J. P. (1997). Revealing family secrets: The influence of topic, function, and relationships. *Journal of Social and Personal Relationships, 14,* 679–708.

VanLear, C. A. (1991). Testing a cyclical model of communicative openness in relationship development: Two longitudinal studies. *Communication Monograph, 58,* 337–361.

Wade, N. (1997, September). Testing genes to save a life without costing you a job. *The New York Times*, p. D5.

Walster, E., Berscheid, E., & Walster, G. W. (1973). New directions in equity research. *Journal of Personality and Social Psychology, 25,* 151–176.

Waring, E. M. (1980). Facilitating marital intimacy through self-disclosure. *American Journal of Family Therapy, 39,* 183–190.

Waring, E. M., McElrath, D., Lefcoe, D., & Weisz, G. (1981). Dimensions of intimacy in marriage. *Psychiatry, 44,* 169–175.

Waring, E. M., McElrath, D., Mitchell, P., & Derry, M. (1981). Intimacy and emotional illness in the general population. *Canadian Journal of Psychiatry, 26,* 167–172.

Waring, E. M., Tillmann, M. P., Frelick, L., Russell, L., & Weisz, G. (1980). Concepts of intimacy in the general population. *Journal of Nervous and Mental Disease, 168,* 471–474.

Warren, C., & Laslett, B. (1977). Privacy and secrecy: A conceptual comparison. *Journal of Social Issues, 33*(3), 43–51.

Warren, S. D., & Brandeis, L. D. (1984). The right to privacy [implicit made explicit]. In F. D. Schoeman (Ed.), *Philosophical dimensions of privacy: An anthology* (pp. 75–103). Cambridge, England: Cambridge University Press.

Waterman, J. (1979). Family patterns of self-disclosure. In G. J. Chelune (Ed.), *Self-disclosure: Origins, patterns, and implications of openness in interpersonal relationships* (pp. 225–242). San Francisco: Jossey-Bass.

Watzlawick, P., Beavin, J., & Jackson, D. (1967). *Pragmatics of human communication.* New York: Norton.

Weitraub, W. (1981). *Verbal behavior: Adaptation and psychopathology.* New York: Springer-Verlag.

Wells, J. W., & Kline, W. B. (1986). Self-disclosure of homosexual orientation. *Journal of Social Psychology, 127,* 191–197.

Werner, C. M., Altman, I., & Oxley, D. (1985). Temporal aspects of homes: A transactional perspective. In I. Altman & C. M. Werner (Eds.), *Human behavior and environment: Advances in theory and research* (pp. 1–32). Beverly Hills, CA: Sage.

West, L. W. (1970). Sex differences in the exercise of circumspection in self-disclosure among adolescents. *Psychological Reports, 26,* 226.

Westin, A. F. (1970). *Privacy and freedom.* New York: Atheneum.

Wheeless, L. R. & Grotz, J. (1976). Conceptualization and measurement of reported self-disclosure. *Human Communication Research, 2,* 338–346.

Wills, T. A. (1985). Supportive functions of interpersonal relationships. In S. Cohen & S. L. Syme (Eds.), *Social support and health* (pp.61–82). New York: Academic Press.

Wills, T. A. (1990). Multiple networks and substance use. *Journal of Social and Clinical Psychology, 9,* 78–90.

Winstead, B. A., Derlega, V. J., & Wong, P. T. P. (1984). Effects of sex-role orientation on behavioral self-disclosure. *Journal of Research in Personality, 18*, 541–553.

Wolfe, M. (1978). Childhood and privacy. In I. Altman & J. Wohlwill (Eds.), *Children and the environment* (pp. 175–222). New York: Plenum Press.

Wolfe, M., & Laufer, R. (1974). The concept of privacy in childhood and adolescence. In S. T. Margulis (Ed.), *Privacy* (pp. 29–54). Stony Brook, NY: Environmental Design Research Association.

Worthy, M., Gary, A. L., & Kahn, G. M. (1969). Self-disclosure as an exchange process. *Journal of Personality and Social Psychology, 13*, 59–63.

Wortman, C. B. (1984). Social support and the cancer patient: Conceptual and methodological issues. *Cancer, 53*, 2239–2362.

Yep, G. A. (1992). Communicating the HIV/AIDS risk to Hispanic populations: A review and integration. *Hispanic Journal of Behavioral Sciences, 14*, 403–420.

Yep, G. A. (1993a, November). *Disclosure of HIV-infection to significant others: A communication boundary management perspective.* Paper presented at the Speech Communication Association meeting, Miami, FL.

Yep, G. A. (1993b). Health beliefs and HIV prevention: Do they predict monogamy and condom use? *Journal of Social Behavior and Personality, 8*, 507–520.

Yep, G. A. (1995). Healthy desires/unhealthy practices: Interpersonal influence strategies for the prevention of HIV/AIDS among Hispanics. In L. K. Fuller & L. McPherson Shilling (Eds.), *Communicating about communicable diseases* (pp. 139–154). Amherst, MA: Human Resources Development Press.

Yep, G. A. (1997). Changing homophobic and heterosexist attitudes: An overview of persuasive communication approaches. In J. T. Sears & W. L. Williams (Eds.), *Overcoming heterosexism and homophobia: Strategies that work* (pp. 49–64). New York: Columbia University Press.

Yep, G. A. (1998). Safer sex negotiation in cross-cultural romantic dyads: An extension of Ting-Toomey's face negotiation theory. In N. L. Roth & L. K. Fuller (Eds.), *Women and AIDS: Negotiating safer practices, care, and representation* (pp. 81–100). New York: Harrington Park Press.

Yep, G. A. (2000). Disclosure of HIV infection in interpersonal relationships: A communication boundary management approach. In S. Petronio (Ed.). *Balancing the secrets of private disclosures* (pp. 83–95). Mahwah, NJ: LEA.

Youniss, J. & Smollar, J. (1985). *Adolescent relations with mothers, fathers, and friends.* Chicago: University of Chicago Press.

# Author Index

# Subject Index

**DATE DUE**